Peter Norton's Official Guide to the Norton Utilities for the Macintosh

Peter Norton's Official Guide to the Norton Utilities for the Macintosh

Peter Norton
Clint Hicks

BANTAM BOOKS

TORONTO • NEW YORK • LONDON • SYDNEY • AUCKLAND

Peter Norton's Official Guide to the Norton Utilities for the Macintosh
A Bantam Book / February 1991

*Throughout the book, trade names and trademarks of some
companies and products have been used, and no such uses are
intended to convey endorsement of or other affiliations with the book.*

*Composed and typeset by Christopher Chabris & Associates
Cambridge, Massachusetts*

For information address: Bantam Books, Inc.

ISBN 0-553-35258-X

Published simultaneously in the United States and Canada

Bantam books are published by Bantam Books, a division of Bantam
Doubleday Dell Publishing Group Inc. Its trademark, consisting of the words
"Bantam Books" and the portrayal of a rooster, is registered in the U.S. Patent
and Trademark Office and in other countries. Marca Registrada, Bantam
Books, Inc., 666 Fifth Avenue, New York, NY 10103.

PRINTED IN THE UNITED STATES OF AMERICA

0 9 8 7 6 5 4 3 2 1

For Our Dads

Acknowledgments

This book was a labor of love. It proved difficult enough to do that we doubt that the volume could have been brought into the world without an abiding affection for the product it covers, one shared by the many fine people who assisted in the delivery.

Principal thanks go to Kevin Goldstein, editor *extraordinaire*, who was quite capably assisted by Scott Clark. Bill Gladstone of Waterside Productions and Steve Guty of Bantam Books also deserve praise for their patience.

The Macintosh Utilities development team at Peter Norton Product Group were of invaluable assistance, and not just because they spent years working on a damned fine product. Marvin Carlberg, Gary Amstutz, John Blackburn, Michael Martz, and technical support representative Steve Forgacs provided a wealth of insights, corrections, and auxiliary material. Thanks especially to Marvin for taking the time to explain the intricacies of HFS and for compiling the material that went into the appendices of this book.

We'd like to take this opportunity to lavish praise on other members of the PNC documentation team, who turned out one of the best users manuals ever seen. Thanks to Allen Reed for very many late, late nights, early early mornings, and weekends trapped in hotel rooms with Macs, LaserWriters, and editors. Thanks also to Larry Colker and Denise Link for their help.

Thanks also to the members of the Engineering Support team at PNC, in particular Kim Lesnansky and Robert Pérez. And no list of acknowledgments would be complete without a tip of the hat to Ellen Kaufman, who provided insights and assistance she doesn't even know about.

Finally, thanks to Rosanna Dill and Angelina, without whose patience and understanding this undertaking would have proved impossible in the end. Love to all.

Contents

Appendix C: Hints and Tips   263

Appendix D: Problems and Solutions   267

I

Basics

1

Introduction and Computer Fundamentals

Why This Book?

The reasons are simple: Product documentation must always be finished long before the software product itself is ready to ship. Disks can be readied and duplicated in a matter of days, if not hours, whereas books require weeks to be printed, allowed to dry, bound, and cut. Print dates must be scheduled months in advance; a delay of even a few days can result in a product's losing its place in the printing queue.

Consequently, during the time between the fateful day (or night) when the manual goes to press and the software itself is finally ready, many changes are apt to occur. Features may be added at the request of respected *beta-testers*, features obviously undocumented. Features may be dropped. Some of these changes may be documented in a so-called *Read-Me* file, but others, especially nifty arcana such as *power-user keystroke combinations*, may be deliberately left out.

Things also get left out because the manual has to appeal to the target sales audience defined by the marketing department. Most people like to know as much as possible about the product they're using, but not necessarily when they want to know how to do some specific thing immediately. The documentation writer has to keep detail to a minimum to keep from obscuring important "how-to" information; users become very impatient with manuals that get in the way

1

at the wrong time. Of course, it's possible to segregate such information into another book, but additional books cost money, and unless you can prove that more people will buy a product because it's there, it's very difficult to get approval for an additional, detailed manual.

Finally, there's the question of tone. Peter Norton Computing has always been known for the light touch applied to its documentation, but even that has its limits. The breeziness of tone appreciated by some is by others singled out for special scorn. So a middle-of-the-road approach is indicated. International marketing imposes additional considerations. Passages that rely on American idiomatic humor to get a point across are going to be deucedly difficult to translate.

It all means this: You never get to do the documentation you really want. There isn't enough time, enough money, or the right audience. But what if there were?

Where No Documentation Has Gone Before

In many ways, this book represents the kind of product documentation that one would do if there were but world enough and time. And more.

We've divided the Norton Utilities for the Macintosh into three groups. The first includes those utilities intended for use in critical periods—when data are threatened. The second group focuses on utilities that may be used to increase efficiency from day to day. The last group has but one member: the Norton Disk Editor, a powerful tool that the novice can use to explore the inner workings of the Mac, and the expert can use to repair damaged files and disks or modify sound ones.

No attempt is made to provide an exhaustive reference to the Norton Utilities for the Macintosh. We take a more goal-oriented approach, showing you how to use the Utilities to accomplish real tasks rather than taking each feature of each utility in isolation. As we encounter topics worthy of deeper consideration, we pause and examine them. This includes the product developers themselves, whom we meet in a series of brief sketches.

Finally, product documentation has to make a uniform assumption about the relative sophistication of the average reader—namely, low. As there isn't time (the *Disk Companion* is a happy exception) to try to make sure everyone is at the same level, many topics must therefore be glossed over or ignored in a typical user's manual.

To get the most out of this book, however (and indeed, out of the Norton Utilities for the Macintosh themselves), you need to know something about the innards of computers in general, the Macintosh in particular, and Macintosh disks most especially. Rather than assume everyone who buys this book knows all this (the number of people who know everything salient about the workings of the Mac is very small), we'll clue you.

The remainder of this introductory chapter is devoted to a little background information about computers in general. Chapter 2 focuses on the Macintosh. We want to make certain that we're all using the same terminology to talk about the same things, if nothing else. In Chapter 3 we make sure you have the Norton Utilities for the Macintosh installed and running properly, because in Chapter 4 we're going to use one of them to peek into a Macintosh disk. And that pretty much sums up this section of the book.

If you feel comfortable with your knowledge of computers, of the Macintosh interface and Macintosh jargon, and have installed the Norton Utilities for the Macintosh already, you may wish to simply review the chapter summaries for the first three chapters and then proceed to Chapter 4.

About Computers in General

It's hard to believe that the digital computer has barely been around for 50 years. Indeed, the theoretical mathematics background of computation itself has largely developed over the last 100 years, thanks to the work of giants such as Boole, von Neumann, and Turing to name but three.

In less than two generations, however, computers (defined broadly) have grown from a few power-hungry behemoths used to calculate tables of numbers for launching ballistic missiles, to the controllers of everthing from automobiles to planetary probes. An industry whose total sales potential was reckoned in the early 1950s to be limited to a few dozen machines worldwide now has sales in the billions. Kindergarteners have computers in their class-rooms.

How many of us know even the first things about these electrical gadgets that fulfill so many important functions in modern life? Indeed, to start with, how many of us could really say, if put to it, what a computer really is, and what it does?

... That Thou Art Mindful of It

What is a computer? Until the personal computer came on the scene starting in the mid-1970s, the term "computer" was apt to conjure up the image of a room-filling collection of data-card munching steel filing cabinets ornamented with rhythmically flashing lights and randomly spinning, tape-laden wheels. New Yorker cartoons depicted lab-coated, bespectacled wizards standing in front of these hulking monstrosities, poring over cash-register tape being emitted by the yard, eagerly anticipating the answer to the question "Is there a God?" To the lay public, the scientific press characterized the computer as an "electronic brain" or a "thinking machine."

In the early 80s at least, it was still possible at certain small state universities to take computer-science courses that required one to feed punched cards to a bureau-sized hunk of metal, complete with flashing lights and chattering teletype. But the lights, switches, and dials are no more characteristic of a computer than the dashboard gauges are of a car, and modern computers look more like desks than dashes. That—forty years and more after the computer's invention—we can barely peer six days into the future to predict the weather is a testament to the computer's lack of success as oracle. And whatever else computers may be, the last two items named in the paragraph above they are eminently not: neither brains nor thinkers. Not the game-playing, chatty WHOPPR of the movie *War Games*, but the so-called "souped-up adding machine" of *Colossus*.

For that, at a basic level, is what a computer really is: a souped-up adding machine. Deep within the guts of the thing, numerical quantities in the form of minute electrical currents are added, compared, and otherwise manipulated and evaluated. A variety of mechanical devices are plugged into these currents, set to respond in certain ways to certain voltage configurations as if to discrete arrangments of a set of on-off switches.

Indeed, in the most fundamental language of computers, there are but two words—"on" vs. "off," "one" vs. "zero"—it matters not how we characterize them. And all other possible meanings in the computer—from the cube root of pi to Elizabeth Barret Browning's *Sonnets from the Portuguese*—are built up from streams and streams of these electrical zeros and ones.

We could go further in our definition of a computer as an arithmetic machine. After all, what is arithmetic? Trust us, it boils down to a set of symbols with rules for manipulating them. So we can say that a computer is a machine that manipulates symbols according to a specified set of rules. What symbols, and what rules, are up to us.

This definition, like many, is so compact that it requires further explanation. There seem to be two avenues to pursue: the symbols being manipulated (also known as data), and whatever is doing the actual manipulation (also known as hardware). We'll look into the nature of computer data first.

Computer Language (the Data)

We implied earlier that computers manipulate data in the form of electric current. (Adding machines manipulate data in the form of positions of toothed wheels and levers.) Now, it's possible to construct computational devices in which data are represented as precise voltage values measured against some reference; such circuits are called *analog*. You could, for instance, represent the number 10 as a current of 10 millivolts. It's relatively straightforward to design a circuit that evaluates the voltage on two separate lines and outputs the sum of their voltages on a third line. However, such circuits tend to be slow and inflexible.

Instead, modern computers relay on *digital circuitry*. In digital circuits, all that matters is whether a current is actually flowing through a circuit. In order to represent numbers greater than one, we need to have more than one circuit.

One of the most fundamental decisions in computer design was how to put circuits together to represent data. (The question is largely settled now.) Since there were only two digits available (0 and 1, off and on), it was logical to choose a *base-2 number system*. This system is called the *binary system*, and operations within it are called binary arithmetic.

Our conventional number system, the one the Arabs copied from the Indians, is a base-10 system. There are 10 possible digits. A quantity is written as a string of digits, like 1990 or 14.95. By convention, each place to the left of the decimal point represents a succeedingly higher factor of 10, starting with 10^0 or 1. Thus, the string "1990" means $(1 \times 10^3) + (9 \times 10^2) + (9 \times 10^1) + (0 \times 10^0)$.

Still with us? Well, a string of binary digits represents increasing factors of 2. Thus, the binary number 1111b (we put a lowercase letter "b" after a binary number to indicate that it should be read as base-2, not base-10) means, in base-10, $(1 \times 2^3) + (1 \times 2^2) + (1 \times 2^1) + (1 \times 2^0)$, or $8 + 4 + 2 + 1 = 15$. So, $1111b = 15_{10}$.

Clearly, though, such a system depends on a reference point: the decimal point referred to above. In the long streams of binary digits that we implied exist within a computer, boundaries have to be marked so we know what factor of 2 each digit represents.

By the way, the term "*binary digit*" is somewhat cumbersome. It gets used so often in computer-talk that an abbreviation has evolved. A binary digit is now called a *bit*.

In the early days, computers worked with groups of binary digits (bits) referred to as *words*. The length of a computer word depended solely on the system and the whims of its manufacturer. Word-lengths still vary from system to system, although 32 bits is fairly standard. Now, 32 bits is quite a lot of data, more than is usually needed, as it turns out. So a smaller unit was settled upon, one of eight bits. This eight binary digit unit is called a *byte*. Simple arithmetic will show that a single byte is capable of representing base-10 numbers from 0 through 255.

All this is fine and dandy and quite enough if all you're ever going to work with is streams and streams of numbers. That's all the first computers ever did. They were built to solve some rather complex problems called differential equations. These problems can't be solved by moving symbols around, like you might solve the algebraic problem $2X + 1 = X + 3$. (The solution, of course, is $X = 2$.) These problems require lots of brute force calculation; essentially, you make a guess at the answer, do calculations to see how far off you are, make another, better guess, and so on until the amount of remaining possible error is small enough to ignore. (The very largest and fastest computers are used for the same purposes to this day. For example, the calculations now being done to determine whether carbon dioxide emissions are causing the earth's atmosphere to warm up—the so-called "greenhouse" effect—require solution of incredibly complex systems of partial differential equations. Billions of arithmetic calculations are needed, and it can take days to come up with an answer. Even then, the numbers are suspect because the grid being used to represent the Earth's surface and atmosphere is very coarse: on the order of one data point for every 10,000 cubic miles or so. No computer on Earth could handle the amount of data that would be required for a really good guess.)

In the early days, the sequence of steps used to solve a problem was wired into the structure of the computer. The flow of data from one problem-solving step to another was controlled via wires and clips. To change the sequence of steps, you had to unclip the wires and move them.

It didn't have to be that way, though. The same kind of switches used to do calculations can be used to control the flow of data from one calculation to the next. In fact, the instructions to do certain calculations can be treated like data themselves, given a suitable scheme for representing instructions like "add" and "compare" via bits and bytes. This was the origin of the stored program. A *program* is simply a sequence of steps, which, when followed in order, solves a given problem. A program can be represented as data and stored in a computer in binary form.

To do so, however, we need a convention for equating certain symbols, say "=", "+", etc., with patterns of bits. And if we're going to represent symbols in that way, why not the letters of the alphabet? The system that has emerged as standard is called *ASCII*: It stands for American Standard Code for Information Interchange. In the eight-bit version of ASCII, 256 symbols, characters, and even instructions to the system are represented by the 256 possible eight-bit binary numbers from 00000000b to 11111111b.

ASCII is a system of codes for both symbols and instructions. The original instruction set was used to control chattering teletype machines. For example, 00000111 rang a little bell; 00001101 returned the type carriage from its current position to the far left margin. Today, pressing the Return key on your Macintosh keyboard transmits this eight-bit message to the insides of your Mac.

It didn't take too long, by the way, for folks to figure out that working with binary numbers was cumbersome. In a world of bytes, base-10 is equally cumbersome. Logically, if we're going to be dealing with eight-bit sequences, we ought to try working with a number system that works on multiples of eight. There are two: *octal* and *hexadecimal*. Octal is base-eight, hexadecimal is base-16. Hexadecimal is more commonly used; and as you'll see it within the Norton Utilities (in particular, within the Norton Disk Editor), it's worth taking a look at.

For a base-16 system, you need 16 different digits. The world has chosen 0–9, A, B, C, D, E, and F. (The world has also chosen, for the most part, to designate hexadecimal numbers with a preceding dollar sign.) Thus, $F is the same as 15 in base-10, $A is 10, and so on.

It turns out that each group of four bits (a unit of data that is one half a byte, or a nibble, if you prefer) can be represented by one hexadecimal digit. So 00000111b becomes $07, and 00001101b becomes $0D. Hexadecimal is more compact and easier to work with, though it is still counterintuitive to those of us (which really means all of us) who learned to do arithmetic in base 10.

So data within a computer consists of current flowing in wires, more or less. The presence of current is taken to mean "1", the absence thereof means "0." A group of eight such current-bearing locations is called a byte, and is the fundamental unit of data. A code called ASCII equates the 256 different possible patterns of current in eight wires with 256 different symbols: commands, letters of the alphabet, and numerical digits. Data can also be interpreted as commands to the computer to perform certain operations—for example, adding two quantities together.

Well, now we know more about what's being worked on inside a computer and how it relates to the symbols we use in the everyday world. But what's doing the work, and how is it accomplished? As a software developer might say, that's a hardware problem.

Nuts and Bolts (the Data Processing Hardware)

Think about what you need to manipulate data. You need a place to put it, especially if there's going to be a lot of it. You need a way to get data into the computer and a way to get results out. And of course, you need something to do the calculating. Each of these parts has, over the years, acquired a name.

The heart and soul (if not brains) of a computer is the calculating engine, which has come to be known as the *central processing unit*, or CPU for short. The CPU is capable of performing a few dozen different operations on a small amount of data. The CPU of a modern personal computer (PC) consists of an amazing piece of complex circuitry called a *microprocessor* and some other support systems.

A microprocessor, of course, is some pretty intricate circuits traced onto silicon and packaged in plastic. Data and instructions are fed into a microprocessor via pins, which are small stiff wires sticking out of the plastic packing. The latest microprocessors deal with data in four-byte (32-bit) chunks.

The microprocessor-based CPU of a PC moves data into and out of storage. It has only a limited amount of data storage itself. The main data storage area of a computer is called memory. These days, we're concerned with three kinds of memory: random access memory, read-only memory, and long-term storage—usually disk memory.

Random access memory, or RAM, is the main working area of the computer while it's in action. Programs and data both are stored therein while the CPU does its work. It's called random access memory because the CPU can read in a chunk of any size it likes from anywhere in RAM by specifying an address. Each byte in RAM has a unique address. Now, since a byte of data can represent, at most, 256 different things, it takes a few bytes to specify an address in a large RAM area. In the case of a million bytes of RAM (a unit usually called a megabyte, abbreviated "meg" or MB), it takes two and a half bytes. A 32-bit CPU is capable of asking for any individual address out of more than 4 billion, however, which is how many storage locations that 4 bytes can reference.

RAM is also changeable. The CPU can read a piece of data from a location, modify it, and then store the new result in the same location. This changeability, however, has certain drawbacks. It makes RAM ephemeral, a quality known in computerese as volatility. To keep remembering a certain piece of data, RAM needs a steady, uninterrupted supply of electric current. If the current to a RAM circuit is interrupted, however briefly, all the data in it are is lost forever. Different kinds of physical materials can be used to make RAMs that are more or less volatile: the RAM in the Mac portable, for instance, needs only a very tiny amount of current to keep remembering.

There are some data, however, that a given computer system needs to remember permanently. There are only a handful of different microprocessors in use. It's much too expensive to design a separate one for each kind of computer. So the kinds of instructions that make each computer unique are stored in a special place called *read-only memory, or ROM*. ROM is non-volatile, meaning it still remembers even when the power is off. As its name implies, however, you can't store new data in ROM—you only read what's already there.

Clearly, a computer needs a storage area intermediate between these two, one that can be read from and written to and is also nonvolatile. On PCs these days, this kind of memory is supplied by disks. Floppy disks, or diskettes, are removable, plastic-housed disks with limited storage area. Hard, or fixed disks have storage media that are sealed into precisely machined enclosures; they can hold much more data than floppy disks.

Both kinds of disks store data as very small magnetized patches on a metal oxide surface. The surface rotates beneath a small detector, which senses the magnetism and converts it into pulses of current that the rest of the computer can read. This detector, called a read-write head, can also generate magnetic pulses and cause data to be stored on the media surface.

On most computers, quite a lot of system-specific instructions are kept on a special disk that must be made available to the computer whenever it is first started up. This special disk is frequently called a system disk. The process of starting up a computer from square one is called booting; this is short for bootstrapping, because the computer is conceived of as pulling itself up into operability by its own bootstraps, as it were.

The third major division of computer hardware, the devices to put data into the machine and get data out of it, are collectively called *I/O, for Input/Output*. Floppy disks, as you probably know, are really a form of I/O whereby relatively large quantities of data can be moved among different computers. Other typical PC input devices include keyboards and mice.

The computer's television screen, or *CRT*, is a major output device. CRT stands for cathode ray tube. In a CRT, a stream of negatively charged particles called electrons ("cathode rays," so called because they come from the cathode, or negative pole of the tube) is made to strike a phosphorescent (literally, "fire-bearing") substance painted onto the face of the tube. Wherever it is struck by electrons, the substance gives off light.

Because electrons are charged, their path can be bent by the application of a magnetic field. Special circuitry within a computer sweeps the electron beam across the screen and down by means of varying magnetic fields. Each sweep across the screen lays down a line called a *raster*. The electron beam can be interrupted, leaving some areas in a raster dark while others are lit. As rasters accumulate vertically, they build up the complete image. A typical electron beam paints the entire CRT screen in rasters several dozen times per second.

Other output devices include printers and plotters. Taken together, therefore, a CPU, storage such as RAM, ROM, and disks, input devices like keyboards and mice, and output devices like CRTs and printers constitute a typical personal computer system. Of course, we aren't really interested in the typical system; we're interested in the Macintosh. That's the subject of our next chapter.

Review

Computers manipulate symbols. These symbols are stored as strings of binary digits, or bits. For convenience, bits are grouped together in units of eight. Such a unit is called a byte. A special code equates the 256 possible values of a byte with 256 different symbols. Data stored in this form can be both quantities to be processed and the instructions for processing such quantities. Although byte values can be represented in binary, or base-2 notation, it is usually more convenient to represent them in hexadecimal, or base-16 notation.

The data-processing part of a computer system is the CPU, or central processing unit, which is where the actual arithmetic takes place. The CPU moves data into and out of memory, which takes the forms of random-access memory (RAM), read-only memory (ROM), and long-term storage (disks). Data is moved into and out of the computer as a whole via I/O devices, such as keyboards and CRT screens.

In Chapter 2, we show how each of these theoretical computer parts corresponds to a part of the Macintosh. After a brief refresher concerning the Macintosh user interface and Macintosh jargon, we talk about how data is manipulated within the Mac. We talk a little about the gross structure of Macintosh disks, in preparation for examing them more fully using the Norton Disk Editor, the subject of Chapter 4.

2

Macintosh Fundamentals

Introduction

Before we launch into any detailed discussion of the Norton Utilities for the Macintosh, it would be prudent to ensure that we're all up to speed on the ins and outs of the total Macintosh experience. For one thing, we're going to be using a lot of Macintosh-specific terminology in the chapters to come. So at this point, we're going to define and explain that terminology, for the benefit of those who may be novice Macintosh users, or may simply want to know more than they do.

What's more, to make the maximum use of the Norton Utilities, you need to know just a few things about how the Macintosh operates. In the last chapter, we introduced some computer fundamentals. Now, we relate those to the specific case of the Macintosh. First, however, let's look at what makes the Macintosh unique among personal computers: the Macintosh user interface.

Desktop Review

Apple has spent a large amount of time and money to make it as easy as possible for a computer novice to open the box in which his or her new Macintosh is so

11

lovingly cradled, read a well-labeled "Getting Started" booklet, plug everything together, and get going. One of the most useful things Apple has done in
its initial product documentation is to take the user through the important
features of computing a la Macintosh.

Thus, we presume that you have been introduced to basic Macintosh
operation and its associated terminology. Still, the topic is worth reviewing to
make certain that, for the purposes of this book at least, we're all on the same
wavelenth.

Mice and Icons

Probably the most notable of all the Macintosh's features is its *graphical user
interface*. This term for a picture-based display and control technology has now
become standard throughout the industry, and is usually referred to via its
initials, *GUI*. Many other computer makers have been scrambling over the last
few years to glom GUIs onto the top of their previous-generation, text-based
display technology. Each new GUI is briefly heralded as the product that will,
at last, bring other machines on par with the Mac. You know what happens next:
It doesn't work out that way. You can't wipe out Apple's six-year lead in
technology overnight. (It is worth noting that Apple did not invent the GUI, but
they did perfect it for the mass market.)

What goes into a GUI? Well, first of all, such an interface is metaphorical:
Each of its features tends to represent something else. Thus, files, which are
independent chunks of data usually corresponding to individual documents in
the real world, are represented by small, labeled pictures called *icons*. Each file
has its own icon. Similar files—documents created by a word processor, for
example—tend to have similarly shaped icons, to make it easy to sort them by
type.

Manipulating file icons in certain ways causes standard computer operations
to be performed upon the files themselves. Of course, this requires a way to
manipulate the icons. For one thing, you need a way to let the computer know
which icon you're talking about. The solution came with the invention of the
mouse. This small mechanical device sits next the computer and can be rolled
about. Doing so moves a pointer on the screen. This pointer is used to
manipulate icons. A mouse usually has one or more buttons. Pressing and then
releasing a button while the pointer is over a specific icon marks that icon in
some way. At this point, we've told the computer that we want it to perform an
operation on the file associated with that icon. What we haven't indicated is
what we want the computer to do.

On a character-based system, you have to type in commands to perform
actions, and then press a key to indicate that you've finished typing and want
the action performed. With a GUI, you use the mouse to point to a command.

Selecting the command in some way, usually by pressing and releasing the mouse button with the pointer over the name of the command, causes some action (example: duplicating a file) to be performed.

Names of commands that perform similar sorts of actions are generally grouped together. These groups of commands are called menus. Like a menu in a restaurant, one can select from them at will. Also like a restaurant, not every command is available at all times (like when they're out of shrimp cocktail). Commands that are currently unavailable are marked in some way.

The Mac, of course, has all these features: icons, mice, and menus. The Macintosh also has a central metaphor that organizes these features into a coherent whole: It's called the *desktop*.

The Macintosh desktop is conceived to be similar to the top of a working person's actual desk. This is the surface where one keeps things that one happens to be working with. For example, documents—it matters not what kind. Most people keep their working documents organized in manila file folders. The Mac desktop has file folders also. Folders may be put into other folders, or nested, just as manila folders may be put into hanging folders.

Most people have tools sitting on their desks, such as scissors, calculators, staplers, and the like. Sitting under the desk is frequently a trash can, into which documents that are no longer needed may be tossed. Before the trash is emptied by the cleaning crew, of course, it's possible to retrieve documents that you suddenly discover you need after all. Indeed, it's even possible, with heroic effort, to recover documents from trash that has been emptied. (That's what Norton UnErase is all about, but more on that later.)

The Macintosh has desktop tools also: They're known as *desk accessories*. They're called up via a special, desk accessory menu. Among other things, there is a calculator, a file-finder, and a keyboard map. (The Norton Utilities for the Macintosh include two desk accessories that replace the last two named items with much more useful and powerful ones.) And of course, there's a trashcan, via which files may be deleted. The trashcan is sometimes thought of as the most Macintosh-like feature of all. For one thing, Apple will sue the pants off anyone who includes a trashcan in their GUI as a metaphor for deleting files.

We also need a way to look into folders and files. This is done via *windows*. A window is an area that opens up onto the desktop and shows us the contents of whatever we've opened. If the window belongs to a folder, we'll see icons for the files that the folder contains. If the window belongs to a document, we see its data, such as the words in a letter or the numbers in a spreadsheet. Windows have controls that are manipulated with the mouse so we can adjust what we're seeing.

We've been talking about manipulating files via icons and windows, but we haven't been specific about what kinds of manipulations are available, and what they're called. Here they are. You probably know these terms already; this is just a review. Again, we absolutely need to all be speaking the same jargon.

Pointer: An arrow used to indicate choices.

Cursor: Sometimes used synonymously with pointer; refers specifically to the exact point where some action will be performed, usually within a document.

Click: Pressing and releasing the mouse button with the pointer positioned over something.

Select: To mark something, usually by clicking it. On the Macintosh, selected items are inverted; black becomes white and vice versa.

Drag: To mark and move something, usually an icon, by holding down the mouse button while the pointer is over it, and then moving the mouse with the button still held down. Dragging an item onto the top of a folder or the trash can will move the item into it.

It is also possible to select items by dragging. If you begin dragging over an unoccupied area, a rectangle appears and grows as you continue dragging. Any icon within the rectangle when you release the mouse button is then selected.

Open: The process of looking into a folder or file through a window. To open an icon, you click it twice in rapid succession. This is called double-clicking.

Application: A file that manipulates documents. So-called because each represents some way in which the Macintosh's features have been applied to the solution of a particular problem. Examples include word processors, spreadsheet generators, and the Norton Macintosh Utilities themselves. Opening an application to work within it is usually called launching.

This should do to go on with. Now that we know what kinds of things can be done within the Macintosh GUI, it's fair to ask, "What's doing the real work?" Let's look at the hardware.

Macintosh Nuts 'n' Bolts

In the first chapter we talked about CPUs, RAM, ROM, disks, and I/O devices. The Mac has all of these, of course. The exact way each is structured and used, however, makes the Macintosh unique. Come along and find out why.

CPU

The central processing unit, or CPU, is where all the computing work is done. Physically, the Mac CPU is housed within the main case of the computer. On compact Macintoshes like the Mac Plus, the SE, and the SE/30, the CPU is housed within the same enclosure that holds the CRT screen and the internal disk drive. On the modular Macintosh II line, the CPU is housed in the same box as the internal drive, the one into which you plug all other modules such as the keyboard, the CRT, etc.

The Macintosh CPU is microprocessor based, as are all personal computer CPUs. Macintoshes use microprocessors built by Motorola Corp. and belonging to that firm's 68000 series. There are different microprocessors in this series. They differ according the amount of data they can work with in one chunk (16 or 32 bytes), the speed at which they operate (faster is better, usually), and special features they may have—such as the ability to store several upcoming instructions directly within the microprocessor itself. (This is called instruction caching; it's one reason the Macintosh IIfx is such a screamer.)

Other devices in addition to the microprocessor make up the CPU. Not all such devices are present in all Macs, and we don't need to worry about them for this book's purposes. Suffice it to say there's more to the CPU than a 68000.

A Macintosh CPU is housed in a module of some sort, as we've said. It needs ways to communicate with other parts of the computer, of course. This is done via connectors called ports. Through these you sort-of "dock" another device with the mother ship, as it were. There are ports for both I/O devices and storage devices. We talk about these devices next. First, storage.

RAM, ROM, and Disks

The CPU needs a place to store data it's working with. Working data is stored in RAM. Currently, all Macs are shipped from the factory with at least eight million binary digits (bits) of RAM. Since bits are grouped into eight-member groups called bytes, that gives about a million bytes (or one megabyte) of memory. As we saw in the last chapter that one byte can be associated with one symbolic character via the code called ASCII, the minimum Macintosh has room to store a million characters of data. At five characters per word (the typist's average), and 250 words per page, that's the equivalent of about 850 typewritten pages, give or take a few dozen.

That's a lot, but not enough, especially when you consider that only a fraction of this RAM space is available for document data. The remainder is taken up with data and instructions that the Mac uses to maintain its interface.

Not all of the Mac interface is maintained in RAM, however. Indeed, most of the heart and soul of the Macintosh interface resides in ROM.

ROM, as we've learned, is memory that may be read from but not written to. It's used to store information that, among other things, pertains to the unique way in which a given brand of computer system operates. Almost all of the instructions to create and maintain icons, windows, and menus (among many other things) are stored in ROM on the Macintosh.

There are now two ROM types in the Mac world. Older machines have ROMs with a capacity of about 128 thousand bytes (128 kilobytes, also written 128K). New Macs have 256K ROMs. On new machines, ROMs are packaged in such a way that they are easy to remove and replace, making it possible to significantly modify the Mac interface in the future.

We've implied that RAM is not enough, when you've less than 800 pages to store stuff in. Worse, RAM is temporary; shutting off the power empties it. ROM doesn't help matters; it's simply a reference library that the computer can't add to. We need a place to store data for the long haul. On the Mac, this storage space is provided by data disks.

Macintosh floppy disks are the 3-1/2", plastic-shielded kind. Older Macs like the Plus can store about 800K of data on such a disk. Newer Macs can store up to 1.4 meg (1440K) on better-quality floppies. Floppies can be removed, of course, meaning you can have any number of them with different files stored on each. Even with 1.4-meg floppies, this gets tedious.

Every Mac sold now has a way to connect a larger-capacity disk storage device to it. We call these devices hard disk drives. They now come in quite a range of capacities: from about 20 megabytes on up to over 600 meg. There are other kinds of disk storage for the Mac, but we don't need to talk about them just yet.

We do need to talk more about Mac disks, as they are a critically important part of any Macintosh system and are the part that the Norton Utilities for the Macintosh are designed to protect and defend. However, we need to finish our discussion of Mac hardware, and talk some about Mac data, before we're ready to dive deeply into Mac disks, so we'll postpone that discussion for a while. Let's finish our tour of Mac hardware first.

Input and Output

Any computer is useless unless you can get data in and out of it. We've indicated that floppy disks can be used to move data into a computer, but of course there has to be a way to get data onto a floppy. And not everyone has a Mac, so we need ways to share our results without resorting to hardware. Well, we have ways to do these things.

The keyboard and the mice are two principal input devices. We've talked about the mouse already. The keyboard is like a typewriter, only instead of causing a piece of metal to strike a piece of paper, pressing a key on a Mac keyboard sends a byte of ASCII data to the CPU. There are other input devices, such as track balls (a nifty mouse replacement), tablets, etc.

While you're working, the main output device you deal with is the CRT screen. This is where the desktop appears. On small Macs such as the Plus and SE, the CRT is housed in the same enclosure as the CPU. On modular Macs, the CRT and the hardware that controls it must be purchased separately. The CRT sits in its own case, like a portable TV. The controlling hardware, contained on a circuit board called a card, is plugged into a slot inside the CPU case. Other Macintosh output devices include laser and dot-matrix printers (the LaserWriters and ImageWriters), pen plotters, video projection systems—the list goes on and on . . .

Summing Up

So that's what's doing all the work. Question still is, how is it being done? Before we can answer that, we have to look more closely at the form data takes inside a Mac.

Macintosh Bits 'n' Bytes

Macintosh data are held in ASCII format, as are the data of all other personal computers currently on the market. As we've seen, ASCII is a standard code that equates different byte values with *alphanumeric* (letter and number) characters and with a few special control codes.

So when you press a key on your keyboard, an ASCII code is transmitted to the CPU. Streams and streams of ASCII bytes are accumulated and stored in RAM. Still, streams and streams of bytes aren't necessarily useful. How do you keep last month's accounts separate from this morning's memoranda?

The solution is to group data into discrete units. These are called *files* in general computer-speak. There are two basic types of files: executable files and data files. Executable files are sometimes called programs; they are essentially sequences of instructions to the CPU intended to accomplish a certain set of purposes. On the Mac, we call them applications, as we've said.

The other type of files are called data files. These files contain the information that an application program accumulates in the construction of a useful piece of work. The numbers and formulas in a spreadsheet, the characters in a letter to your aunt, the picture elements (*pixels*) in a drawing; all these are data in a data file. Carrying the desktop metaphor still further on the Mac, we refer to data files as documents.

Actually, there is a separate class of executable files that are very important to the Macintosh. We call these system files, and they have a special icon of their own, one that resembles a compact Macintosh in outline. System files such as the Finder manage the desktop; they contain the broad instructions to do the actual work of drawing icons and windows, opening documents and launching applications, and the like. The system files as a whole are middlemen for you, the user, and your applications. Data that you input is passed through the system on its way to your word processor, or whatever.

(By the way, all computers have these kinds of files, ones that manage all activity on the computer. Collectively, they are sometimes known as the computer's operating system, or OS for short.)

For one thing, the system records everything that happens in a special area of RAM. This area is called the event queue. Keystrokes, mouse clicks, disk insertions—all these are *events* that the Mac keeps track of. In the case of mouse clicks, the Mac notes where the pointer was on the screen when the click occurred. Events are handed off to whatever application (including the Finder) or window happens to be *active*. You can tell which one this is by the horizontal lines at the top of the window. The topmost, or title bar area of an inactive window is blank except for its name.

Unlike the routines in ROM (which are used extensively by all applications and system files, of course; nothing like not having to reinvent the wheel, or more appropriately, the window), system files change quite frequently. Sometimes Apple Computer introduces new ones, like Multifinder a few years back or the files in System 7.0. Thus, they are kept on disk, where they can be replaced relatively easily simply by copying new files onto the top of old ones (or by inserting new information into the old files).

System files are so important that they are needed and called for as soon as the Mac starts. Indeed, it is not possible to boot the computer without them. Because of this, a special disk is needed, without which the Macintosh can't be started and used. And that brings us back to disks.

Macintosh Disks and Why They're Important

One of the first things a Macintosh does when you turn it on is to ask you for a disk. If there is no hard disk drive connected and no floppy disk inserted into a drive, a small icon of a floppy disk appears on the screen, with a flashing "?" in it. The Mac will sit like this until doomsday, unless a valid system, or *startup disk* is inserted.

A startup disk contains all the files that the Macintosh needs to get up and running and ready to open documents and launch applications. When a disk is inserted at startup time, the Mac checks to see if it contains the right files. If not, the disk is rejected and the Mac keeps waiting.

Disks, of course, have importance beyond serving as the repositories of the operating system files. For the vast majority of Macintosh users, disks are where all files are kept safe and sound; remember, RAM is not very useful in that regard (except on the Macintosh Portable and even there it isn't forever). Disks are where data are preserved and kept safe, and sadly, disks are where sometimes data are lost or corrupted.

Since disks are so important, and since the Norton Utilities themselves are mainly intended to work with disks and their data, we ought to look at them a little more closely.

Disk Basics

A data storage disk is very similar to magnetic tape like that inside a tape cassette, DAT, or VHS. To a plastic support surface, or *substrate*, is applied a fine powder of metallic oxide particles, which are made to adhere to the substrate with the appropriate chemistry. The difference is, a disk is a single circular piece of oxided plastic rather than a long ribbon. It spins round and round rather like a record or a CD.

As it spins, areas on the disk are carried past a fixed observer called the read/write head. This gizmo senses pulses of magnetism on the disk surface and converts them into electric current, which is passed on the rest of the computer system to be converted into data.

Just as with streams of data in the rest of the computer, an undifferentiated stream of magnetic pulses is not very useful; how do we know where one group of data begins and another ends? Disks are marked off into discrete segments, each of which is stamped with an address (vaguely similar to the way RAM is addressable byte by byte). In the case of disks, which are intended to store large amounts of data, the segments are comparatively large—on the order of 512 bytes. The process of laying down all these segments and readying a disk for use is called formatting, and it's important enough to warrant a section of its own.

Formatting

As they come from the factory, disks are more or less totally blank. It's the job of a particular computer system's operating software and hardware to ready the disk for use. Preparing a disk in this way is called formatting, and there are essentially two kinds thereof.

The more fundamental of the two is physical, or hard formatting. Hard formatting divides the disk into manageable data segments. Around the circumference of the disk, tracks are laid down, one inside another. Each track is made just wide enough to reliably hold a stream of bits. The better the equipment, the narrower the tracks can be. On an 800K disk there are 80 tracks on each side, starting at the inside and leaving off just short of the center.

Tracks in their turn are divided into segments called sectors. A sector is an arc of fixed length along a track. Sectors usually hold 512 bytes of data. In addition, a sector contains a brief header section, into which is recorded the address of the sector. In that way, the computer system can always tell what sector happens to be passing under the read/write head at any given moment. The header sort-of says "Hey! I'm sector number so and so." (By the way, all of this is covered in more detail in the *Disk Companion*, which accompanies Norton Utilities for the Macintosh.)

Whenever a file is recorded onto a disk, its data is written into one or more sectors. There's no splitting sectors between files, either. Because there are quite a number of sectors available (upwards of 1600 on an 800K floppy disk alone), we need a way of recording which sectors belong to what files. It would be tedious and time consuming to search through every sector as it passed to look for a particular file, like canvassing an entire neighborhood to find someone's house. Better to have a directory of some sort.

Mac disks contain several directory areas. The process of recording these areas onto a disk is another form of formatting, sometimes called logical, or soft formatting. It is even occasionally referred to as initializing, although Apple Computer itself is not consistent in how it applies this term. (Sometimes "initialize" is used to refer to hard formatting.)

The distinction between the two types of formatting is clear. Hard (physical) formatting is done to make a disk usable by a particular kind of hardware; 800K floppies and 1.4-meg floppies are formatted differently on the Mac. Soft (logical) formatting, on other hand, is done to make a disk usable by a particular kind of software—in this case, the Macintosh OS. All Macintosh disks are logically formatted in an almost identical way. And this way of creating directories and other file managment structures is so important, it warrants a chapter of its own. A long one.

Review

We've seen how the parts of a Macintosh correspond to the parts of any computer: the CPU, storage, and input/output devices. We've toured the Mac desktop, examined its central metaphor, and reviewed the definitions of a few key Macintosh operating terms. Finally, we looked more closely into Macintosh disks, their importance, and a little of their physical structure.

Now we're almost ready to examine the structure of Macintosh disks in detail, using the Norton Utilities for the Macintosh. Before we do that, we have to make certain that you've installed and configured the Utilities correctly. That happens to be the subject of the next chapter.

3

Installing the Norton Utilities for the Macintosh

Introduction

Before you can use the Norton Utilities for the Macintosh with a hard disk, you have to install and configure them. Perhaps you've done this already, perhaps not. In any event, we're going to review the procedure here. That way, we'll all be starting from the same place when we get to the important work in the next chapter.

Using the Installer

Installing the Norton Utilities for the Macintosh is not difficult; you could do it on your own without much trouble. You simply have to copy the various files included on the three distribution diskettes into the appropriate places on your hard disk. (Floppy-disk-only users see note below.) But no-brainer tasks like these are what a computer does best, so the entire procedure has been automated for you—without sacrificing flexibility, we might add. You can still pick and choose what parts of the Utilities to install and where to put them.

Floppy-Disk Users: If you do not have a hard disk, it may seem nonsensical to talk of "installing" the Utilities. There is, after all, not enough room on a 1.4-meg diskette (much less on an 800K one) to copy all of the Utilities and have any room left over for your System file, the Finder, etc. However, it makes eminent sense to install Norton FileSaver protection on your startup floppy disks. These are the System and (probably) Finder-containing disks you use to bring your computer to life. FileSaver, on the other hand, is an INIT (a small program that is run at startup time, and sits in RAM until you restart) that watches for certain actions, such as emptying the trash, and intervenes to take steps that safeguard data. You may also want to install the Norton desk accessories "FastFind" and "KeyFinder."

The installation program, aptly named "Installer," is contained, surprise, on the Installation diskette. Before we have you proceed, however, let's stop to make sure everything is in shape. Better a little advance preparation than having to interrupt the entire procedure to clean up a few details. What kind of details? We'll show you.

Advance Preparation

Before proceeding, you need to make sure that there is enough room on the disk or disks that you'll be installing onto. If you intend to install the whole shooting match, including the on-line help system, you need to have about 1.5 megabytes of space free on your hard disk.

If you don't intend to install everything (you have that option), you can get away with less room. How much less is impossible for us to predict, however, without knowing you personally. So we give the sizes of the different pieces of the Utilities and let you make up your own mind.

Module Name on Disk	Size
Norton Utilities main program (volume and file recovery, disk editor)	550K
Help	330K
Directory Assistance* (**Open...** dialog enhancer)	99K
DiskLight* (disk read/write indicator)	13K
Fast Find* (replaces Find File DA; faster; view, open files)	97K
FileSaver* (data protection INIT)	57K

KeyFinder*   32K
    (replaces Key Caps DA; easier; more features)
Layout Plus   57K
    (changes Finder desktop appearance, more)
Speed Disk   157K
    (disk optimizer, increases operation speed)

* Items marked with an asterisk are of special interest to users without hard disks. These must be installed on your startup disk(s) in order to function. All other modules may be run from the distribution diskettes or, better yet, from backup copies thereof.

When you've cleared off enough space, you next have to give thought to the number of desk accessories (DAs) you're currently running. You see, the current 6.0 and earlier series System only allows you to have 15 DAs, no more. If you already have 14 or 15 installed, you'll have to remove one or two using Font/DA Mover (a utility program included with Apple's system disks). Ideal candidates for removal are Apple's own Find File and Key Caps, which the Norton DAs will replace, and then some.

Removing DAs is fairly straightforward. You need to copy Font/DA Mover from Apple's System Tools disk to the startup disk that has the DAs you want to ditch. Double-click the Font/DA Mover icon to launch the utility. Make certain the **Desk Accessories** *radio button* is selected (not **Fonts**). The names of your DAs will appear. Click the name of the DA you want to delete and then click **Remove**. Repeat the procedure if necessary. Choose Quit from the File menu when you've finished. If you need more information, consult Apple's documentation.

One last thing. For safety's sake, it's best to work with copies of your Norton diskettes, rather than with the originals. If anything should go wrong, you'll have the orginal diskettes to go back to. This will save a call to Norton Customer Service and a few days while you wait for new disks to arrive.

Slide the write-protection tabs UP on all the distribution diskettes (the ones that came in the Norton box) if this hasn't already been done. Find three blank diskettes. Copy the protected disks as usual. One-floppy-drive systems will have to swap diskettes in and out. (To copy, make certain both floppy icons are visible on the desktop. One-drive users will have to eject one diskette using Command-Shift-1 before inserting the second diskette. Drag the Norton disk icon onto the copy disk icon. Follow the screen prompts.)

Copies made? Good. Put the originals away. You're now ready to go. Insert the copied Installation disk into an available drive. You'll see the Installer icon. Double-click it to launch the Installer. An introductory screen will appear.

Click the Yes button at the bottom right corner to proceed with installation. This is what you'll see (Figure 3.1).

The scrolling area (to scroll is to move up or down) to the left explains a little about each part of the Utilities; it has no other function. The area to the right explains the buttons at the bottom of the *dialog box*. If you want to know more, you can click Help to access a small help screen.

Above the buttons, a small legend indicates which drive the Utilities will be installed onto if you proceed immediately. It will feature the name of your startup disk unless you change it. Cycle among all available drives and disks by clicking the Drive button until the name of the appropriate drive appears.

If you want to install all the Utilities, click Install at this point. Follow the screen prompts the rest of the way and you'll be all set. Otherwise, you have some choices to make.

Making Choices

If you want to install only a portion of the complete Utilities (perhaps because you only want to install the DAs and the INITs on a startup floppy disk), click the Customize button on the screen shown in Figure 3.1. The following appears (Figure 3.2):

Notice on the screen (Figure 3.2) that all the items shown in the three major areas to the left are checked or marked in some way. Clicking on an item's name toggles its selection. Thus, to disable installation of the three applications in the Utilities (the main program, Speed Disk, and Layout Plus), click on each icon.

On the right of the screen are other controls. You can specify whether to install the on-line help and the color icon resources. On a black-and-white

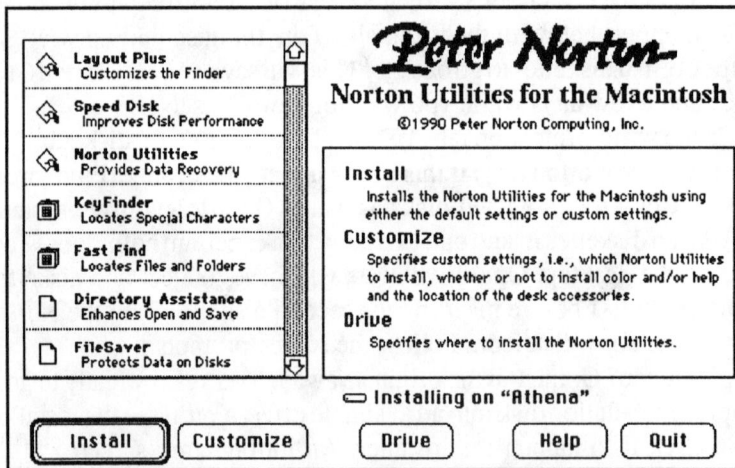

Figure 3.1 Norton Installer main dialog box

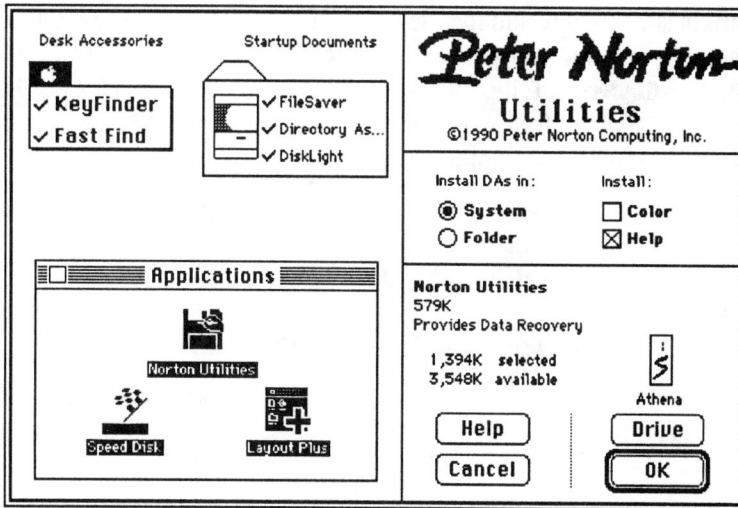

Figure 3.2 Customize dialog box from Norton Installer

system, the Installer senses the lack of color; this option appears unchecked. However, you may not want to install color even on a color system, to save room.

Finally, you have a choice as to how to install the desk accessories, if you'll be installing them. This applies only to users of so-called "resource optimization" applications such as Suitcase II. With Suitcase, you keep your fonts, DAs, etc. in folders; you don't have to install them into the System file with Font/DA Mover. If you choose to install DAs in this manner, you'll have to activate them later using the procedure outlined in your resource optimizer's documentation. Of course, even if you use a resource optimizer, you can install the DAs directly into the System file if you wish. Click the option you desire.

When you have the Installer configured like you want, including selecting the disk you'll be installing onto, click OK to proceed, and follow the screen prompts from there.

Getting Started with the Norton Macintosh Utilities

No matter how you install the Utilities, there are a couple of things you should do before you use them. In the following procedure, we're going to assume that you've installed everything.

First and foremost, you need to restart your computer using the startup disk onto which you installed the Utilities. Three of the Utilities—FileSaver, Directory Assistance, and DiskLight—are INITs. An INIT is a small program that runs at startup time and then remains in memory. It usually modifies your Macintosh's operation in some way. Used to be, INITs had to be installed directly into the System file, like fonts and DAs. Now, INIT files need only be present in the System folder of the startup disk. They are loaded into RAM as part of the normal booting procedure.

You can see that INITs are being loaded during startup, by the way, by looking at the bottom of your Mac's screen. Usually, an INITs icon is displayed as it is loaded. INITs are loaded in alphabetical order. FileSaver's INIT looks like a life preserver ring, Directory Assistance's like a highly miniaturized and modifed Open... dialog box, and DiskLight's like a disk drive.

Even after you've restarted, you're still not quite ready. There are a few more tasks to attend to.

Activating FileSaver

FileSaver installs a hidden protection file on all disks for which it has been activated. This file is used to make a backup of critical bookkeeping info. We'll be introduced to this information in the next chapter, where we'll also see why it's so very important. For now, suffice it to say that only one copy exists on each disk. Sometimes, that's not enough.

FileSaver is activated and controlled via the Control Panel, which is an Apple Desk Accessory. Choose Control Panel from the Apple menu. Find and click on the FileSaver icon in the scrolling area to the left. You'll see this (Figure 3.3):

Make certain the three radio buttons are clicked "On." You can set the value for saving files (bottom of screen) to any value you like up to Max (about 500), although the actual number of files protected will depend on how much free space you have on your drive(s). Click Save to install protection on the disk shown above the Drive button. You install protection on additional disks by (in the case of floppies) inserting them into an available drive and pressing Save. You can cycle among available disks with the Drive button as well and install protection on each.

Once installed, FileSaver updates the protection file every time a disk is ejected or the entire system is shut down. It also is activated when you delete a file. You can see when it's working; the pointer briefly changes into a small life-preserver ring.

Oh, and another thing . . . .

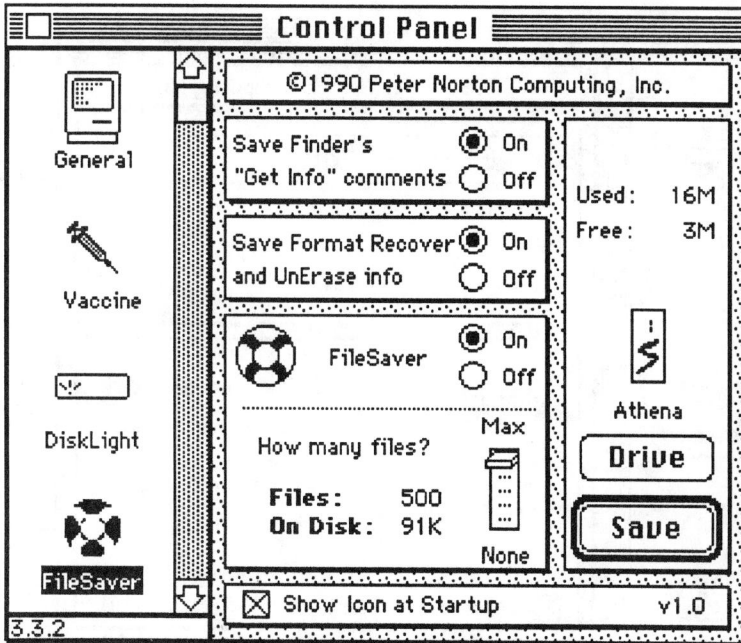

Figure 3.3 FileSaver control panel device

Using DiskLight

DiskLight is another INIT that you activate via the Control Panel. DiskLight is not critical or important or flashy, merely convenient. With DiskLight active, a small icon of a disk flashes at the far left or right (your choice) of the menu bar whenever a disk is being read from or written to. When information is being written onto a disk, a small letter "w" appears below the DiskLight icon.

Why should you care? Well, suppose you notice that your disk is being written to, without your having done anything to cause such action. This may be a clue that something nasty is going on; something like a virus, for instance. Sometimes you can intervene before something dreadful happens.

To activate DiskLight (once it's been copied to your System folder and you've restarted your Macintosh), choose the Control Panel from the Apple menu and then click the DiskLight icon in the scrolling area at the left. DiskLight's control area is shown in Figure 3.4.

Starting DiskLight couldn't be simpler: Just click the radio button corresponding to the position where you want the light to appear. Click the close box to proceed.

Now you're really all set, right? Yes, unless you feel like you now want or will soon be needing some additional help. To that end, let's introduce the

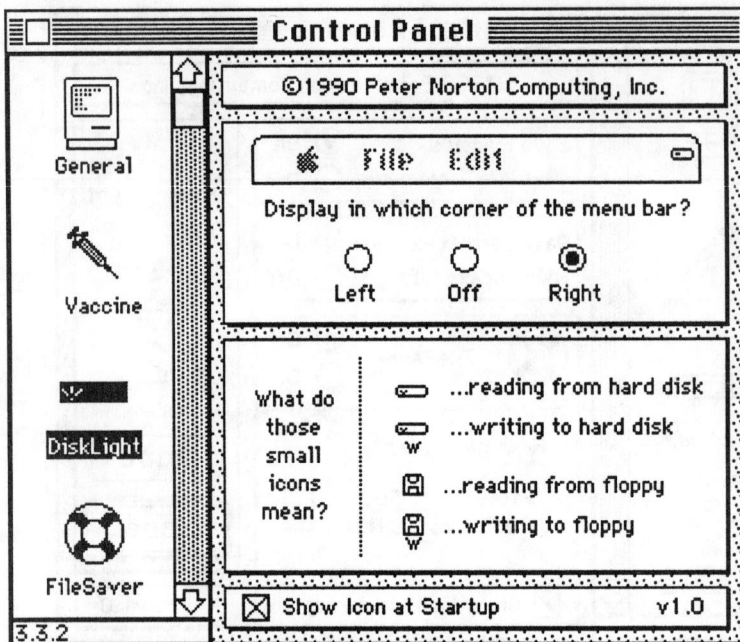

Figure 3.4 DiskLight control panel device

Norton Utilities for the Macintosh on-line help system before we review this chapter.

Getting Help

A pretty sophisticated, hypertext-like help system is available within all of the Norton applications. These include the main program (Disk Doctor, UnErase, Format Recover, Disk Editor), Speed Disk, and Layout Plus. To access help while you're working with any of these applications, choose Help from the Apple menu. The help window appears as shown in Figure 3.5. The Help has some pretty nifty features. Most of it's controls are arrayed across the top of the window.

Topics: This returns you to the Topics screen, which is shown above. When you position the pointer over a topic's name, it changes into a small representation of a magnifying glass. Clicking at that point takes you to a screen with information on the selected topic.

Glossary: A screenful of terms. Click on a term to see its definition.

```
┌─────────────────────────────────────────────────────────┐
│ ▤ □ ▤▤▤▤▤▤ Norton Utilities Help ▤▤▤▤▤▤ ▣▣ │
├─────────────────────────────────────────────────────────┤
│  ┌───┐  ┌───┐   ⇦    ⟲    ⇨   ┌────┐  ┌────┐            │
│  │📁 │  │ A │                  │ 📖 │  │ 👁 │            │
│  │   │  │ Z │                  │    │  │    │            │
│  └───┘  └───┘                  └────┘  └────┘            │
│  Topics Glossary              BookMarks  See Also        │
├─────────────────────────────────────────────────────────┤
│                       Topics                              │
├─────────────────────────────────────────────────────────┤
│         Utilities:  Norton Utilities (Main Menu)    ⬆    │
│                     Norton Disk Doctor                   │
│                     Norton Disk Editor             ▓    │
│                     Format Recover                 ▓    │
│                     Speed Disk                     ▓    │
│                     UnErase                        ▓    │
│                     Layout Plus                          │
│                                                          │
│  Desk Accessories (DAs):  Fast Find                      │
│                     KeyFinder                            │
│  Startup Documents (INITs):  Directory Assistance  ⬇    │
│                     File Saver                           │
│                     DiskLight                      ▣    │
└─────────────────────────────────────────────────────────┘
```

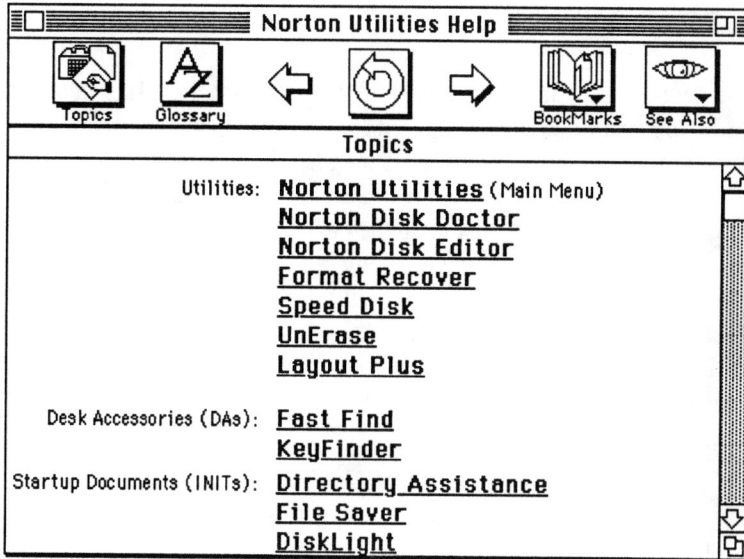

Figure 3.5 Norton Utilities on-line help

The center three buttons take you back in the topic list, cycle through all the screens you've been through, and take you forward, respectively.

Bookmarks: These are really neat. If you click and hold the mouse button with the pointer on this button, you'll see a menu of topics, and also the items Set and Clear bookmark. When you find a page with information you will want to return to, you can choose Set Bookmark and then a number. The bookmark will then appear in the menu.

See Also: There may be other topics of interest related to the one you're currently perusing. If you press and hold this button, you'll see a list of topics relevant to the one you're currently viewing.

If you see a term on a topic screen that you want to know more about, move the pointer over it. If the pointer changes into a magnifying glass, information is available on that term. Click directly on the word to see information about it. To return to the topic you were previously examining, click the cycle button at the very center of the button area.

If you want additional help with the Help, click the last topic on the Topics screen: "How to Use This Online Help." You may have to scroll down to see it. (Click the lowermost arrow on the scroll bar until it appears.)

Now you know everything you need to know to get started with the Norton Utilities for the Macintosh. What do you know? Let's review and find out.

Review

We've seen how to install the Norton Utilities for the Macintosh using the Installer application on the so-named Installation disk. We made certain there was enough room (approximately 1.5 meg) on the target startup disk(s) and that there were fewer than 14 active desk accessories on that disk.

We showed you how to install all the parts of the Utilities and how to choose which parts to install. Finally, we showed how to activate certain parts of the Utilities, in particular the very important FileSaver INIT. We looked at the on-line help system, in case questions arise in the future.

At this point, you're ready to find out even more about the Macintosh that you saw in Chapter 2. This time, however, we're going to use the Norton Utilities to do it.

4

Behind the Scenes

Part One: Exploring the Mac with the Norton Disk Editor

We know your type. You're the inquisitive sort: the kind of person who wants to know "what's going on in there?"—the kind of person who buys a book entitled *Inside the Norton Utilities for the Macintosh*. Now in the preceding chapter, we took you through the basics of Macintosh operation, more to make sure we were all speaking the same language than anything else. In this chapter, we attempt to satisfy your curiosity about what makes it all tick by taking you inside a Macintosh disk. In the process, we introduce you to the Norton Disk Editor, one of the tools included with the Norton Utilities for the Macintosh.

If you'd like to follow along with your Mac, launch the Norton Utilities. When the Main Menu screen appears, choose **Norton Disk Editor** from the **Utilities** menu. You'll be asked to specify which volume to explore; choose your current system disk. Now you're all set. (We'll explain a little more about what you see on your screen later, after we've covered some background material.)

Background

Previously, we talked a little about disks. (This subject is also covered in the *Disk Companion* booklet that accompanies the Norton Utilities for the Macintosh.) Now it's time to go into more detail, exploring how that information—documents, applications, etc.—is organized. Disk organization is vitally important: Even slight damage can render all the data on a disk inaccessible.

Consider this example. Suppose someone asked you to retrieve an important document from a locked filing cabinet. All you know for sure is where the filing cabinet is located; you don't know where the key is, or anything else. So you go to your department's administrative assistant, that underpaid font of all knowledge, intending to ask "Ellen, can you get me such-and-such document from the files?" Alas, this usually reliable person took the day off. Dejected, you go the filing cabinet, thinking "Perhaps a crowbar . . ."

All is not lost. Knowing that someone might need to get into the files, Ellen has left a typed note taped to the first file drawer. It says "If you need to get into the files, ask Personnel for the key."

You obtain the key and unlock the files. You find drawer after drawer jammed with documents in folders, each folder labeled with a number. Great. How do you find the document you want? You could look through every folder, but it could take hours if not days to find the right document. What you need is some sort of directory that explains what the numbers mean and how to find files using them.

As luck would have it, the first folder in the first drawer is marked "Directory." Looking within, you see that each folder number refers to a specific client. You remember that these numbers are established by Accounting to aid with billing; each new client is assigned a specific number. Your department also references specific projects by client-number.

You happen to know which client is referred to in the document you've been asked to find. You look up the client's name in the directory list and find the correct number. Looking at the labels on the front of the file drawers, you can see that the file you want is in the third drawer. You open the drawer and find the appropriately labeled hanging file. There are actually three, each containing a great many manila file folders. Finding the document you want could still be time-consuming if you had to look through every folder.

But you don't. At the front of the first hanging folder is a list associating individual projects done for that client with project numbers. Each manila folder is marked with such a project number. You know what project the required document refers to, so you look up the project name in the list. Armed with the project number, you select the correct folder. In less than a minute of searching you find the document. Leaving a placemarker to show that you're currently using the document, in case someone else comes looking for it, you close the files and return to the boss triumphant.

This thought-exercise demonstrates more than just the importance of administrative assistants and well-organized files. It also shows what kind of information is needed, and where it, in turn, needs to be stored for a basically ignorant person to be able to use the filing system.

The organization of information on a Macintosh disk is conceptually very similar to the filing-cabinet example just discussed. Your documents and applications (files) are referenced by name and by folder number. A highly structured set of directories keeps track of this information. A special area at the very front of the disk acts as a "key" to all the remaining information on the disk, be it an 800K floppy or a 600-meg hard disk.

Disk Structure

When you start up your Macintosh, it's in the same position as a person confronted with a locked filing cabinet. Your startup disk, whether it's a floppy or a hard disk, contains information that your Mac has to find before it can start: for example, the location of a valid System file and Finder. Your Mac, however, knows where to find the key to your startup disk. It's called the *boot blocks*, and it's found at the very beginning of the disk.

Recall from Chapter 3 that we described the process of starting a computer from nothing as booting, which is short for bootstrapping. The ROMs in your Mac contain much of the program code that is used in this process. Past a certain point, however, your Mac needs additional information that is not stored in the ROMs. Apple wisely kept a large portion of the Macintosh operating system separate from the ROMs; it's stored on disk instead. Rather than replacing the unmodifiable ROMs (read *only* memory, remember?) to update the System, you copy a new version to a startup disk. It's much easier to update that way. Imagine having to crack open the case every time you wanted to update the System file.

However, when your Mac first starts it doesn't know where the System file is. There are many things about the current startup disk that it doesn't know and can't assume at first. Think of all the different kinds of disk drives there are available. There are 400K floppies (still), 800K and 1.4-meg floppies, SCSI hard disks from 20 meg on up, Write Once Read Many (WORM) optical drives, CD-ROMs, and even fully erasable Optical disks. You'll recall we mentioned physical formatting in the last chapter. Well, each of these disks can have a slightly different physical formatting structure—the size of the smallest chunk of space available on the disk, for example. (This chunk is called an allocation block, by the way.) Your Macintosh needs to know all this before it can finish booting. The information it needs to unlock the startup disk is found beginning with the boot blocks.

Return to the Disk Editor for a moment, if you're running it. We promised we'd explain a little about the interface before we used it; now's the time to do it.

When you've chosen a volume to explore (Volume means disk, in general), you're presented with a window containing a hierarchical view of the files and folders on your disk. At the top of the window are buttons. Pressing one while a file or folder name is selected activates a particular function.

As with all Macintosh applications, the Disk Editor's menus are found along the menu bar at the top of the screen. The one most important to this chapter is the **Objects** menu, which contains commands to view the various parts of a Macintosh volume. These parts come up in windows separate from the directory window.

Choose **Boot Blocks** from the **Objects** menu. You should see something similar to the screen shown in Figure 4.1. Note that the information shown is contained in *absolute* sector 0; that is, the very start of the physical disk. Measurements made relative to the physical disk are called absolute measurements. Sometimes it's convenient to refer to another beginning point, say, the start of a second partition. The distance between the physical beginning of a disk and the start of (in this case) a second partition is called the volume offset. Offset is a handy concept to remember. You'll see it pop up in several places. For example, the difference between your current position within a file and the file's beginning is also called the offset. It's shown in the Figure 4.2.

Note also that the information shown in Figure 4.1 is in a neat, organized fashion, with explanations of each item. This is *not* the way this information is stored; the labels and interpretations are supplied by the Norton Disk Editor. To get a better idea of what the hard disk version of the data really looks like,

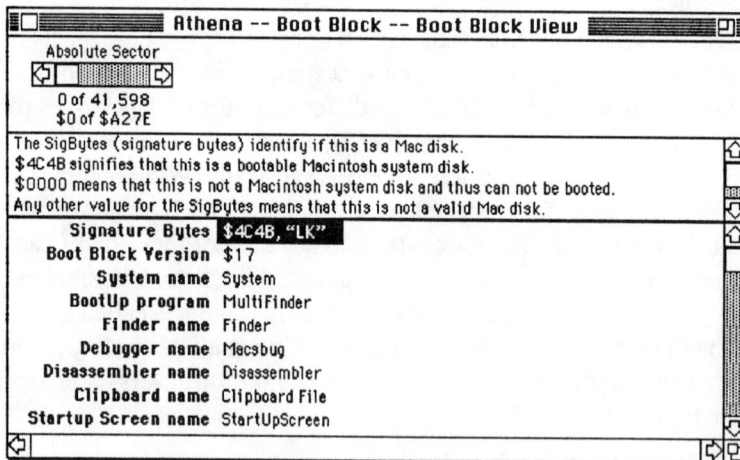

Figure 4.1 Boot Blocks on hard disk Athena (interpreted)

choose **View in Hex** from the **Display** menu. You'll see something like this Figure 4.2.

The rows of hexadecimal digits (0–F) are simply convenient ways to represent the long strings of 0's and 1's that are actually present. Recall from Chapter 2 that each byte (eight bits) of storage within the computer disk can be represented by two hexadecimal digits. Thus, "11111111" in binary is the same as "FF" in hexadecimal, and "01100001" is the same as "61". To the far right, next to the four columns of hexadecimal data, is an ASCII interpretation of that data. Remember that ASCII associates a single alphanumeric character or control code (e.g., "a" for **Return**) with each of the 256 possible values a byte can represent. $FF stands for the diacritical mark "˝". This is ASCII character 255 (numbering starts with 0, not 1). $61, on the other hand, stands for the lowercase letter "a".

All data on a computer are stored this way. The labels are not provided because they're understood. The computer expects to find data of a certain kind at specific locations on a disk or within an individual file on that disk. There are no marks to tell where one piece of data leaves off and another begins. The length has either been settled beforehand (i.e., the affected program knows how much data to retrieve) or is stored as part of the data.

We humans have a limited ability to look at data in the same way. For example, if we told you that 1015551234 was a United States telephone number, you'd be able to pick out the area code, even though it isn't separated out. It's 101, of course. Likewise, many people can look at a zip code, say 87501, and say what part of the country it refers to (in this case, the Southwest).

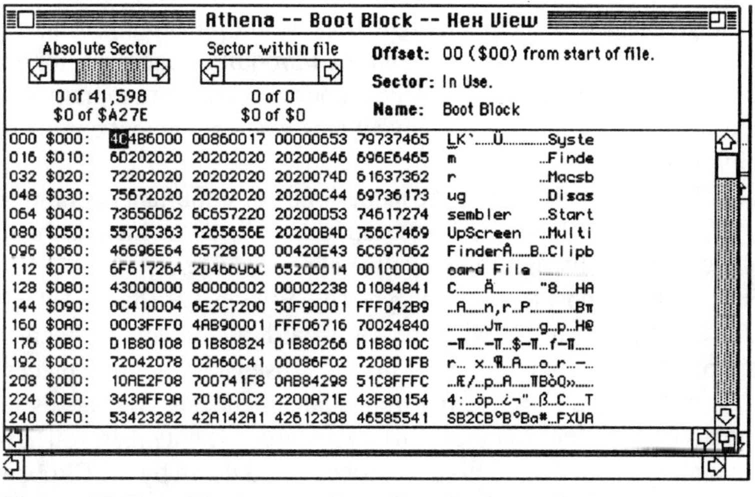

Figure 4.2 Boot Blocks on Athena (hexadecimal view)

The difference is, a computer looks at nothing but long strings of numbers, much longer than we ever encounter. In a way, it's like trying to read a book in which there is not only minimal punctuation, but no spaces between words. Worse than Proust, by far.

Fortunately for us, the Norton Disk Editor knows as much (or more) about the long streams of data on a disk as the Mac does itself. We can rely on it to interpret things for us.

So what does it all mean? For that, we switch back to the interpreted view. (We call this feature AutoView.) Choose **View As... Boot Blocks** from the **Objects** menu. You're returned to a view similar to that shown in Figure 4.1.

First, your Mac wants to know if this disk is usable by a Macintosh. The very first bytes on the disk—the *signature bytes*—tell it so. These are shown at the top of the boot blocks display. A value of $4C4B means the disk is supposed to be a valid Macintosh system disk. A value of $0000 means the disk is formatted for Macintoshes but isn't a system disk. If the Mac finds any other value here, it rejects the disk: A floppy disk is ejected, a hard disk ignored.

Once your Mac has determined whether it can work with the disk, it wants to know more. It needs to know, for example, what version of the bootstrap code is being used. This number tells the Mac whether to use the program code in the boot blocks or in ROM. With 256K ROMs, most of the bootstrap code is in ROM, although the operating system can be told to ignore the ROM code and use the bootstrap code in the boot blocks.

The boot blocks also tell your Mac the name of the operating system file ("System"), the name of the Finder program, and the name of the startup program (in this case "MultiFinder"). Note that the Macintosh does not automatically assume the names of any of these important operating files, even though they've all been an integral part of the Macintosh for years—in the case of the System and the Finder, right back to the beginning. This provides flexibility for the future. It's been rumored for quite some time, for example, that Apple is thinking of replacing the Finder with another program. Under the current setup they can do so and give it a new name, without confusing older Macintoshes.

Your Macintosh also learns the names of other important operating system files from the boot blocks on the startup hard disk. These include the name of the debugger, the disassembler, and the clipboard file.

Fine, we now know their names, you say. But what are they? Actually, you should be fairly familiar with the Clipboard file if you've been using a Macintosh for any length of time. This file is used to store those pieces of text or graphics that you **Cut** or **Copy** from a document. The Mac needs space on disk to store these pieces, as they can be very large. (Remember, you have more disk memory than RAM.) This disk space is held down by the Clipboard file.

Your Mac simply needs to know the exact name of this file in order to find it when it needs to store a cut or copied piece of information.

The other two items are of interest mainly to software developers. A debugger, for instance, is a programming tool that allows you, among other things, to verify the contents of any location in RAM, check the values contained within the CPU's memory registers, and the like. You can also "step" through a program, running it one line at a time. In this manner, you can discover exactly what is causing the nasty bug that prevents your long-labored-over program from being a salable commodity.

Several different debuggers are available, with different sets of features. Most can be set to "jump in" whenever a program crashes, showing the contents of memory and the exact place where your Mac gave up. The debugger can also be accessed at any time by pressing the rearmost of the two "programmer's switches" on the left side of the Mac—the ones we're told not to install unless we know what we're doing. In any case, your Mac needs to know the name of the debugger it's going to be using (even if it's just the debugger built into ROM); so that vital piece of data is stored in the boot blocks.

The disassembler is a trickier and more arcane feature and one that is rarely used. Suffice it to say that a disassembler can take the *machine code* capable of being run by a computer (and which looks like long strings of numbers and characters—remember the hexadecimal view of the boot blocks we looked at earlier?) and turn it into *assembly code* that can be read (and perhaps understood) by a human being. This has its uses (the most famous being rather unscrupulous), so the Mac wants to know the name of a disassembler at startup time. Most systems don't actually have a disassembler installed.

By the way, if you're curious about any item shown on the Norton Editor's object view screen, click on its name to select it. The legend above changes to an explanation of the currently selected item.

The Mac also looks for the name of a startup screen, if any. This screen is shown just after the "smiling Mac" that appears during startup, after the Mac has found a valid system disk to boot off of. Usually, it's just the "Welcome to Macintosh" screen with the Picassoesque lineart representation of a Mac. However, you can substitute any other Macintosh graphic, provided it's in the correct format. The application Superpaint, for example, will save graphics in "startup screen" format, and will allow you to edit them, also. Using the Norton Disk Editor, you can then change the name stored in the boot blocks under "Startup Screen" to the name of your graphic. As long as a graphic with the correct name and format is stored in the system folder, it will be displayed at startup. (Using the Norton Disk Editor to actually modify data can be tricky at times. We show you how to do so in a later chapter, by which time you should know enough to make direct data editing far less risky. Just changing the name of the startup screen, however, won't cause any problems.)

The remainder of the information stored in the boot blocks is fairly technical and of limited interest. The value stored for MaxFiles indicates how much memory should be set aside for the *File Control Blocks (FCBs)* that are used to keep track of open documents. FCBs are stored in RAM. Each contains, among other things, the exact location of the file on disk, the current position in the file (this is like a bookmark), and so on.

The Event Queue size value tells the Mac how many events—keystrokes and mouse-clicks—to remember at once. You see, the Macintosh stores every keystroke that you type and every mouse-click that you press in a memory location called the Event Queue. Events are stacked up one after another in the order in which they are received. Programs such as your word processor check the event queue to find out what they should do next. If a word processor sees a keystroke in the queue, it will enter the character associated with it at the current insertion point in your document. If it sees a mouse-click, it will check to see where on the screen it happened, perhaps executing a menu command (if you chose one).

The value in Event Queue size determines how far ahead you can type (or click) while your Mac is doing something else before characters start to be lost. Generally, about 20 events can be stacked up in the queue before the oldest ones get pushed off and forgotten. Fast touch-typists have discovered that, if they start typing while the Mac is busy elsewhere—say, saving a document—they're apt to lose the first several characters they typed. It's best to wait and take a sip of coffee while the watch-cursor is on.

Finally, the Mac learns from the boot blocks where the actual bootstrap program code begins and what it contains. In our example (Figure 4.3), the bootstrap code begins at memory location 8Ax, or 138 in decimal notation. You can switch the view of the boot blocks in the Norton Editor to Hex View as we did before if you'd like to see what the boot code looks like.

Next Things Next

After reading the boot blocks, your Mac knows much about your current setup, but it still doesn't know enough: not enough for you to begin working, in any case. The information it needs is specific to the particular disk volume being used as startup disk and is contained, curiously enough, in the volume info block, which immediately follows the boot blocks on a nonpartitioned hard disk.

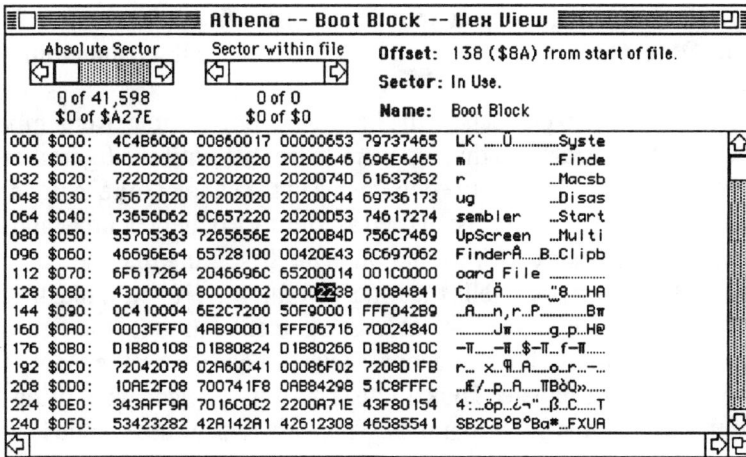

Figure 4.3 **Boot blocks with cursor set at beginning of bootstrap code**

▼ Partitions

Just as it's more convenient to divide up a large filing cabinet into a number of drawers, it's sometimes easier to work with a large hard disk if it has been *partitioned* into a number of disk *volumes*. Recall from the last chapter that we briefly touched on the difference between physical and logical formatting (this information is also covered in the *Disk Companion*). Partitioning is a form of logical formatting. It divides a single hard disk into a number of volumes. A volume is a logical entity, which the Macintosh operating system treats as if it were a separate disk. You could, in principle, partition a single 100-meg hard disk into one 40-meg volume and two 30-meg volumes. Each would appear on the desktop with a separate name and icon. Each disk volume has its own volume info block and directory information. Damage to this information can render data inaccessible; thus, partitioning is a way of protecting data on a large hard disk: Damage to the directory information for one volume will not affect other volumes. In this case damage is limited to a single volume on the disk. Having partitions can also speed up your computing on a large hard disk, if you organize your data well. You could place all your applications on your startup volume, and keep other volumes for documents. When searching for a particular document, you need only look at the appropriate volume (if you organize, say, by project), rather than at the entire disk. The time savings can be significant when using small partitions on a very large disk.

If you're following along at your Macintosh, choose **Volume Info Block** from the **Objects** menu in the Norton Disk Editor. You'll see something similar to Figure 4.4.

The volume info block acts as the key to the disk volume. Remember from our filing-cabinet example that we were in trouble until we figured out what system had been used to file the documents in the cabinet? We learned that all documents in the cabinet had been filed according to Client number and Project number. Well, this kind of information is the first thing that the volume info block (VIB for short, ok?) tells the Mac. (By the way, if you'd like to see how the information really looks—or at least close enough to it—you can choose View in Hex from the Display menu as we did earlier for the Boot Blocks.) Notice the first line, labeled **Disk Type**. This tells the Mac what filing system has been used for this particular disk. There are two, although one is virtually extinct.

When the 128K Macintosh was introduced in 1984, files on its 400K diskettes were organized by the Macintosh Filing System (MFS). This "flat" filing system was like a filing cabinet with a fixed number of storage folders already built in—in this case 128. Thus, MFS could keep track of 128 folders, applications, and documents, which of course was far more than you could get onto a single 400K disk.

It didn't take adventurous types very long to hack into Steven Jobs's closed machine. They quickly discovered how to connect a hard disk via the serial ports (the connectors for modem and printer), a possibility that Jobs had rejected. Almost immediately, folks discovered that 128 files wasn't nearly

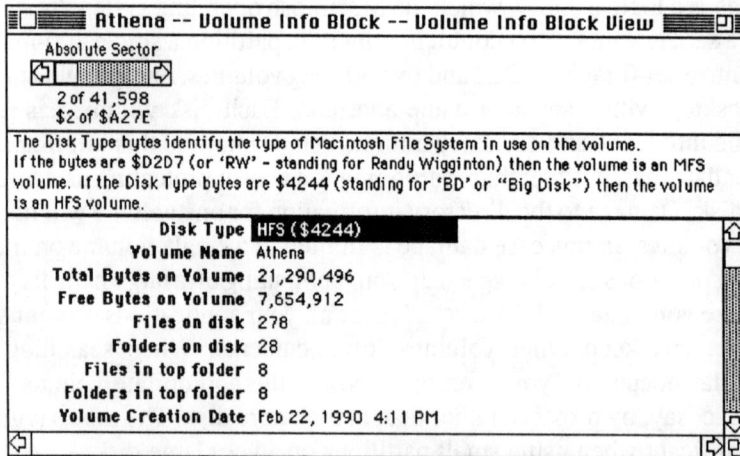

Figure 4.4 Volume Info Block on hard disk Athena (interpreted)

enough on even a 5-meg hard disk, and that trying to store more than that invariably resulted in bad system crashes. Usually, all folders were lost.

In the meantime, Apple had a change of heart (and eventually, of course, a change of helmsman). By adding a Small Computer Systems Interface (SCSI) port to the Macintosh Plus, they made it possible to easily connect a hard disk drive to the machine. With the new machine came a new filing system, called HFS. This Hierarchical Filing System promised to keep track of a near-limitless number of files, and to make it faster to find them, too. We'll look at HFS in more detail when we examine the directory information stored by a Macintosh disk volume—specifically, the catalog and extents b-trees, which keep track of the exact location on disk of each file or piece thereof.

Thus, the first bytes in the VIB tell the Mac whether the volume in question is MFS or HFS. Only the old 400K floppies are formatted MFS. The Norton Utilities for the Macintosh are not designed to work with MFS disks, so we won't discuss them any more.

As you can see, the VIB provides quite a bit of information about the disk volume being examined, starting with its name. Also shown are the volume's exact size in bytes. You may find it interesting to note that, in the case of hard disks, this value will not be the same as what you were told when your disk was sold to you. The (small) 20-megabyte hard disk used in this example actually contains almost 21.3 megabytes of usable space. Even if you multiply 1024 bytes x 1024 bytes (which is how much a megabyte really is—slightly more than a million) times 20, you only get 20.9 meg. Thus, we've got 400K for free here. As it turns out, most hard disks contain more than the advertised amount of space in order to make up for any damaged (and therefore unusable) areas that the disk may have at the beginning or acquire through service. The actual disk media on which information is stored is by far the cheapest part of the whole drive. It doesn't cost the manufacturer much to throw in a little lagniappe. That little bit is an investment in customer goodwill: Wouldn't it tick you off to discover that your 40-meg hard disk only had 39 meg of useful space?

The VIB also indicates how much of the volume's space is free, that is to say, not currently occupied by files. Also shown are how many files and folders are currently stored on the disk. A count is maintained of how many files and folders are contained within the top folder (the window that opens when you double-click the volume's icon). We refer to this folder sometimes as the disk window.

Other useful information includes the date the volume was created (initialized). Initialization prepares a disk volume for use. During the process, the essential bookkeeping areas discussed in this chapter are created and set to their initial (first) values, hence the term initialize. Sometimes the term format is used interchangeably with initialize (even Apple, in its documentation, does so), but strictly speaking the two are not the same. Formatting is a lower-level process that prepares a disk surface for use by a particular operating system. Most hard disks come pre-formatted, meaning they are ready for the Mac to use.

Warning about formatting: Low-level formatting destroys all information on a disk. The **Erase Disk** *command in the Finder's* **Special** *menu will do this to a floppy, although it merely initializes a hard disk without destroying data. Most hard disks come with a utility program that also destroys data in the process of preparing a volume for use. There is no way on Earth to recover data from a disk that has been formatted with such a program. It's best not to use this kind of utility unless the disk you've selected for formatting contains no useful data.*

Other information that the VIB knows about the current disk volume includes the date it was last modified. Modification means creation or deletion of a file or folder, anything that causes the disk volume to be written to (i.e., have information recorded on it). Deleting or erasing information also involves writing, as zeros are written in the place of the previously recorded bookkeeping information for a deleted file.

The VIB also knows the date the disk volume was last backed up. Which reminds us: The example hard disk, Athena, is in sore need of a backup. We shan't launch into a sermon about backups just yet, but do remember: A reliable and current backup is your last line of defense against data loss, which can range in tediousness from merely annoying to financially ruinous, depending on what's lost and what you meant to do with it. If nothing else, keep important documents backed up onto floppies (that's what we did with the working documents for this book) and keep the original disks for all your software locked and stored safely. (To lock a diskette, slide the small tab in the upper left corner of the diskette's back **up**.) A small icon representing a lock appears on the far left of the status bar in a locked diskette's window, as shown in Figure 4.5.

Back once more to our program: Again, if you choose the **View in Hex** command from the **Display** menu, the interpreted view of the data in the VIB changes to a hexadecimal view of the "raw" data. Probably the only thing you'll recognize is the ASCII representation of the volume's name. Well, it may all look like Greek to you, but it's Gospel to the Macintosh.

Now, a value of particular interest in this Gospel according to Macintosh is the Allocation block size. You see, the space on a disk volume is divided up into sections (some find it convenient to think of them as similar to the pages in a book) called blocks. The allocation block size determines the relationship between these logical (that is, software-defined) entities and the physical disk entities called sectors. A sector is a discreet, physically addressable area on a

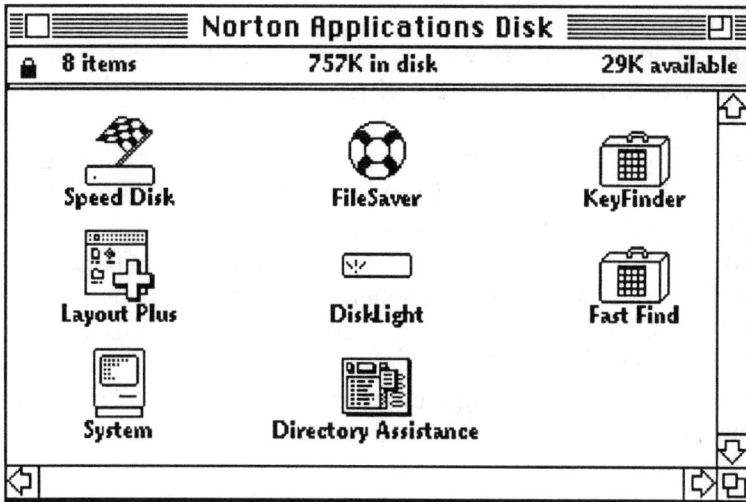

Figure 4.5 Window of locked diskette

disk occupying 512 bytes. On our example disk, allocation blocks are one sector in size. On larger disks, they can be two or even four sectors big.

Each file on your disk occupies a whole number of blocks; they cannot be split between files, so unused space at the end is temporarily lost. Of course, this unused space can be particularly useful in the future, say if the file should be modifed and require more room. Actually, to facilitate this process, the Macintosh adds a clump of extra blocks onto the end of a file when it's first created. The clump size value stored in the VIB tells the Mac how much such space to add.

Of course, there's more to file creation than simply assigning the right amount of space. For one thing, you have to keep track of that allocated space. It wouldn't do, after all, to store a file's information on disk without recording where that information was stored. Returning to our filing system analogy from earlier in the chapter, it would be helpful to have some sort of scheme to group related files, perhaps under some common number. This is, indeed, what the Macintosh's Hierarchical Filing System does. Numbers are assigned to folders (indeed, to all files) as they are created. Thus, each file within a folder can be referenced by a combination of its name and its number. (By the by, this also allows you to store files with the same name in separate places on your disk without one destroying another through overwriting. This wasn't possible under MFS.)

Now obviously, if you're going to assign numbers to folders, you want to make sure to assign a given number to one and only one folder. So you need to keep track of what numbers have been used. The Next File Number variable in the volume info block keeps track of the next number available to be assigned to a file or folder. When a new file or folder is created, the appropriate number is assigned to it and the variable is increased by one.

Volume Write Count   This number catalogs the number of times the volume in question has been written to since it was initialized. This number is of no pressing or particular interest, except that if it is *very* high it indicates an older or heavily used volume that may (we say *may*) be subject to failure. We don't know of any software that uses this number, but some disk repair experts do. It some cases, it is necessary to fully back up, format, initialize, and restore a very heavily used volume that has been giving trouble. This number can give the disk repair expert (meaning you, perhaps) a clue as to the condition of a disk volume under examination, and whether it might require such treatment.

Backup Sequence Number   This number is almost always zero, except in the case of a set of floppy disks that have been used to back up another disk volume. The number identifies which position in the backup sequence is occupied by the diskette in question. The first backup diskette is one, the second two, and so on. When you restore data from a backup set, this number is checked to ensure that you've inserted the correct diskette from the backup sequence. It's faster than checking the diskette name or, God forbid, its actual contents.

New File Allocation Pointer   This number points to the place on the disk volume where the Mac should begin checking for free space whenever it wants to create a new file. In this particular case, the pointer is set to zero, meaning the file system on the Mac will begin checking for free space at the very beginning of the disk volume's file data area. The data area, of course, is where files are actually stored; it comes after all the bookkeeping stuff we're talking about now. If the front part of your disk volume is completely jam-packed full, this number is set higher to reflect this fact. This saves just a shade of time when a file is being created, although the file system does not scan the actual data area when looking for space, but rather a sort of map thereof, as we'll discuss later on in this chapter.

▼ **Pointers**

A useful term to know, if you're going to go about snooping into the work of programmers such as those that created the Macintosh system (or even the

Norton Utilities themselves) is *pointer*. Pointers are variables used to keep track of data whose locations are apt to change. Pointers also allow data storage to be allocated at need, rather than when a program starts up. They do all this by allowing a program to make reference to data indirectly, rather than by its exact location. This is how it works:

You know, of course, that the data a program uses is kept in memory. In a higher-level programming language such as Pascal or C, the data can be referenced by a name, say "Window." Window must be defined, or set up, at the beginning of the program. At that time, a certain specific location in RAM, with predetermined length and beginning point, is set aside for it. A special table shows where to find Window's data, which in the case of an actual Macintosh window includes its title, size, and so on.

Suppose, however, we want to have more than one window. Suppose, indeed, that we don't want any specific limit to the number of windows we can create within the program, as long as there's RAM available for them to be stored in. We could set up a separate variable for each potential window, but as they must be defined at the beginning of the program, we have to decide on a maximum number of windows. What's more, all those potential windows will be set up at the beginning of the program's execution, meaning all that RAM must be set aside for them. This isn't at all efficient if you only rarely work with the maximum number of windows.

There's another problem with this method. You see, the Macintosh operating system (OS) likes to move programs and data around to make maximum use of the available RAM space. If you quit one program, all of the RAM it was occupying becomes free. Now, to keep all its free space in as few chunks as possible, the OS is likely to want to move up everything after the just-terminated program. In effect, it squeezes the freed-up RAM to the end of memory. Otherwise, you soon end up with little open spaces all over memory, which are difficult to keep track of and inefficient to use.

But remember that we said that, with pre-declared variables such as "Window," the program keeps track of the data's beginning address. What happens if the OS decides to move our program lock, stock, and barrel? The OS doesn't know from window data; it just moves everything in one heap (no pun intended, Mac buttonheads). Thus, the OS doesn't know to change Window's beginning location. And the program doesn't know to change it, either, since there's no way for it to know that it's even been moved. In this case, the program ends up trying to get to window data that's no longer there. Know what happens? "Sorry, System Error."

To take care of both these potential problems—inflexibility in creating new variables as needed and inflexibility in moving them around without confusing programs—we need a way of referring to data by something other than its exact address, a way that lets us create variables on the fly and reference their data no matter where they are. To see how this might be done, consider a rotary card file.

A properly maintained Rolodex file is a way of keeping track of a varying number of individuals. Simply by knowing the name of the person you want, you can locate that person's telephone number and address, and then contact the person. Each card in such a file is in the same format: The card is headed by the person's name and contains the phone number, etc., in a recognizable format. When you want to add an individual to the list, you type up a new card according to the pattern, with a new name and locating information.

A pointer, it turns out, is rather like a Rolodex card for a program variable. It points to the place in memory where the variable's data is currently stored. Now, just as an office Rolodex is kept up by a trusty secretary (perhaps the famous Ellen we spoke of earlier), pointers are kept track of by the operating system. When you want a new variable, you tell the OS what kind of variable you need. It sets aside the space in RAM, creates a pointer that contains the beginning address of this RAM data space, and then finally comes back and tells you where the pointer is. When your program wants to work with (contact) a specific window, it looks up that window's pointer, finds out where the window's data is, and accesses it.

This allows the OS to move data around without upsetting things. Indeed, it can move programs and data independently, since the OS knows what chunks are pointer-referenced data (it created them, remember, by request from the program). Also, you don't have to decide at first how many windows you want and then set them all up. You can manage the creation (and destruction) of windows (and other types of data, of course) as your program needs them.

To summarize: A pointer is a location in RAM that contains the RAM address of another variable, such as a window definition. Pointers allow variable storage areas to be created as needed out of templates, and they allow data to be moved around by the operating system without compromising a program's operation.

The New File Allocation Pointer in the VIB is a specific location that contains the first address on the current volume that is available to contain a new file's data. Rather than looking directly for potential free space, the Mac OS checks this pointer, which tells it where to begin looking.

Volume Attributes   This variable keeps track of the disk volume's status. It is two bytes (16 bits) long. Each bit refers to an attribute, each of which is like a switch that may be set "on" or "off." The Finder checks these switches (flags, in computerese) to see if a volume is eligible to be operated upon in certain ways. The flags include:

Bit 15 set: Volume is locked by software; it cannot be modified in any way.

Bit 14 set: The volume cannot be copied. This is a very simple form of copy protection and is obviously very easy to defeat; you just have to change this single bit back to zero.

Bit 8 set: The system was shut down properly last time the power was interrupted or the Mac was otherwise restarted. If this bit is not set, then the Mac was interrupted without being properly shut down via the **Shut Down** or **Restart** commands in the **Special** menu of the Finder. In this case, there is considerable disk housekeeping to do before the volume is ready for use.

Bit 7 set: The volume is hardware locked. In the case of floppies, the little tab on the disk's back has been pushed up. The volume cannot be modified: Documents and folders cannot be created or deleted and changes to windows will not be remembered when the volume is ejected.

Bit 6 set: The volume is in active use by another application. You'll just have to wait your turn.

Bits 0 through 2 set: Problems were found during the bootup file system check. The volume can't be used. This sounds like a call for the Norton Disk Doctor (see next chapter).

It's best to leave these attribute flags alone.

Blessed Folder   This location in the VIB contains the file number assigned to the folder containing the currently active System file. You can tell by looking in the Finder which is the "blessed" folder; it sports a small Mac icon of the same sort used to represent system files. Using this number, and the system file name found in the boot blocks, the Macintosh OS can locate the System file. We'll show you exactly how just a little later in this chapter.

Startup Application Folder   This tells the OS where to find the application that will be run whenever the booting process is complete—in effect, the application that your Mac starts up into. The name of the startup application itself is contained in the boot blocks. The number in the VIB tells the OS what folder the startup application is in. Usually, the startup application is either the Finder or MultiFinder. However, you can of course set your Mac to start up into any application you like using the **Set Startup** command in the Finder's **Special** menu.

(It is possible to change startup applications; we must therefore define the "Finder" as the application that all other applications quit to. Remember that the name of the Finder is defined in the boot blocks, hence, it's possible to have another application be the one that all others quit to. If that particular application doesn't let you launch applications and open documents, however, it can be very troublesome to reconfigure your Mac: How can you launch the Finder itself, for instance? Best not to change the name of the Finder program in the boot blocks to anything not "finderish.")

Bit Map Starts at Sector   You'll recall that earlier, while discussing the New File Allocation Pointer (prior to the sidebar on pointers), we said that, when checking a volume for free space, the Mac OS does not scan the actual data area, but a map thereof. Well, this particular area in the VIB tells the OS where that map begins on this particular volume. In the current example, it happens to be sector 3. (Remember, as sectors are numbered starting with 0, this is actually the fourth sector on this volume.)

The volume bit map is an interesting creature. It is, in effect, a sort of hotel directory saying which rooms are taken and which are available. Each bit in the volume bit map corresponds to an allocation block on the disk volume containing the map. Blocks that are "taken," that is, that belong to files, are marked with ones in the bit map. Blocks that are available are marked with zeros.

Of course, we're not interested in areas that are obviously already taken, such as the boot blocks, the volume info block, and indeed the volume bit map itself, which occupies several sectors. The next variable in the VIB, First Sector in Bit Map, lets the OS know what allocation block is referred to by the first bit in the volume bit map.

Let's look at the bit map and see if we can decipher what it tells the Mac OS. Returning to the Norton Disk Editor, make sure the window containing your disk's volume info block is active (click on it). Note the horizontal scroll bar labeled "Absolute Sector" in the upper left of the window. Click on the scroll bar's right arrow until the number shown below is the same as that shown for the beginning of the volume bit map. (On a hard disk with one sector block, you need only click once.) You'll see something similar to the screen shown in Figure 4.6.

Notice all the "F"s? If you recall that each pair of hexadecimal digits refers to a single byte (eight bits) of data, then it's clear that each "F" refers to four bits that are marked "taken." (1111=F=16). Based on that, you can see that the first part of volume Athena is jammed full. We'll have to look farther. (Note: Your disk volume may not be quite so full, although the amount of data shown is equal to about 2048 sectors, or one megabyte.)

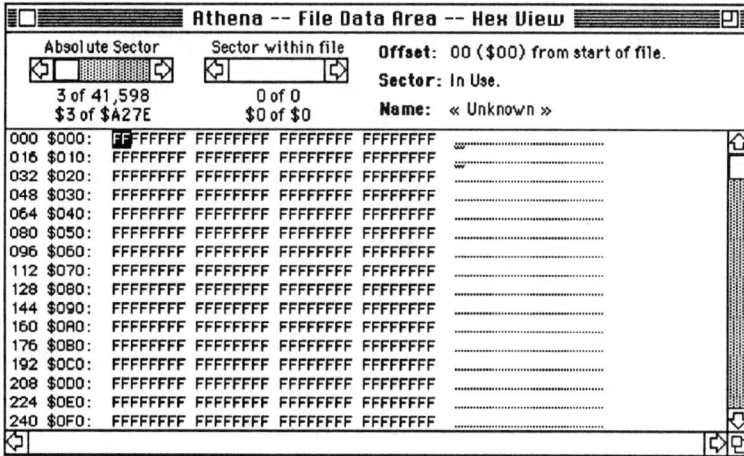

Figure 4.6 Hex view of volume bit map on volume Athena

As it turns out (see Figure 4.7), we have to go quite a way in on Athena before we find any free space.

So it seems that byte number 280 of the third sector in the bit map shows free space. (Anything not marked "FF" indicates free blocks.) Well, for starters, $FC=B11111100. That's six blocks in there. Now, we've come two full sectors and 280 bytes of another; that's 1304 bytes (512+512+280). Each byte in the volume bit map accounts for eight blocks, so that makes 1304*8=10432 blocks. Plus 14 blocks, because that's how far in the data area begins, plus the six blocks

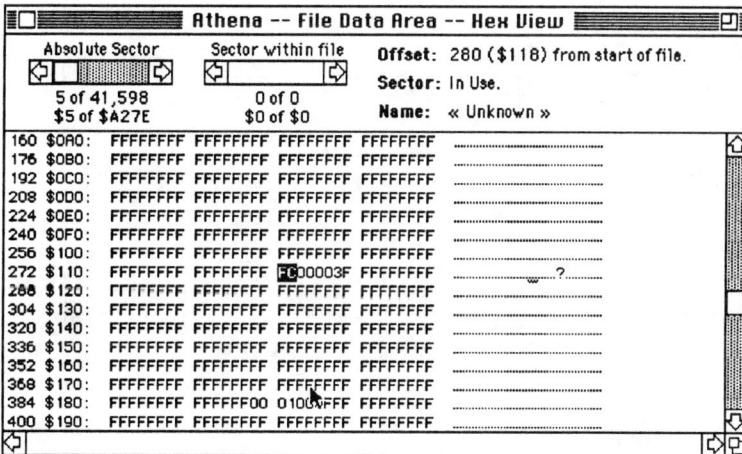

**Figure 4.7 First free blocks on volume Athena, as shown
by volume bit map**

Read What: ◉ **Decimal**
                                   ○ **Hex**

◉ **Sector Number**   [10452]
○ **Allocation Block**   [10438]
○ **Catalog B-Tree Node**   [   ]
○ **Extents B-Tree Node**   [   ]
○ **Byte Offset within file**   [.......]

[**Read**]   [**Cancel**]

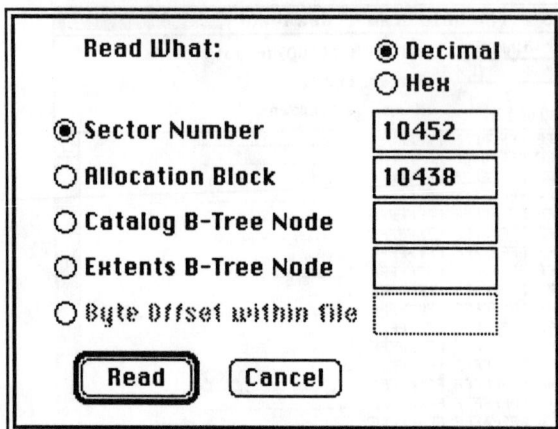

**Figure 4.8 Read Sector... dialog box from
Norton Disk Editor Objects menu**

we started with, gives a final offset of 10452 blocks. On this volume, there's
one sector per block. We use the **Read Sector...** command from the **Objects**
menu in the Norton Disk Editor (Figure 4.8), enter the number 10452, and sure
enough, we get the screen shown in Figure 4.9.

Note that the legend **Sector:** at the upper right of the window indicates this
sector is unused by any file. Note further that the sector is not empty;
something, perhaps a PICT, has gone here before. This, as it turns out, is crucial
to the successful operation of Norton UnErase, as we'll see in Chapter 6.

Well, it seems a shame to come this far and not leave behind a record of our
presence. We'll just type a little message (Figure 4.10).

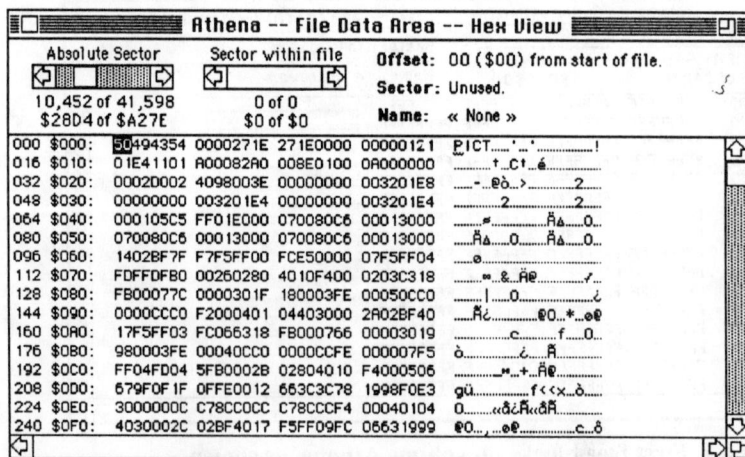

```
▤▢▦▦▦▦▦▦ Athena -- File Data Area -- Hex View ▦▦▦▦▦▦▢▤
   Absolute Sector    Sector within file    Offset:  00 ($00) from start of file.
  ⬅▢▨▨▨▨▨▨➡   ⬅▢       ➡          Sector:  Unused.                    ʃ
  10,452 of 41,598       0 of 0            Name:   « None »
  $28D4 of $A27E        $0 of $0
000 $000:  50494354 0000271E 271E0000 00000121  PICT...'...'.............!
016 $010:  01E41101 A00082A0 008E0100 0A000000  .....†.c†..é..........
032 $020:  0002D002 4098003E 00000000 003201E8  ...-..eò..>.........2
048 $030:  00000000 003201E4 00000000 003201E4  .........2.........2
064 $040:  000105C5 FF01E000 07008006 00013000  ....æ...........Ã▲...0...
080 $050:  070080C6 00013000 070080C6 00013000  .Ã▲...0...Ã▲...0...
096 $060:  1402BF7F F7F5FF00 FCE50000 07F5FF04  ...ø...................
112 $070:  FDFFDFB0 00250280 4010F400 0203C318  ....&..Ãê..........ʃ..
128 $080:  FB00077C 0000301F 180003FE 00050CC0  ...|...0..............¿
144 $090:  0000CCC0 F2000401 04403000 2A02BF40  ..Ãċ........ê0..*..eê
160 $0A0:  17F5FF03 FC066318 FB000766 00003019  .......c......f...0..
176 $0B0:  980003FE 00040CC0 0000CCFE 000007F5  ò........¿...Ã......
192 $0C0:  FF04FD04 5FB0002B 02804010 F4000505  .....,..+..Ãê........
208 $0D0:  679F0F1F 0FFE0012 663C3C78 1998F0E3  gü...........f<<x..ò....
224 $0E0:  3000000C C78CCCCC C78CCCF4 00040104  0....«ôċÃ«ôÃ........
240 $0F0:  4030002C 02BF4017 F5FF09FC 06631999  ê0...,...eê...........c...ô
⬅                                                               ➡▢
```

Figure 4.9 Contents of volume Athena at absolute sector 10,452

```
▐▐█▐▌▒▒▒▒▒▒▒▒▒▒▒▒█ Athena -- File Data Area -- Hex View █▒▒▒▒▒▒▒▒▐▐▐▌▐
   Absolute Sector       Sector within file    Offset: 09 ($09) from start of file.
 ◁▐▒▒▒█▒▒▒▒▒▒▒▒▌▷   ◁▐▒▒▒▒▒▒▒▒▒▒▌▷   Sector: Unused.
   10,452 of 41,598         0 of 0       Name:  « None »
   $28D4 of $A27E          $0 of $0
 ┌─────────────────────────────────────────────────────────────────┐
 │000 $000:  48692074 68657265 211E0000 00000121   Hi there!█.........!   ▲▲▐
 │016 $010:  01E41101 A00082A0 008E0100 0A000000   .....†..C†..ê..........▐
 │032 $020:  0002D002 4098003E 00000000 003201E8   .....-..êò...>.........2....▐
 │048 $030:  00000000 003201E4 00000000 003201E4   .........2.............2.....▐
 │064 $040:  000105C5 FF01E000 07008006 00013000   ......ᴂ........Ãᴧ....0...▐
 │080 $050:  07008006 00013000 07008006 00013000   .....Ãᴧ....0....Ãᴧ....0...▐
 │096 $060:  1402BF7F F7F5FF00 FCE50000 07F5FF04   .....ø..................▐
 │112 $070:  FDFFDFB0 00260280 4010F400 0203C318   .....÷..&..Ãᴇ.........√..▐
 │128 $080:  FB00077C 0000301F 180003FE 00050CC0   ....|....0...........¿▐
 │144 $090:  0000CCC0 F2000401 04403000 2A02BF40   ...Ã¿.........ᴇO...*..oᴇ▐
 │160 $0A0:  17F5FF03 FC066318 FB000766 00003019   ........c.....f....0...▐
 │176 $0B0:  980003FE 00040CC0 0000CCFE 000007F5   ò.......¿..Ã............▐
 │192 $0C0:  FF04FD04 5FB0002B 02804010 F4000506   .......=..+..Ãᴇ.......▐
 │208 $0D0:  679F0F1F 0FFE0012 663C3C78 1998F0E3   gü.......f<<x..ò.....▐
 │224 $0E0:  3000000C C78C0CCC C78CCCF4 00040104   0.......«ᴀ¿Ã«ᴀR.......▐
 │240 $0F0:  4030002C 02BF4017 F5FF09FC 06631999   ᴇO..,...oᴇ............c...ᴃ ▼▼▐
 └─────────────────────────────────────────────────────────────────┘
 ◁▐                                                              ▷▐▐▌
```

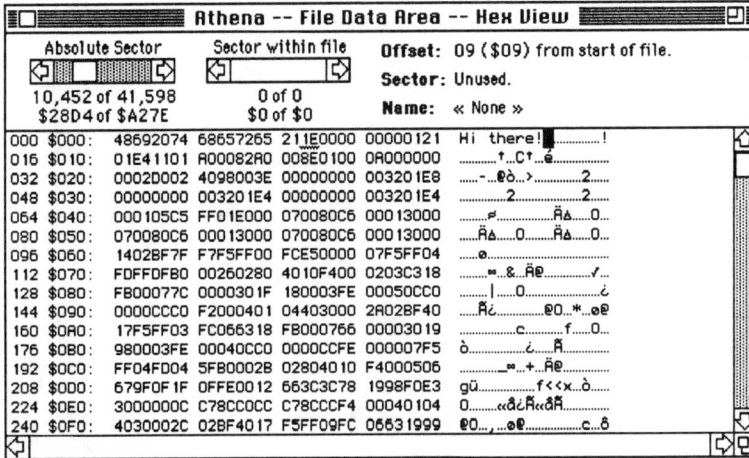

Figure 4.10 The message "Hi there!" left in an unused sector on volume Athena

When we return to absolute sector 2 (the volume info block), the Norton Disk Editor asks if we want to save changes, and we say "Yes." We'll find our little message using Norton UnErase in Chapter 6.

In effect, we've used the Norton Disk Editor to find the first free sector on this volume, using the volume bit map just as the Macintosh OS would. We'll be using a similar method to locate files. First though, we have to wrap up our tour through the wonders of the volume info block.

Extents and Catalog Tree Sizes and Clump Sizes   The next four data in the VIB are used to set up some of the most critical bookkeeping areas on the entire disk, ones that we'll be examining at length in the second part of this chapter. For now, suffice it to say that the extents and catalog trees are data structures used to keep track of the exact location of file data on the disk volume. The data here in the VIB tell the Mac OS how big each structure is and how much space to add if it either fills up and has to be expanded.

The last two data in the VIB tell the Mac OS where each of these data structures, the catalog tree and the extents tree, begins and how big it is. This information is very important when it comes to locating files on disk. We'll note in particular that the catalog tree begins at sector number 324 (Figure 4.11); we'll use this fact shortly.

```
 ▤□ ▆▆▆ Athena -- Volume Info Block -- Volume Info Block View ▆▆▆ ▣▯▤
    Absolute Sector
    ◁│▯▐░░░░░░▌▕▷
     2 of 41,598
     $2 of $A27E
 This is the First extent of the Catalog B-Tree. This extent starts with allocation block 324,
 and the extent is 324 blocks long, which means that the extent occupies sectors 338 through
 661 (sectors $152 through $295).

        Startup App Folder  19                                    ⇧
    Bit Map starts at sector  3
      First sector in Bit Map  14
           Extents Tree Size  165,888
     Extents Tree Clump Size  165,888
          Catalog Tree Size  165,888
     Catalog Tree Clump Size  165,888
          First Extent Extent  $E..$151
          First Catalog Extent  ▐$152..$295         ▌         ⇩
 ◁▯                                                        ▷▯
```

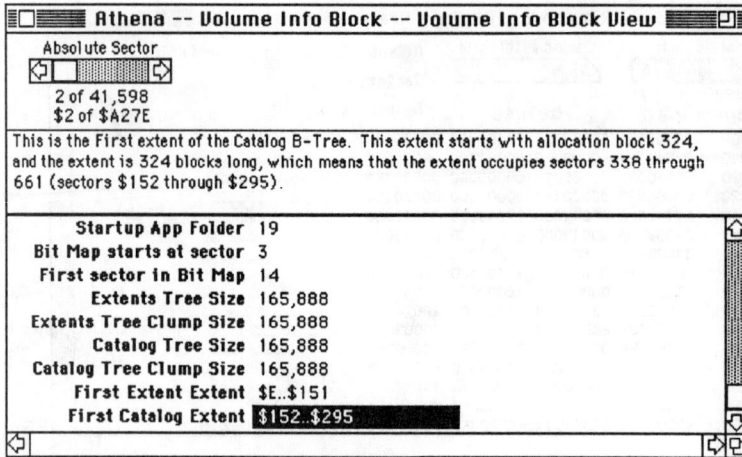

Figure 4.11 **Location of first sector in Catalog Tree,**
as recorded in volume info block

Part One Review

Whew! We've covered quite a lot of ground. It's probably a good idea to pause here, catch our breath, and just briefly review what we've seen so far.

We've looked in turn at each part of the boot blocks and the volume info block, which we said act as key to the system and key to the startup disk volume, respectively. We've seen what kinds of information the Macintosh OS needs to pull itself up by its bootstraps, and the kinds of information that are needed to make the data on a disk volume accessible. We saw how to use the volume bit map, an area of about 12 sectors found after the volume info block, to locate free space on a disk volume. Along the way, we discussed partitions and pointers. We saw that partitions are the way to make one physical disk into more than one volume, and that pointers are a way to locate data in memory in such a way that its location may change without upsetting program operation.

Now that we've gotten through the preliminaries, let's see how the Macintosh really works. Specifically, let's see how files are located. Knowing this, besides being interesting in its own right, will help us make best use of the other features in the Norton Utilities for the Macintosh, particularly the Norton Disk Doctor, Norton UnErase, and Format Recover.

Part Two: The Macintosh Hierarchical Filing System: What's In It and How It Works

Having slogged our way through the boot blocks, the volume info block, and the volume bit map, we're now in the same position your Macintosh is in after it finishes booting up and proceeds to launch the startup application, which in most cases is either Finder or MultiFinder.

Well, almost. It turns out the Mac has to locate and read-in (load) part of the System first, so it knows what the heck the startup application is talking about when it starts making the impertinent and imperious requests that all applications do: Make me a window, draw me a menu, etc. We saw earlier that the Mac knows the name of the system ("System"), and the ID number of the folder it's in (the so-called "blessed" folder). How, exactly, using only these two things, does the Mac go about locating the System's data in preparation to loading it?

The answer to this question turns out to be important, because the name of a file and the ID number of its folder are all the Macintosh File System ever knows about any file; be it a system file, an application, or a document. These two data are enough to locate any file.

The Catalog Tree

At the beginning of this chapter we introduced you to a problem: How do you find your way around a locked filing cabinet with files that are in an unknown order. We showed that in a well-organized system the order can be determined and the files accessed. We stated that the order used in our locked-file example is similar to that used by the Macintosh Hierarchical Filing system—similar to, but not identical.

Now, the process of searching for files is easiest, of course, if you've organized the files yourself, like the engineers at Apple did with HFS. If *you* had to organize several thousand files, how would you do it? There are any number of ways, we suppose. As it turns out, however, the way a disk is structured imposes limits on how data can be organized. Let's review these conditions. Your filing cabinet (disk) has a fixed number of slots; each can hold exactly one 8-1/2" x 11" sheet of paper—no more, no less. Each such slot is numbered. You have to organize the slots so that each file is easy to locate, and so that files may be added to or deleted from the filing cabinet without too much trouble.

The simplest approach, of course, is to alphabetize files by name, like the videocassettes on the shelves of your local rental place. Our slot requirement, however, creates a deuce of a problem in that regard. What happens when we want to add a file somewhere near the beginning, say in the B's? In a regular set of files, you just shove everything back and stick the new file in. That doesn't work here, though. The slots are hard, cold, steel and numbered to boot. There's no shoving these babies back, nor adding any in the middle.

What we have to do, then, to maintain alphabetical files, is to move everything that's going to come after our new file back by the appropriate amount, leaving enough space for the file in the B's. Which means, of course, moving umpteen thousand sheets of paper one at a time. What a drag!

It probably comes as no suprise to you that there isn't a computer system we know of that organizes files this way. The overhead that a physical alphabetizing system would consume is simply staggering. On average, any addition to the disk volume would require that half of its contents be moved back by the size of the addition. Consider that this means 10 megabytes on even a small hard disk, and you get the point.

But there are more ways of alphabetizing than just by alphabetizing, meaning that it isn't necessary to have things in physical order. Suppose instead we maintain an alphabetized list, one that shows what slot each file begins in and how long it is. Well, in that case, we just have to keep the list alphabetized; we can have the actual files in any order we like so long as we record where each begins and how long it is. To add a new file, we stick it at the back of the file cabinet, record its position, and retype the file list.

This is about the way the original Macintosh Filing System (MFS) worked. Naturally the filing cabinet slots (one per page of data) in our example are the same as sectors on a disk, each of which is numbered (from 0 out to over 41,000 on a 20-meg hard disk, although MFS only worked on 400K diskettes). MFS kept an alphabetized list of all the files and folders on a disk.

Problem was, the list itself was a fixed length. It could hold about 128 names. More than that, and things got funky, as we've hinted elsewhere. Well, it's simple enough to make a bigger list, you may suppose. That's true enough, except using and maintaining such a list gets to be a bore. Consider a 5000-name list. You could easily have that many files. Well, searching through a 5000-name list, even a well-alphabetized one, can be time consuming, especially if you haven't any idea where each letter begins. A computer doesn't. Unless we tell it otherwise, it starts at the beginning and looks at each entry in turn till it finds one that matches. Not very smart.

It gets worse. Imagine realphabetizing the list every time you add a new filename. Remember, the list itself is also in the slotted filing cabinet that constitutes a Macintosh disk volume. To keep it physically alphabetized, we have to shove things around a lot—messy and time consuming, although less so than keeping a whole volume physically ordered. We stopped by giving up on ordering the volume. Could we do that with the list? And how can we make the list easier for a computer to search?

The first trick is to finesse the order the list is kept in. The computer is still going to look at one entry, and then the next, and then the next. We just change the definition of "next," that's all. We do that by having each entry in the list tell the computer which entry is *logically* next. This results in a *virtually* organized list, as opposed to a physically organized one.

Let's consider a very simple example: Someone gives you one entire suit of playing cards, say the Ace, King, Queen, Jack, Ten on through the Deuce of Diamonds. The cards are handed to you face down in a stack. You're told that the cards are "in order," and are asked to find the Jack, while trying not to turn over any card that isn't the Jack.

Simple, right? You count down four cards and turn over the Jack. Now suppose you're told the cards are not in any physical order. Not so easy. Indeed, you pretty much have to proceed at random; on average you turn over six or seven cards that aren't the Jack before you find him.

Suppose, however, that someone has penciled in instructions on the back of each playing card. Indeed, suppose also that the stack of cards is accompanied by a little note that says "The Ace is second." Counting down two cards, you find the Ace, the back of which says "The King is fifth," and so on. Although somewhat more complicated to search than the physically ordered list, you still have to examine only four cards before you find the Jack.

Structures like these are important to the inner workings of computer operating systems, so important that they've been given a name. They're called linked lists. Each element in such a list contains a piece of data and a link: The link indicates which element is logically "next" in the list.

Linked lists are easier to maintain than straight lists, especially if each element holds a lot of data. To sort the list, you simply determine the new order and update the links; you don't have to move data around. Adding elements to or deleting elements from such a list is easier. Again, you update links. A newly added element can actually be at the physical end of the list, as the long as the appropriate link points to it, indicating its correct position.

It works like this: When you add a new item, you store all its data in an available slot, marking down its location. Then you scan the list, looking for the place in line where the new item should go. You're looking for the item that the new element should follow. When you find it, you update that element's link, pointing it to the newly added element. The old link, which now points to the item following the new element, becomes the new element's link. Elementary.

We seem to have solved the problem of making the list easier to maintain, but it still isn't any easier to search. In fact, it's actually more difficult. On average, you still have to search through about half the number of items before you find the correct one. If only you didn't have to start at the beginning each time . . . .

You don't. Think of an alphabetized filing cabinet again. Usually, they're equipped with tabs showing where the A's begin, where the B's commence, where the C's take off, etc. If you're looking for an entry that starts with the letter M, you don't start looking at the very first entries in the file. Instead, you go to the entries marked with the "M" tab and start there. That saves a lot of looking.

This principle has been adapted to computer list-management. However, we have to introduce a couple of subtleties, especially to preserve the requirement that any such list be easy to maintain. Also, it's one thing to put tabs into a physically ordered list. Putting such tabs, or indexes in computer-talk, into a virtually organized structure such as our linked list is another matter.

Well, what we really want to do is make the list easy for a computer to search. So let's try to think like a computer. That means doing things in binary: zero or one, yes or no, first or last. Remember, we're trying to tell it where to begin searching for the desired item. Thinking in binary, then, should the computer begin searching in the first half of the list or the last? Now, what about that half? Is the desired item in the first half, or the second? Proceeding in this way, you can narrow down the position of an item in a 1000-element list in no more than 10 searches, each progressively halving the field of search.

To give the Macintosh the ability to search through a linked list of file data in the way described above, we have to add new elements to the list. In so doing, we turn it into a new entity, one called a b-tree. Two such trees are maintained by the Macintosh Hierarchical Filing System (HFS): the catalog tree and the extents tree. The catalog tree is the more important of the two, though both are vital.

We also have a new name for the elements in the linked list. From here on, we'll call them nodes. Confusingly enough, the topmost node of all is called the root node. This node points to other nodes below it. In the case of the Macintosh, this node doesn't just point to the first or second half of the linked list it's designed to catalog. In fact, it can point to 11 other nodes; in effect, it can point to what node the desired entry is in. The exact details vary from system to system, and depend on its unique history. On hard disks, no two b-trees are ever alike. (Unless, of course, one is a backup of another.)

It might be helpful to think of a b-tree as a stack of linked lists, each node in a higher layer pointing to nodes in a layer below. In effect, there are links between layers. The bottommost layer is the original list containing the desired data, in this case the exact location of each piece of every file on a disk.

This is also where the numeric ordering-scheme that we introduced at the very beginning of the chapter (the one designed by our trusty Ellen) comes in. Files are referred to by name, but they're also referenced by folder number.

Recall that we introduced folder numbers while talking about the volume information block (VIB). To see how it works, it's probably best to look at the real thing. For that, we return to the Norton Disk Editor.

Presuming you have the Norton Disk Editor up and running on your Macintosh, choose Catalog Tree Header from the Objects menu. Your screen changes to show something like Figure 4.12

The header, which provides the Macintosh filing system with essential information about the catalog b-tree, is the very first node in the tree. Its location is specified in the volume info block (VIB), in this case absolute sector #352.

The header knows how many nodes there are in the tree *in toto*; in this case 338, of which 165 happen to be empty at this time. There are a total of 512 leaf records in the tree. A record is another name for the complete set of data that is stored about each file. There is one leaf record for each file.

Leaf records are stored in leaf nodes. Each such node can store at most four file records. Since the root node is at the very top of the catalog tree, it shouldn't be surprising that the leaf nodes are at the bottom.

The header node indicates that this particular b-tree has a depth of 4. This means there are four layers of linked lists in this tree. The topmost layer, of course, has only one item in it; namely, the root node. The next two layers below it are index nodes used to locate specific file information. Index nodes store index records, each of which points to one and only one node at the next level down. It's by bouncing from index record to index record that HFS locates files, as we'll see.

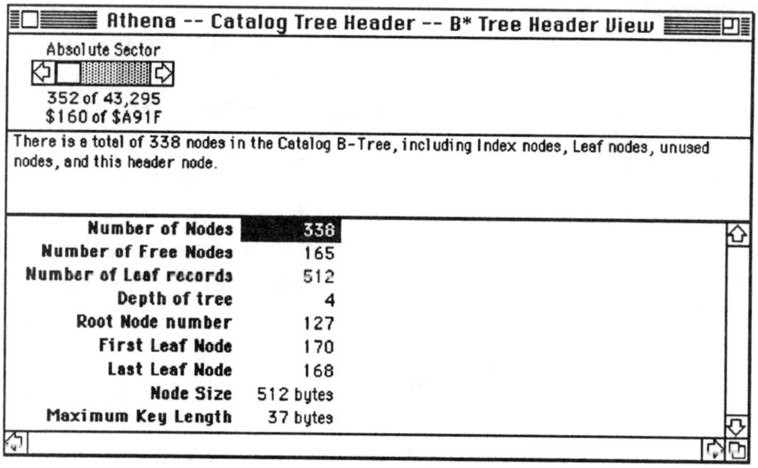

Figure 4.12 Catalog Tree Header on volume Athena

The bottommost layer, as we've said, consists of leaf nodes, each of which contains the leaf records that actually store file information.

▼ Record versus Node

Before we go bandying about these high-powered terms like "record" and "node," we ought to explain a little more about them, don't you think? Try thinking of a node as a file folder, and of a record as a piece of paper within that folder. In the case of index records, each points to an entire node on the next level down. In the case of leaf records, each contains all HFS needs to know about a file in order to retrieve it from its place on disk.

To sum up: Nodes contain records, and records contain data. In some cases, the data point to the location of other nodes. In others, the data point to a location on disk where a file may be found. In all cases, the exact interpretation of data depends on what type of node—index, leaf, or thread—is being viewed. If the node type is off, then everything is off. Something to think about.

One of the most important pieces of data stored in the catalog tree header is the location of the catalog tree's root node. Without this essential information, the Mac's Hierarchical Filing System cannot locate files. Period. In this case, the root node is said to be node #127. Recalling that the catalog b-tree begins at absolute sector #352, this means the root node is at sector #459. Over the life of a disk, the root node can actually change as the disk fills and expands. There is thus no rhyme or reason to the root node number, which is why it is so vitally important that it be kept track of in a place where HFS can find it easily.

On this particular hard disk, we find another example of the fractured physical state of a disk underlying the logical order. Note that the first leaf node in the catalog tree is said to be node #170. The last leaf node is #168. Without links to tell it where to go to find each node, the Mac would quickly get lost.

The last two items in the catalog tree header provide some technical information that is mainly of internal interest. The node size is obviously important, so that the Mac knows where one node leaves off and another begins. The maximum key length refers to the longest name in the tree.

Now we've worked our way through the header to the catalog tree. Want to see it in action? We can do that and show off some of the nifty features in the Norton Disk Editor that make the job easier for us. All we need to do is pick a file to locate. Harking back to the bootup process, we could do what the Mac does first. Let's try to find the System file.

You'll recall from our examination of the boot blocks and the VIB that the Macintosh determines the name of the active system file ("System") and the ID number of the folder it's in (the so-called "blessed" folder). In the particular case of volume Athena, the blessed folder bears ID number 19. (If you're following along with your Macintosh, the ID number of your blessed folder is undoubtedly different.)

Like HFS itself, we must start our search with the root node of the catalog b-tree. However, we don't have to do any fancy calculations in order to find it; we simply use the Norton Disk Editor. Return to the **Objects** menu and choose **Catalog B-Tree**. The view in the window switches to the screen in Figure 4.13.

You'll notice several differences between this window and those we've seen before; it's worthwhile to pause for a moment and describe the features of this catalog tree view window. In the upper-left corner is a scroll bar, similar to the one featured in other windows, that lets you move from sector to sector on the disk.

In the upper middle of the window is a feature unique to the catalog and extents b-tree views. The four navigation buttons grouped there allow you to move among nodes in the tree following the tree's established links. Up moves you toward the root (when you're at the root node, this button is dimmed and inactive, obviously). Down moves you to the next level of nodes. Exactly where you go in that level depends on what name you have highlighted in the field below (more on this shortly).

Left and Right move you to nodes on the same level that are left and right respectively of your current location. Nodes to the left are numerically lower in the file-numbering scheme; nodes to the right are higher. That, by the way,

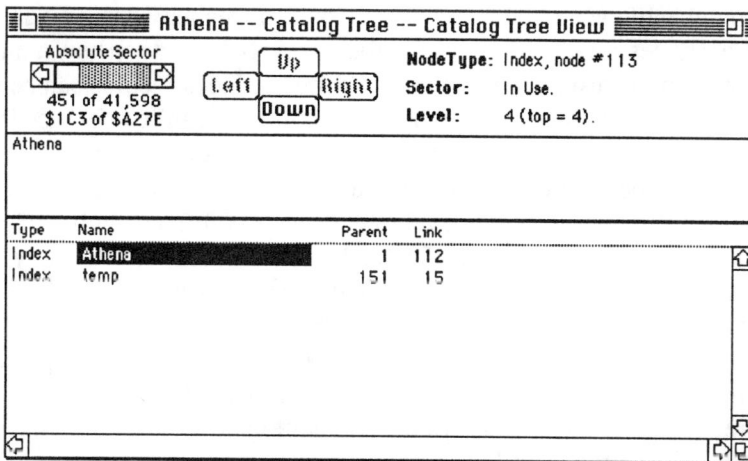

Figure 4.13 Root node of Catalog Tree on volume Athena

is why both these trees (catalog and extents) are called b-trees. "B" means "balanced," with origin left and ending right, as in any orderly progression of arabic numerals written in the English style from left to right.

If you'll recall that the actual physical layout of the catalog tree is quite different from its logical structure, which can only be deduced from the links preserved in each node of the tree, you'll see that this navigation scheme saves a lot of trouble moving around the tree. You don't have to reconstruct it yourself. As with the labels and interpretations supplied for various data within the boot blocks and VIB, the Norton Disk Editor provides you with a human-readable form of the catalog and extents trees.

To the right of the navigation buttons are three fields that explain a little about the currently visible node. The topmost indicates what type of node is being viewed and what it's position is within the physical layout of the tree. In this particular case, the root node is stored in the 113th allocation block (same as a sector on a small hard disk like this) from the start of the catalog tree. The scroll bar to the far left reveals this to be the 451st absolute sector on the volume. (113 from the tree's start + catalog tree starts at volume data sector 324 + 14 sectors for bit map = 451).

There are, by the way, three types of nodes: index nodes, which are used to locate information based on folder number and file name; leaf nodes, which sit at the bottom (!) and store the actual file data such as the location of the file's data on the disk and of the file's icon on the desktop; and thread nodes, which are a navigational aid that we needn't bother ourselves with here.

The Sector field reveals that this node of the catalog tree is in use. The catalog tree is allocated in large chunks—324 sectors, actually. Not all of these sectors are in use as nodes. Sectors not yet in use are marked.

Finally, we're told what level we're at. In this case, the root is at level 4. The level number of the root node is always shown, no matter where you are in the tree. Leaf nodes are at level 1. The number of levels depends on how many files are stored on the disk. Recalling that 11 different index records can be stored in each index node, the maximum number of files that can be referenced within a tree becomes a geometric function of the number of levels. Thus, a three-level tree can reference 121 folder numbers (around 480 files); a four-level tree can reference 1331 folders; a five-level tree, over 14,000. The number of folders that can be referenced decreases if more than four files are stored in any folder; it decreases by one for each such case, and for each additional four files in any one folder.

A large System (blessed) folder, with 100 files, can thus take up about 25 folders worth of space. Three index nodes in the catalog tree will be taken up with references to the contents of the System folder.

Now, as we stated a little earlier, the area at the bottom of the window is where the names of individual records within a node are displayed. In the case of index nodes, the full contents of each record are displayed. In the current example (Figure 4.14), there are only two such records in the root index node. Each is identified by type ("index" in both cases) and by filename (used to locate files in large folders, where there is more than one possible path down the tree).

"Parent" actually refers to the *first* file ID number that this record references. "Link" is the node number in the tree that this record points to. Thus, the index record named "Athena" references the main disk window (or root window, if you prefer) and points to node number 112 in the tree. This node is on the third level.

So how does HFS find file data using this setup? Well, at last, let's try it out ourselves. We want to find the System file, whose folder ID number is 19. Like HFS, we begin by examining each record in the root node in turn. The first references folder IDs *starting with* number 1 (the distinction "starting with" is critical). The second record, called "temp," references IDs starting with 151. That's too high. We must want the previous record. We click on it to select it.

Now, the job of an index record is to tell us what index node to examine next. Like an accurate map of a dungeon, the record shows us the way down. The Macintosh itself would read the "Link" field of the record, determine which node number to examine next, and then read in the contents of that entire node in preparation to repeat the procedure. All we have to do is ensure that the "Athena" record is selected and click the Down button.

We find ourselves at the leftmost index node on level 3 of the tree. (We can tell that because the Left navigation button is dimmed.) We examine index records in turn. The folder ID of the first is 1, of the second is 2. Aha, the folder

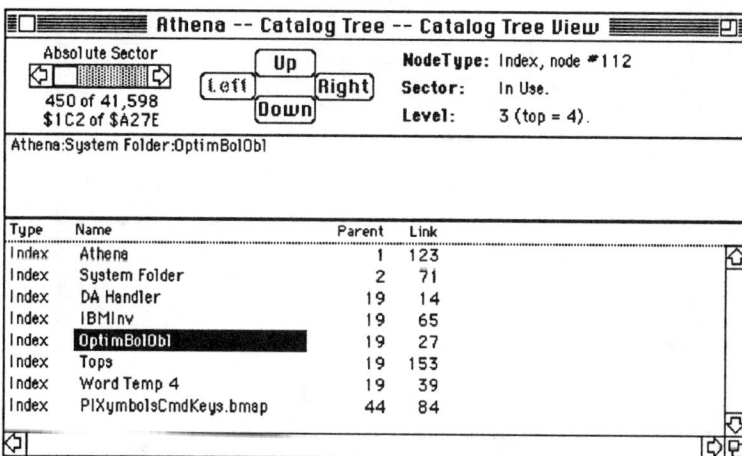

Figure 4.14 Spelunking down the catalog tree—Third level node

ID of the third is 19, which is what we want. Or is it. Examining further, we find that the ID of the next record is also 19. What do we do now?

This is where the filename business comes in. Refer to Figure 4.15. You'll notice that the names are in alphabetical order. Remember, the tree is contructed in an orderly, balanced manner. So let's start comparing names to the name we want, namely "System." When we get to "Tops," we see that we've gone too far, just as we did with numbers at root level. So we select the previous record, which references files with folder ID 19 and names starting with OptimBolObl. (That happens to be the name of a laser font, by the way.) Again, we click the Down button to move to the index node pointed to by this record—namely, node number 27.

Here we see that indeed, this node refers to files in folder number 19 whose names begin at "OP" and end prior to "TO". We scan down (Figure 4.16) until we find another "begins with" name that is later in the alphabetical sequence than what we're looking for (namely "System"); click on it to select it (turns out to be "Suitcase II" here); and click the Down button for, as it turns out, the last time.

We say the last time, because of course moving down from level 2 takes us to level 1, the lowermost level of the tree, and the residence of the deep data denizens we're after: the leaf records. (We will admit that it is overpoweringly odd to think of leaves as "deep," but . . . there it is.) At this point, we need only examine each record (there will be no more than four) to find an exact match to the name we seek. In this example (Figure 4.17), "System" turns out to be the third and final record in the node.

You may have noticed that the window is now different; an additional space has opened up between the node area at the bottom and the control area at the

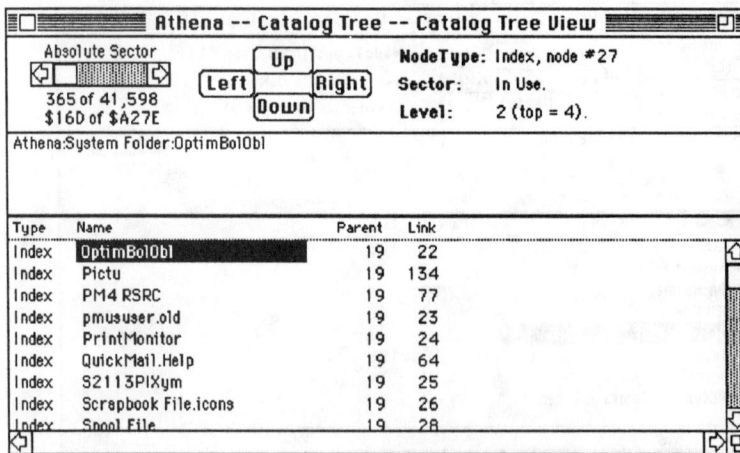

Figure 4.15 **Further adventures in the catalog tree—Node at level 2**

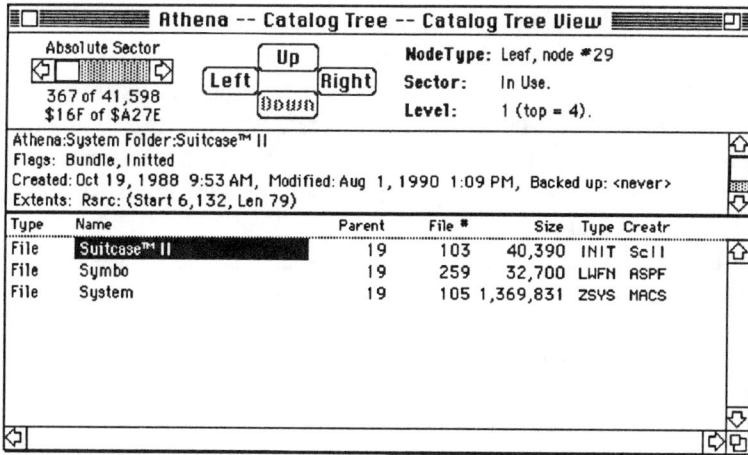

Figure 4.16 Still searching the catalog tree: The Last Node

top. This is where the actual data from each leaf record is displayed. Thus, when we click on the name "System" to highlight it, the data in the center changes to show facts about the file "System." This is what we came all this way for.

As you can see, this leaf record seems to know quite a bit about the file "System." It shows the path to the file on the desktop. You should know that this means what volume it's on, what folder within that volume, what folder within that folder, and so on down to the name of the file itself. Notice that the different parts of the pathname, as it's called, are separated by colons. This notation is significant to the Mac and is why you can't have a colon in a file's

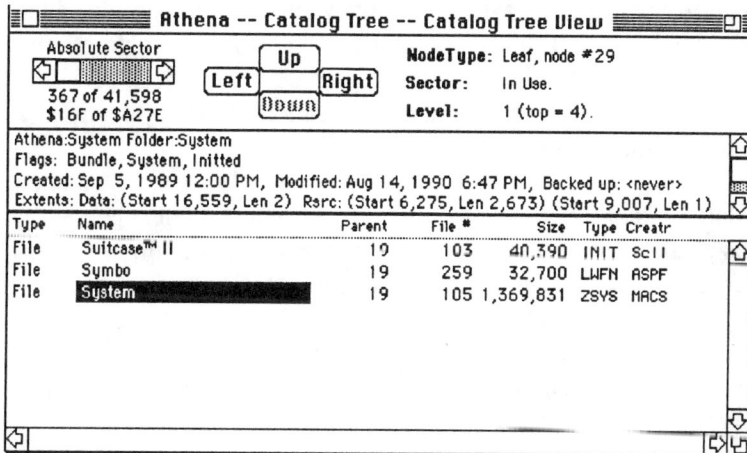

Figure 4.17 Leaf record for file "System" on volume Athena

name. (Try to name a file with a colon in the name; the OS won't let you—you'll get an alert box telling you it can't be done.)

The file's leaf record also knows which of the Finder flags are set. You may recall we introduced the notion of flags earlier, when talking about the volume info block. As it turns out, there are 16 flags that may be set for each file on a disk. We'll look at them in a later chapter, when we learn about using the Norton Disk Editor to repair or modify files.

The leaf record tells us when the file was created, when it was last modified, and whether it has ever been backed up (Ooops!). Again, though all of this information is shown in an easy-to-read format in the Tree View window, switching to Hex View will give you a closer approximation of what the Macintosh "sees."

Some of the most important data stored in a file's leaf record are shown on the last line of the data area in the screen shot in Figure 4.17. This is where the actual location of a file is recorded. We ought to say location*s*, because there can be more than one. Here's why:

To maximize the efficiency and flexibility of the Macintosh, its designers early-on made a distinction between changeable data such as the contents of a letter or a database, and more nearly permanent data such as a screen font; a program's instructions, dialog boxes, etc.; and text strings such as "Welcome to Macintosh!" Recognizing that keeping these two types of data separate would, among other things, make application programs much easier to localize (i.e., translate into an overseas language for an international market, like France), engineers divided every file on the Mac into two *forks*: the resource fork and the data fork.

Into the resource fork go references to (or copies of) each piece of permanent data that a file uses to contruct its part of the Macintosh interface. Thus, an application program has a large resource fork, containing all of the dialog boxes, window definitions, text messages, and program instructions that the application needs. Individual resources can be modified, in general, without affecting other resources or the actual operation of the application. (At least, that's the way it supposed to be.)

Changeable, file-specific data are kept in the data fork. Documents have large data forks. In fact, the resource fork for a document is generally empty.

This system allows things such as windows and dialog boxes to be kept centralized and to be shared among applications. This can increase efficiency, as only one copy of certain *resources* (the name for the items kept in the resource fork; there are many kinds) is needed for an entire volume; not a separate copy for each application using it. Also, these data can be located quickly and made ready, without having to scan through large amounts of other, unrelated data.

Now as it turns out, each fork of a file, be it an application or a document, can itself be divvied up into pieces. This however, though provided for by the Macintosh's HFS filing system, is an accident of use rather than a specific plan. The technical term for this sort of division is fragmentation. Here's how and why it happens:

Let's confine ourselves to the data fork of a document for a moment. Suppose we create a 5K document on an otherwise empty floppy disk. The data fork of the document will occupy 10 sectors of the disk. Now we create a second file of length 2K. The Mac scans for free space to store the file starting at the first available location. Thus, the file's data fork is stored in the four sectors immediately following the 10 already occupied by the first file. So far, so good.

The complication comes in when we modify the first file. Suppose we open it and add data to it, adding say 4K. Where is that 4K (eight sectors worth) stored? Obviously it can't go immediately after the data already present; four sectors of that space is already occupied by the second file. The solution: The Macintosh places the new data in the first available place, namely, after the second file. The data fork of the first file is now in two separate pieces on the floppy disk: one 10 sectors long, the other eight. The file is fragmented. There is a name for such fragments in MacSpeak: They're called extents (perhaps because they extend across the disk).

In the course of operation, it's clear that a file could become pretty badly fragmented, especially if other files are often being created and deleted. Given that the location and length of each piece has to be recorded, it follows that a flexible place is needed to keep track of them. This is where the extents tree comes in, though we'll hold off looking at it for a while. Suffice it to say that the extents tree keeps track of badly fragmented files—that is to say, ones whose resource and/or data forks have more than three extents each.

Back to the catalog b-tree leaf record for the System file: You can see from the illustration (or from your Macintosh's screen if you're following along with the Norton Disk Editor) that the leaf record stores the starting location and length of the extents (pieces) belonging to the data and resource forks of the System file. In this particular case, the data fork has only one extent. The resource fork has two; hence, it is fragmented. Because the resource fork and data fork aren't contiguous (one doesn't begin after the other), the System file on this disk is actually in three pieces—one for the data fork and two for the resource fork.

Before we try to use this information to locate the System file on disk, we ought to mention that there is other information stored within the file's leaf record as well. The length of both file forks is known. Note that two figures are given: the physical length and the logical length. The physical length is how long each fork actually is; the logical length represents how much disk space the fork occupies. Since the Mac can't split sectors between files, the logical length is slightly longer than the physical length. The discrepancy represents unused space that is, alas unavailable for use. (The technical name for this unused space is *slack*. In contrast to other aspects of modern life, we don't want the Mac to cut us much slack. It just goes to waste.)

Also stored in the leaf record are data important to the Finder's desktop. The leaf record knows exactly where within its window the System file's icon is located. This is given in a coordinate system. The icon to use is also specified— in this case Finder ICON #0. (ICON is the shorthand that the Mac OS uses for icon resources. There are many such four-letter mnemonics.) A comment ID is also specified.

The remainder of the fields within the leaf record are mainly of technical interest. In this case, they all contain the value 0 and are thus ignored.

Now we know what the catalog tree knows about the System file. Armed with that knowledge, let's try to locate the System file's data fork.

Now, the leaf record says that the System file's data fork begins at volume data area sector #16,559 on this hard disk. We know that we must add 14 to this figure to get the exact sector number, because the data area actually begins at the fifteenth sector, the first 14 being taken up by the boot blocks, the volume info block, and the volume bit map. This means we should be able to find the data fork to the System file at absolute sector number 16,573.

Note: Remember that, strictly speaking, the numbers in the leaf record and elsewhere refer to allocation blocks, not sectors. On small hard disks such as the one in this example, the correspondence is one to one; there is one sector per allocation block, so the two terms are virtually synonymous. However, on larger hard disks there may be two or more sectors per allocation block. In these cases, you must multiply the allocation block number by the number of sectors per block, then add the volume offset to get the absolute sector number.

We choose Read Sector... from the Objects menu again. Hmmm. Now wait a minute. We've been going through all this rigamarole, adding up block numbers to get sector numbers. Yet we see several fields available in this dialog box, one of which is labeled "Allocation block." Let's double-click on it to select it.

So far, so good. Now, we'll type in the exact number from the leaf record: 16,559. We note that, as we type, the other fields are filled in as well. In particular, we note that the sector field at the top acquires the value 15, 573 when we finish typing. (See Figure 4.18.) So we don't have to calculate the exact value after all; the Norton Disk Editor does it for us. This applies to a hard disk with two-sector (or more) allocation blocks as well, and eliminates all that figuring. Then we press Return or click the OK button on screen.

```
================================================================
▤▭▭▭▭▭▭▭▭ Athena -- File Data Area -- Hex View ▭▭▭▭▭▭▭▭▭▭▯▤

   Absolute Sector      Sector within file   Offset: 00 ($00) from start of file.
   ◁▧▭▭□▭▧▧▭▷          ◁▭□▭▧▧▭▷            Sector: In Use.
   16,573 of 41,598        1 of 2            Name:  System (Data fork)
   $40BD of $A27E          $1 of $2

 000 $000:  40516369 6E746F73 68205379 73746556D   Macintosh System
 016 $010:  2046696C 65202056 65727369 6F6E2036    File Version 6
 032 $020:  2E302E34 0D0D0DA9 20417070 6C652043   .0.4......9 Apple C
 048 $030:  6F6D7075 7465722C 20496E63 2E203139   omputer, Inc. 19
 064 $040:  38332D38 3920200D 416C6C20 72696768   83-89 ..All righ
 080 $050:  74732072 65736572 7665642E 20202020   ts reserved.
 096 $060:  20202020 20202020 20202020 20202020
 112 $070:  20202020 20202020 20202020 20202020
 128 $080:  20202020 20202020 20202020 20202020
 144 $090:  20202020 20202020 20202020 20202020
 160 $0A0:  20202000 00000000 00000000 00000000   ................
 176 $0B0:  00000000 00000000 00000000 00000000   ................
 192 $0C0:  00000000 00000000 00000000 00000000   ................
 208 $0D0:  00000000 00000000 00000000 00000000   ................
 ◁                                                              ▷▯
================================================================
```

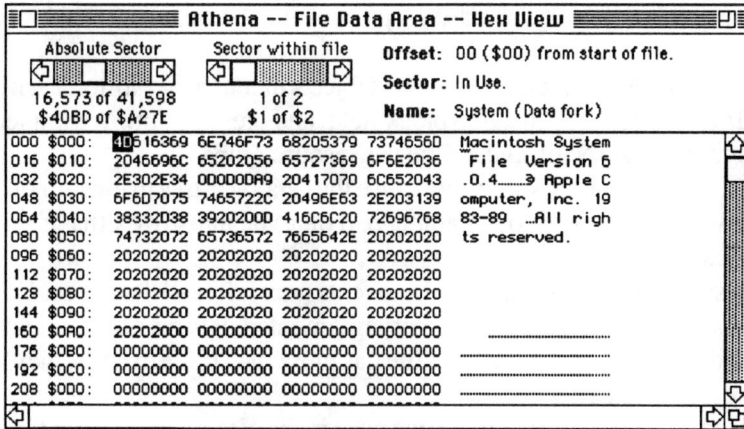

Figure 4.18 First Sector in Data Fork; System File on Hard Disk Volume Athena

Voilà! We're immediately taken to the first sector in the System file's data fork. Finding the Resource fork extents is just as easy. Again, we choose Read Sector..., type in the Allocation block number, and press Return.

That's all there is to it. Of course, a lot goes on behind the scenes whenever the Mac's file system locates a file. In particular, a number of data structures are set up in RAM to manage the newly found file and its data. Each opened file has a File Control Block (FCB) assigned to it in RAM. We talked about these earlier in the context of the boot blocks. An FCB is used to remember a file's location on disk, once it's been determined. It also maintains a sort of bookmark in the file, to let any application using the file know where it left off reading data into RAM, or writing it out to disk. However, as the FCB and other data structures are RAM phenomena, and the Norton Utilities are designed to work with disks and their data, we won't worry about them any more.

Just to make sure we know what we're doing, let's try to find another File. How about the Finder? We know that the Finder file is in the "blessed" folder, whose file ID number is 19. Its name, specified in the boot blocks, is "Finder."

Returning to the Disk Editor, we choose **Catalog b-tree** from the **Objects** menu. As before, we choose the first index record shown, which catalogs file IDs from 1–150, and click the **Down** button.

Again, we see several index records in this node that have catalog file ID #19. We want the one in correct alphabetical sequence. The first #19 name shown is DA Handler; that should do it. We click the Down button.

On the next level we find Finder Startup, but not Finder. We click on the previous record name, Easy Access, and click Down.

We scroll to the last record, as the Finder file is the last leaf record in this node. The leaf record says that the resource fork begins at allocation block number 16,240. There are no data present for the data fork; this means its empty.

We choose Read Sector... from the Objects menu in the Norton Disk Editor, type 16,240 into the Allocation block field, and press Return. We immediately move to the first sector in the Finder's resource fork.

So that's it. Now we know how to use the catalog b-tree to locate a file's data on a disk. There is now no remaining part of a Macintosh disk that is unknown to us. Except perhaps the Extents tree . . . .

We said earlier we'd examine the extents b-tree. Recall that we said it's there to manage files that happen to be very fragmented. It turns out that if either the data fork or the resource fork of a file has more than three extents, they're kept track of in the extents tree.

The reason for this is simple. Each node in the catalog tree (and in the extents tree, for that matter) is but one allocation block long. There is a limited amount of storage area there. In particular, there's only enough room in a one-sector wide node to store four leaf records, where extents data is ultimately kept.

Now, in principle, there is no limit to the number of extents that a file can be fragmented into. Well, each of these fragments must be kept track of, and with the kinds of numbers involved, each extent requires more than a byte of storage. More like four bytes, in fact. What's more, not every byte in a leaf record is available to store extents data. There has to be room saved for other data like the file's desktop location, creation date, etc. Twenty-five extents require more than 100 bytes to store. If there are four records in a 1024-byte sector, that means there are about 256 bytes per record. Clearly there isn't room there to store 100 bytes of extents data. What do we do?

The answer, of course, is to create another data structure on the disk to dynamically manage heavily fragmented files. That entity, appropriately enough, is called the Extents b-tree.

If you're following along with your Mac, return to the Norton Disk Editor and choose Extents Tree Header from the Objects menu. You'll see a screen like Figure 4.19.

Note first of all that the extents tree begins immediately after the volume bit map. This has always seemed slightly strange to us; we wondered why the catalog tree, which is a more important structure, doesn't appear first.

It may be because the extents tree is very unlikely to grow, whereas the catalog tree very well might. If the catalog tree appeared first, the extents tree following would "box" it in, leaving no room for contiguous expansion. The catalog tree, if it had to grow, would become fragmented. Of course, even at the end of the system area the catalog tree is stilled followed immediately by file data, and it will probably have to fragment anyway. So your guess is as good as ours. It just is.

```
┌──────────────────────────────────────────────────────────────────────┐
│▓□▓▓▓▓ Athena -- Extents Tree Header -- B* Tree Header View ▓▓▓▓□▓│
├──────────────────────────────────────────────────────────────────────┤
│  Absolute Sector                                                        │
│  ◁□▓▓▓▓▓▓▓▓▷                                                            │
│  14 of 43,295                                                          │
│  $E of $A91F                                                           │
├──────────────────────────────────────────────────────────────────────┤
│ There is a total of 338 nodes in the Extents B-Tree, including Index nodes, Leaf nodes, unused │
│ nodes, and this header node.                                           │
│                                                                        │
│                                                                        │
│        Number of Nodes ▓▓▓▓    338                                 ⇧   │
│     Number of Free Nodes      336                                      │
│    Number of Leaf records      17                                      │
│           Depth of tree         1                                      │
│       Root Node number          1                                      │
│        First Leaf Node          1                                      │
│         Last Leaf Node          1                                      │
│             Node Size    512 bytes                                     │
│     Maximum Key Length     7 bytes                                 ⇩   │
│◁                                                                   ▷▢│
└──────────────────────────────────────────────────────────────────────┘
```

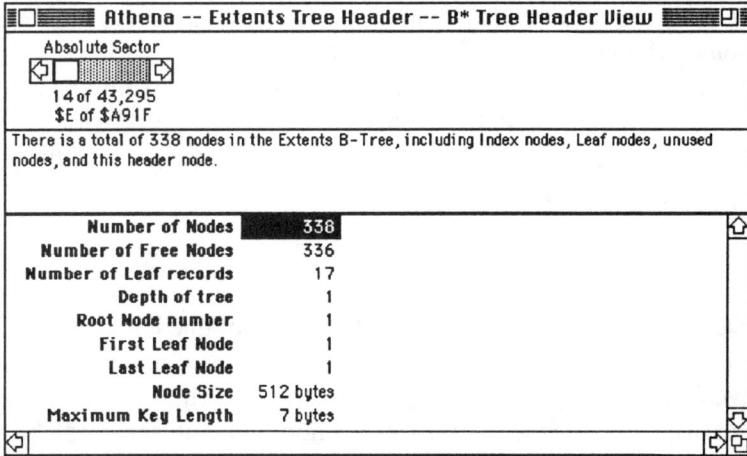

Figure 4.19 Extents tree header on volume Athena

From the contents of the header, you can see that the extents tree is much less complicated than the catalog tree, at least in the case of volume Athena. (The same will be true for all regular users of Speed Disk, as we shall see in a later chapter.) Although the extents tree has been allotted 338 sectors, it only occupies two of them. It is but one level deep, having indeed only one node, which obviously is the root node, as well as being both the first and last leaf nodes. How compact of it. To examine it further, we choose Extents b-tree from the Objects menu.

Hmmmm. These data are singularly unfriendly. Everything is referenced by file number; there are no names. (This is the first proof we've seen that the Macintosh filing system assigns numbers to all files, not just to folders. Documents and applications receive numbers as well.) It's clear enough, though, that stored here is the same sort of extents data that we found in the leaf records of the catalog b-tree. The question is, how does the Mac find it?

Indeed, how does the Mac know it even needs it? There has to be a way to show that a file has more than three extents in one or both forks. (Recall that three extents each can be managed in the catalog tree.) Wouldn't it be logical to mark that fact right there, in the catalog tree leaf record? That's exactly what the Mac does.

Proving it is not so hard. Although it may not seem so easy finding a file merely by its file number, the Disk Editor lets us cheat. The name of the file is shown in the area above whenever you select an extents record. Returning to the catalog tree to find the file, now that we know its name, we find what we are looking for: a mark.

As it turns out, there is a field at the end of the extents area in the leaf record that can be marked to show that there are more extents in the file. This immediately signals HFS that it must look through the extents tree to find the additional pieces.

If the extents tree has more than one node, HFS parses it similarly to the way it parses the catalog tree. In this case, however, it only needs the file number. When there's only one node, as in this example, it's easy to find the match.

Part Two Review

Believe it our not, that just about does it for our introduction to the Macintosh way of storing data on disk. In the process of learning these arcana, we discovered a little about the Norton Disk Editor, as well. What we learned will stand us in good stead when we turn our attention to the other parts of the Norton Utilities for the Macintosh and when we return to the Disk Editor at the end of this book.

This is what we've learned: A disk is divided into small areas of equal size called sectors, each of which is numbered and marked. This is the only physical formatting that exists; the rest is purely logical. As such, the Macintosh needs a number of bookkeeping areas to help it unlock a disk. These are found in predefined areas.

The first of these are the boot blocks, which are found at the very beginning of the disk. From reading the information in the boot blocks, the Mac determines where other bookkeeping areas are located, and what important files are called.

Immediately following the boot blocks is the volume info block. Each disk is divided into one or more volumes, which are the logical equivalent of separate disks. The volume info block, which is found at the very beginning of the volume, lets the Mac know where the volume's bookkeeping information is, how big it is, and so on.

Following the volume info block is the volume bit map. This multi-sector area is a directory showing which blocks on a volume are currently assigned to files and which are free. Each byte in the bit map corresponds to eight blocks on the disk. Blocks that are taken are marked with 1, blocks available are marked 0. In hexadecimal notation, FF indicates eight occupied blocks; 00 indicates eight free blocks.

To achieve maximum flexibility and to minimize the time it takes to locate important information, the bookkeeping data on the Mac is organized in a highly structured way. Files are not kept in physical order. Their beginning locations and their lengths are tracked in data structures called the catalog and extents b-trees. These structures are themselves logically ordered via links, rather than physically ordered, to make them easier to manage.

To find a record of a file's location on a disk volume, the Mac's Hierarchical

Filing System (HFS) needs to know the file's name and the ID number of the folder it's contained in. ID numbers are assigned to both files and folders as they are created; the next number available to be assigned is recorded in the volume info block.

The process of searching through a b-tree to find data is called parsing. Parsing the catalog b-tree involves first locating the header node, which is pointed to by the volume info block. The header node points to the root, or top node. This node contains two or more records that point to other nodes at the next level down in the tree.

By comparing the file's directory ID number and/or name, HFS can determine which node to examine next. The procedure is repeated until HFS finds the lowest level, or leaf node, that contains the file's bookkeeping information. This information is stored in a leaf record.

Files are divided into forks: a resource fork, which contains things such as text strings, dialog boxes, and icons; and a data fork, which contains changeable data such as the contents of a letter. Each fork may be divided into separate pieces on a disk, and hence be fragmented. Fragments are called extents.

A leaf record can keep track of three extents for each fork of a file. (One of the forks may be empty, but never both. There would be no file in that case.) If the file is more fragmented than that, its leaf record is so marked. This mark tells HFS that it must look at the extents b-tree to find out the location and length of the other extents.

It's possible to use the Norton Disk Editor to find a file's data. Once its extent locations have been determined, these allocation block numbers (for such they are) can be typed into the appropriate field of the Read Sector... dialog box to jump directly to the appropriate sector. A scroll bar allows one to move around within that extent.

Now what?

We didn't bring you all this way for nothing. Now that you've seen inside a Macintosh disk volume, you're in a really good position to understand what can go wrong with one. As the Norton Utilities for the Macintosh are designed to repair such damage (and more), knowing how things work will give you a leg up on how to fix them, or at the very least will give you an appreciation of the art that goes into automatic fixes such as the Norton Disk Doctor, which is the subject of the first chapter of the next section (Chapter 5).

Want to know more?

If you want to know more (and you haven't already done so), you ought to read the *Norton Disk Companion for the Macintosh*. This free (!) booklet is sent to all registered users of the Norton Utilities for the Macintosh. It'll be forwarded to you within a few weeks after the Peter Norton Computing product group of Symantec Corporation receives your product registeration card. The booklet comes highly recommended. We agree. We wrote it.

II

Critical Operations

Remember the *Hitchhikers Guide to the Galaxy*, the game by Infocom? It was one of the first games for the Mac. (It migrated there from other platforms.) A button came in the package. It said: Don't Panic. Good advice.

Perhaps we should have included such a button with this book, or persuaded PNC to put one into the box with the Norton Utilities for the Macintosh. Indeed, the idea of remaining calm during an apparent crisis motivated our choice for the title of this section. We could have called it "Emergency Operations," but somehow that implies chaos, loss of control, uncertainty. Messy.

No, we chose "Critical Operations." Think of a patient in critical condition. He or she needs expert care, the best technology, and sound, sober judgment. From time to time you may end up with a disk or a single file in need of such care. Data in critical condition needs expert help. The Norton Utilities for the Macintosh provide it, in the form of the Disk Doctor, Norton UnErase, and Format Recover.

The three chapters in this section show you how to use each of these programs to best advantage. Norton Disk Doctor, for automatically repairing damage to entire volumes; Norton UnErase, for recovering files that have been deleted, either intentionally or accidentally; and Format Recover, for restoring erased hard disks.

Note: In the case of very pressing and immediate problems, you may wish to consult the blue-bordered pages of the Norton Utilities user's manual.

Carrying our medical metaphor to it logical extreme, we'll start with the Disk Doctor.

5

Housecalls

Repairing Disk Volumes with the Norton Disk Doctor

Introduction

In Chapter 4 we examined several critical parts of a Macintosh disk. We hinted that damage to some of these parts could render a disk inaccessible. Now it's time to explain what we mean, and show how such damage need not necessarily be fatal to your data.

In the process, we'll introduce you to the Norton Disk Doctor, an important part of the Norton Utilities for the Macintosh. We'll show you how and when to use it to repair damage to floppy and hard disks.

Just a Bit Off

Computers, as they stand now, are literal and prosaic things, and the Macintosh is, you may be surprised to learn, no exception. When a computer encounters a piece of data, it takes it at absolutely face value. Suppose, for example, it encounters the name "Brpwn" in its rambles. You or I might immediately recognize this as a mistyping of "Brown," but to a computer, "Brpwn" is as different from "Brown" as peas are from apples, or at least as one number is from another. Because that's all there is to a computer: streams and streams of numbers. Binary numbers at that.

As we've seen, the improbable code called ASCII associates binary numbers of one byte each with characters and control codes. If we represent these binary numbers in hexadecimal notation (for neatness sake, as we'll see), then Brwpn is represented by $427270776E, while Brown is given by $42726F776E. Translate to binary, and you get 01000010011100100111000001110111011011101b versus 01000010011100100110111101110111011011101b. You can see that the twentieth through twenty-fourth bits are flipped opposite each other. Five bits is a lot of difference to a computer. *One* bit, in exactly the wrong place, can make a lot of difference to a computer.

There are a lot of wrong places for such errors, and a lot of ways such errors can creep, undetected, into your computer system and onto your disk. Start with the boot blocks. Remember from the last chapter that we said the Mac, while booting, expects to find information of a very particular sort in previously agreed-upon places. For example, the very first two bytes on a disk tell the Mac whether a disk is a system disk or not. But it isn't, alas, a simple yes or no (that could be stored in one bit, after all). $0000 means not a system disk, $4C4B means system disk. Anything else—$0001 or $4B4B even—and the Mac will absolutely refuse to deal with the disk in question, even if the rest of it is in picture-perfect condition.

In fact, just about any error anywhere in the boot blocks can cripple a disk. The same is not true of the volume info block, although there are important data there that will crash a system if altered. The location of the catalog and extents tree headers is an example. And within these headers, an error in the location of the root node of the tree will make a disk unmountable and hence unusable. (To mount a disk is to make it visible on the desktop.) One flipped bit—a zero where there should be a one, or vice-versa—and the location of the root node will be off by from one to 128 sectors. HFS expects to find information of a certain format in the root node. If it's surprised by something different, because it's been sent to the wrong place, it will simply refuse to work with the disk. It won't go hunting around to try and find the correct node.

There are other errors, less serious, more subtle, but still dangerous. An error in the volume bit map, for example, can cause part of a file to be assigned to another file. Or it can make the Mac think that some stray fragment, unwanted by anyone, is actually part of a file and deserving of protection (a tedious problem on a *very* full disk, to be sure). There are, as it turns out, just loads of places on a disk where a very small amount, indeed a single bit, of data damage can make a volume very, very sick.

Well, clearly such minor damage ought to be reparable. If, after all, the Mac can recognize when something is wrong, such as when it has been steered to the wrong place while looking for a catalog tree root node, then it ought to know when something is right, and be able to correct things.

True, this knowledge exists. Some of it is even written down. You could, in principle, nose your way into a damaged volume, examine it minutely for discrepancies (the Mac doesn't tell you exactly what's wrong, even though it knows what made it give up on a disk), and fix them, perhaps even using the Norton Disk Editor. You could. But it would be tedious. Besides, 'tis said that whosoever operateth upon him/herself hath a fool for a patient.

What you need, you see, is an automated diagnosis and repair program. Something that checks out the potential problem areas, looks for errors, and fixes them. What you need is the Norton Disk Doctor. If you own the Norton Utilities for the Macintosh, you already have it.

Calling the Doctor

It ought to be clear from the discussion above that it isn't all that difficult to damage a disk beyond apparent recall. We can do it with the Norton Disk Editor, in fact. Let's damage a floppy disk, and then see if the Disk Doctor can get it back.

The following, by the way, is the procedure used at trade shows to demonstrate the Norton Disk Doctor feature of the Norton Utilities. Except Marvin Carlberg cheated and added a menu item to the Disk Editor called **Crash a Disk.** *Many viewers found this disconcerting, though they were repeatedly assured that this feature is NOT in the product on the shelf. Although a relief to most, that fact actually disappointed a few.*

We launch the Utilities and select Norton Disk Editor from the Utilities menu. When the Choose Volume dialog box appears, we insert a floppy disk. Any old floppy. We're going to be perverse and use an old beta Norton Utilities installation diskette; you should use any floppy you have that contains nothing you need.

When the directory window appears, we choose Catalog Tree Header from the Objects menu. Next we choose View In Hex from the Display menu. This changes the header node to an editable form. We hold down the zero key until the first few lines of data are completely wiped out. Then we click on the hex view window to close it. A dialog box asks if we wish to save changes; we say yes. We quit the Disk Editor.

Now what? Nothing terrible seems to have happened to the disk, we can close it and open it in the Finder without apparent difficulty. Let's eject it using the command key sequence Command-Shift-1.

Now we reinsert it. Ugh, what a nasty message! We certainly do not want to initialize this disk, damaged though it may be. Initializing a floppy disk completely erases it, for good. This disk might have data we want. But how are we going to fix it? The Mac doesn't even seem to want to let us insert the disk, let alone try to deal with it.

Launching the Utilities again, we click the Norton Disk Doctor icon. A Choose Volume dialog box appears, similar to the one we saw in the Norton Disk Editor. We reinsert the damaged floppy. The Finder intervenes temporarily, informing us the disk is damaged. We click OK to dismiss the dialog.

A hopeful sign immediately appears. The Disk Doctor knows the name of this disk. We click OK to proceed.

The Diagnosis screen appears. We click Diagnose. The Disk Doctor analyses the disk for a few moments and then reports a problem. Well, what do you know, the catalog tree header is damaged. Who'd've thunk it? We give our consent for the problem to be fixed. Later, we're told that the header references the wrong node number for the root node. We choose to fix that problem, too.

In a minute or so, the Disk Doctor has repaired the damaged floppy. It even appears on the desktop. All of its data is intact and accessible. How about that.

Using the Disk Doctor

The preceding example was interesting (perhaps even exciting, we dare say), but you may protest that it is hardly practical or representative. Maybe so, maybe not. The real purpose was to show that very minor damage—damage that you could cause yourself—could render a disk unusable, and that the Disk Doctor could repair such damage. So what about real life?

Real life is not so very different, although there are many, many problems that can affect an entire disk volume, or infect individual files on it. The Disk Doctor fixes over 40 of these. Naturally, we can't (or won't, better still) tell you them all; that's a trade secret. The problems do fall into broad categories, however, and these we can talk about. We can also talk about appropriate times to use the Disk Doctor, about preventative maintenance, and what to do with seemingly unsolvable (mainly hardware-related) problems. We can also show you how to stay out of trouble.

Disks, especially floppies, do seem to fail, and who knows why. From time to time, you may insert what you thought was a perfectly healthy floppy disk, only to be informed "This disk is damaged. Do you want to initialize it?" This is a tedious message if the disk has important data on it. Such a disk is a candidate for Disk Doctor diagnosis.

Now, if the Finder refuses to mount a disk, displaying instead the message above, you have to finesse the disk past it and into the Disk Doctor. Do as we did in the example: launch the Utilities, open the Disk Doctor, and then insert the disk when the Choose Volume dialog appears. You may have to get past a Finder alert box, as we did in the example, but that doesn't matter. (Of course, we'll discuss these kinds of topics more later in the chapter, when we tell you what kinds of disks are eligible for Disk Doctor repair and how to proceed with them.)

As you can see from the main Disk Doctor screen, the program diagnoses six major areas on a disk.

Checking Volume Info

Here, the Disk Doctor checks the integrity of the boot blocks and the volume info block. Fields are cross-checked to make sure they're telling the truth when they say that data appear in a certain place.

If your Mac starts refusing to boot off a previously bootable system disk, chances are the Disk Doctor will find the problem here.

Analyzing Directory

Here, the Disk Doctor is looking at the catalog b-tree. As we saw from our little example earlier, the catalog tree is susceptible to damage—damage that can render the entire volume inaccessible. This is especially true if you're using MultiFinder, or if you've activated disk caching. (Caching is to retain in RAM certain frequently needed data that normally reside only on disk and are only called up to RAM when needed.) The Disk Doctor checks to make certain the root node can be found and that the catalog tree is in good shape.

Note, however, that the Disk Doctor cannot ensure that the information stored therein is correct. There is, in principle, no way to ensure that the extents referenced in the catalog tree actually belong to the files they're supposed to. Fortunately, this kind of damage is very uncommon.

Checking Hierarchy

Here, the Doctor goes spelunking around the catalog and extents trees, to make sure they're in good order.

Checking Allocation

This series of tests focuses on the volume bit map. Recall that the bit map records which allocation blocks on a volume are occupied and which are available.

An error here, as we've intimated before, can have one of two effects. If a sector is marked free that is actually part of a file, then the Mac filing system may assign it to another file in the future, thinking it available. New file data will be assigned to it, destroying the old data. Two files will end up believing each owns the errant sector. One will be correct, the other mistaken. The "mistaken" file may be damaged so that it is unopenable, or a section thereof may simply be garbled data actually belonging to the second file. Any changes made to the damaged file at this point run the risk of damaging the second file, and so on.

Second, a sector may be marked as "taken" that is actually not a part of any file. This kind of error is less serious. However, if a whole block of sectors is so marked, it might indicate a file whose bookkeeping data has been lost. Or it may simply indicate some sort of tampering with the volume bit map.

When checking allocation, the Disk Doctor is actually looking to make sure that each allocated sector (that is, each one marked as "taken" in the volume bit map) belongs to one and only one file. Errors are, of course, reported.

Looking for Lost Files

This area addresses the second of the two volume bit map problems addressed above. Areas that are marked in the bit map, but not referenced in the catalog or extents b-trees, are checked to see if they might actually be long lost files. Candidates are restored to file status, and the appropriate information is recorded in the catalog.

Checking Files

Among other things, this set of procedures checks for common viruses. These are becoming all too common, we fear. Those who use only commercial software have little to dread. However, shareware, bulletin boards, networks, and the dreaded "sneaker net" (i.e., sharing files via floppy disks) are all potential sources of infection. Most viruses enter the Macintosh OS as resources; usually CODE resources or INITs. They like to attach themselves to other files.

Other things checked by this step include a file's creation and backup dates (nonsensical dates are questioned; a file can't have been backed up before it was created, for example) and any icon resource bundled with it.

Reporting Damage

As we saw in the example, whenever the Disk Doctor locates a potential problem, it reports the problem to you. Included is a brief explanation of the affected area and the problem involved, what you can expect if the problem is not corrected, and a recommendation regarding repair. You may choose to repair or ignore any problem. You could, for example, merely diagnose a problem disk, choosing not to repair any problems revealed. Based on the number and severity of problems discovered, and on the importance of the data on the disk, you could then make a judgment about whether to attempt repair. This is important because, in the case of very severe damage, it may be best to leave the disk alone and try other ways of recovering data from it, such as UnErase and Format Recover.

If you choose to fix problems, the Disk Doctor will comply and will indicate whether it succeeded or failed.

At the end of the diagnosis, you can obtain a report of the problems found, the repairs attempted, and the results thereof. This report includes pertinent information about the affected disk, including its type, size, creation date, and so on.

A Few Things to Know

One important thing to realize is that the main Norton Disk Doctor screen behaves more like a dialog box than a window. Thus, you can't switch out of the Disk Doctor in MultiFinder. This is an important safety feature, not a limitation. (Ever heard the old programmer's excuse: "That's not a bug, it's a feature!"?) Switching over to another application during a repair could result in very serious damage. So the Disk Doctor doesn't let you even try.

Another thing to keep in mind is that, though it is very powerful, the Norton Disk Doctor is not omniscient. There are some problems that it cannot correct, and some disks that it cannot repair. In most cases, such disks are literally beyond repair, though services exist that have the ability to recover data. It's also possible to recover data from some disks using UnErase or Format Recover. We'll show you how later.

Most important in that regard, the Disk Doctor fixes software problems, not hardware problems. If the problem is with a disk's media, perhaps because the metal oxide surface has been scratched, worn, or contaminated (beer, for example, will take the oxide right off), or if the problem exists somewhere in the mechanical parts of the disk drive (read/write heads especially are prone to fail on Mac floppy drives; we've been told that a couple of years of slamming disks into the slot will do their business as sure as shootin'), then the Disk Doctor won't be able to do anything. The drive itself is at fault, and must be taken to a certified technician for diagnosis and repair.

Keeping these limitations in mind, you may ask "What kinds of disks are candidates for Disk Doctor repair, and how exactly do I use it?" Let's find out.

Potential Patients

Startup Disks that Won't Start   As you probably know by now, a startup disk is one containing a System file and a startup application (usually, but not necessarily always, the Finder). A floppy disk can be inserted into a drive prior to turning on the power; startup hard disks must be connected to the SCSI port.*

Floppy disk symptoms of trouble are pretty limited: The Mac simply spits the disk out without doing anything. You still see the "insert disk" icon on the screen; that's the picture of a floppy disk with a flashing "x" in it.

With a damaged startup hard disk, your Macintosh will probably do nothing at all when you start the power. After the startup RAM test (which can take several seconds on a 4-meg Mac Plus, by the by), the disk activity light on your drive may flash briefly, but you'll end up seeing the "insert disk" icon on your screen.

In either case, if you make it to the "Welcome to Macintosh" screen (or whatever startup screen you happen to have installed, if you've a different one) then the problem does not lie with the boot blocks, the VIB, or even the catalog tree, but likely with the System file itself. The startup screen is only shown when the System file has been found and is being loaded. So remember this: If the Disk Doctor cannot fix a disk so that it starts up, it could be that the disk's System file is damaged and in need of replacement.

Disks that Won't Show Their Faces   The floppy we damaged earlier is an example of this type of problem. In these cases, your Macintosh has successfully started off another disk. You attempt to insert a floppy disk: The problem disk is either immediately ejected (in the case of floppies) or you see the message "This disk is damaged, do you want to initialize it?" (Obviously you must click Eject to prevent the disk from being even more severely compromised by an overly zealous Finder.) Disks that are immediately ejected without comment are very severely damaged and may be unrecoverable. With disks that you're asked regarding initialization, it may be that the disk has never been formatted, or that it belongs to another computer type. This can happen in offices where both IBM PC-types and Macintoshes are in use.

Unmountable hard disks are frequently just ignored, although this can indicate other, hardware related problems. You must always check the power and the cabling before you assume the problem lies with the disk itself, especially with the disk's data. More on this later.

---

* There are older hard disk drives that connect to the serial (modem and printer) ports, but these all require startup floppy disks to become active. There have been a couple of hard disk designs that plugged into the external disk drive port.

Patient Conscious

It is possible for a damaged disk—hard or floppy—to be only moderately compromised and appear otherwise usable. In these cases, the disk is mountable (indeed, you may be able to boot the system off it), but strange and unsettling things happen during the operation. It's impossible to catalog them all, but such damage can include viral infection. If Finder operations seem to be taking an interminable amount of time, you may suspect viral infection of the Desktop file itself. (This type of damage can be temporarily cured by rebuilding the desktop; hold down the Command and Shift keys while booting.)

Trouble in deleting, finding, launching, opening, or otherwise manipulating certain files may indicate damage that is Disk-Doctor diagnosable, if not fixable. The Disk Doctor cannot fix damage to file data, although it can detect it and advise you thereof. In these cases, you must rely on a backup.

How to Proceed

In any event, damaged disks fall into four broad catagories, with variation therein. Obviously we can discriminate between floppies and hard disks. Another useful distinction is between damaged startup disks and damaged data disks.

A damaged data disk can be a startup disk; it just happens to be the case that you aren't using it as such at the time. The important point here is that you've successfully started your Macintosh using another disk, one we presume is your accustomed startup disk. That you could potentially start off the damaged disk is not important.

Thus we have four types of damaged disks: startup floppies, data floppies, startup hard disks, and data hard disks.* Let's look at how to proceed with each of these in turn.

Startup Floppy   If you're starting up with floppy disks, odds are that you don't have a hard disk. This can be tedious. (Exception: you have a serial hard disk connected to either the printer or modem port, and the floppy you must use to boot the entire system appears damaged.) The most tedious situation of all

---

*   In the case of hard disks, wherever we say "disk" we really mean "volume"; it's possible to partition a hard disk drive so that it contains more than one volume. The Macintosh OS will treat each of these volumes as if it were a separate disk, giving each its own icon, window, and all. A single damaged volume on an otherwise usable multi-volume hard disk is perhaps the most hopeful sort of damage of all. It means there is no problem with the disk drive hardware, although there could be media (disk surface) trouble at the exact site of the damaged volume.

is when you have only the internal disk drive to work with.

Petit sermon—If you have but one floppy drive, and no hard disk, at the very least you ought to treat yourself to an external floppy drive. These have come down to the $200 range, which is only twice what you paid for the Norton Utilities for the Macintosh and this book combined. Small hard disks start at about $350 and go up from there. The time you save and frustration you avoid by not having to swap disks, if nothing else, will amaze you. Sermon over.

Have the problem disk handy. Insert the Norton Emergency Disk into your internal drive slot and start your computer. You'll start up immediately into the Norton Utilities. Click the Disk Doctor button, which is the topmost one. When the Choose Volume dialog box appears, either insert the damaged floppy into your internal drive or Eject the Norton Emergency disk and insert the damaged disk in its place. Click Start to proceed.

One-drive users should expect to have to swap disks an interminable number of times—maybe 50 to 100. Dreadfully sorry, but those are the breaks.

From this point on the procedure is the same for all users.

Data Floppy   There are a couple of ways to proceed here. Everything depends on the kind of configuration you have. If you're using data floppies with a hard disk system, we presume you've installed the Norton Utilities for the Macintosh on your hard disk. If you have no hard disk, things are trickier. Your best bet, in all probability, is to ignore your startup floppy and restart your computer with the Emergency diskette. Follow the instructions for "Startup Floppy" above.

There isn't much point in installing or copying the Norton Utilities main program (which is where the Disk Doctor hangs out) onto a startup floppy, even if you have room there—which is highly unlikely even in the case of 1.4-meg disks.

For hard disk users with floppy trouble, once you've launched the Norton Utilities for the Macintosh by double-clicking the icon, the procedure is the same as for damaged startup floppies.

Startup Hard Disk   Here we presume that you have but one startup hard disk volume; otherwise the situation is the same as a damaged data hard disk, described below. Again, start your computer using the red Norton Emergency Diskette and click the Disk Doctor button. Now you must click the Drive button on the Choose Volume dialog box until the your damaged hard disk appears.

Note that it may not appear by name, especially if the boot blocks and/or VIB are damaged. The Disk Doctor may refer to it by SCSI ID number. This is worth an aside.

▼ SCSI IDs

You may know that you can connect more than one SCSI device to your Macintosh. Most such devices have two ports, one of which may be connected to your Mac, the other of which is available for another device to be connected to. This kind of configuration is called a daisy chain, and the process of setting one up is called daisy-chaining. The first device is connected to the Mac, the second is connected to the first, the third to the second, and so on.

The Mac needs a way to know which device is which. Thus, each device in a chain must have a unique ID number, generally from 0 to 9. Whenever the Mac wants to send data to or read data from a particular SCSI device, it prefaces the request with the appropriate ID number. In that way, all devices on the chain know who is supposed to be talking to whom.

On most currently made SCSI devices, from advanced floppies to scanners, it is possible to set the SCSI device number via a small switch on the back of the unit, near where the power cord plugs in. You can also read what number the device is set to. In the case of hard disks, the device number is important to know. SCSI hard disks usually get the lowest number; 0 in the case of startup hard disks. There is only one ID number per drive, by the way; SCSI doesn't care if the disk happens to be partitioned in multiple volumes.

However many devices are daisy-chained off your Mac, it is vitally important to have proper termination for the chain. A SCSI chain needs a "plug" at the very end, almost as if to keep data from "leaking out" and being lost. Many devices are self-terminating. This means that, if only one of the two SCSI ports on the back of the device is actually plugged to something, then the free plug acts like a terminus. If, however, you plug a cable into the free port, termination will likely be broken.

Symptoms of improper SCSI termination are easy to recognize: The Mac simply freezes. It won't start off of or communicate with any device in the chain. You must either remove any cable that happens to make up the very end of the chain (i.e., is plugged into the last device but no other) or ensure that the last device in the chain, if not self-terminating, has a SCSI terminator plugged into the unused SCSI port. These terminators are available at your hardware dealer; some software dealers also stock them.

Note also that you cannot put a "loop" into your SCSI chain. This means that the last device in the chain cannot be plugged into another device in the chain, forming a circuit. Doing so risks damage.

So you must click the Drive button until either the name of the damaged hard disk volume appears or you see the appropriate SCSI ID number. If the ID number is not seen, you should suspect a hardware problem. Check the SCSI cabling for tight fits and proper termination. If doing so does not render the disk drive visible in the Choose Volume dialog (you may have to reboot the entire system to get any effect), then probably there is damage to the disk drive controller. You must take the drive in for service.

Once the main Disk Doctor diagnosis screen appears, the procedure is the same for all types of disk volume. Details of that procedure follow.

Data Hard Disk   This is perhaps the easiest to deal with of all. We presume that you have installed the Norton Utilities for the Macintosh onto your startup hard disk; if not, you should do so (see Chapter 3). Launch the Norton Utilities and click the Disk Doctor button. Click the Drive button until the name of the damaged hard disk volume appears. (See the note on SCSI devices above if you have trouble locating the volume. If the damaged volume is in a partition on the startup hard disk and is not visible, it may not be recoverable.)

With all types of hard disks, you must make certain that the disk is soundly connected to your Mac and that the power is on. Be certain to shut down and power off your entire system before making any changes! Messing with the cables while the system is up and running risks severe damage, possibly even to you. Review the sidebar on SCSI ID numbers above if you have questions or are unsure.

Diagnosing and Repairing Damage

At this point, we presume that the damaged disk—startup or data, hard disk or floppy—has been successfully recognized by the Norton Disk Doctor and that the main Disk Doctor diagnosis screen, shown in Figure 5.1, is visible.

Now all you have to do is click the Start button at the bottom right of the screen. The Disk Doctor icon appears, to show you what part of the disk is being diagnosed. He moves from panel to panel as the diagnosis progresses. (See Figure 5.2.)

If a problem is discovered, a window will open up over the diagnosis screen. Within the window will be a text explanation of what kind of problem has been found. The affected area of the disk is identified and its importance revealed. The problem is briefly explained, its symptoms given, and a prognosis made presuming the damage is not repaired. A recommendation is made regarding whether to fix the damage.

In general, you should let the Disk Doctor repair any damage that it finds to the boot blocks, volume info block, volume bit map, and catalog and extents b-trees. These areas are vital, and damage usually renders the disk inaccessible.

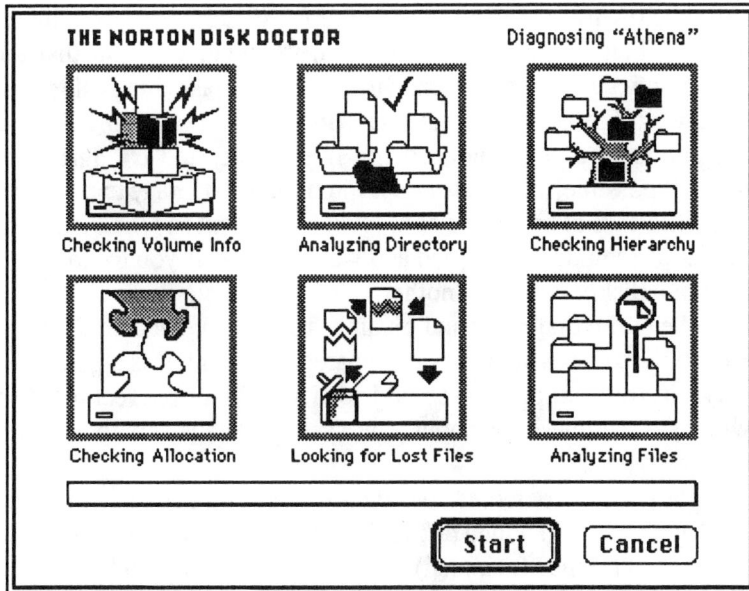

Figure 5.1 Disk Doctor ready to Diagnose

You must use your own judgment when being asked whether to repair individual files. If you have a relatively recent backup of the file, then there is

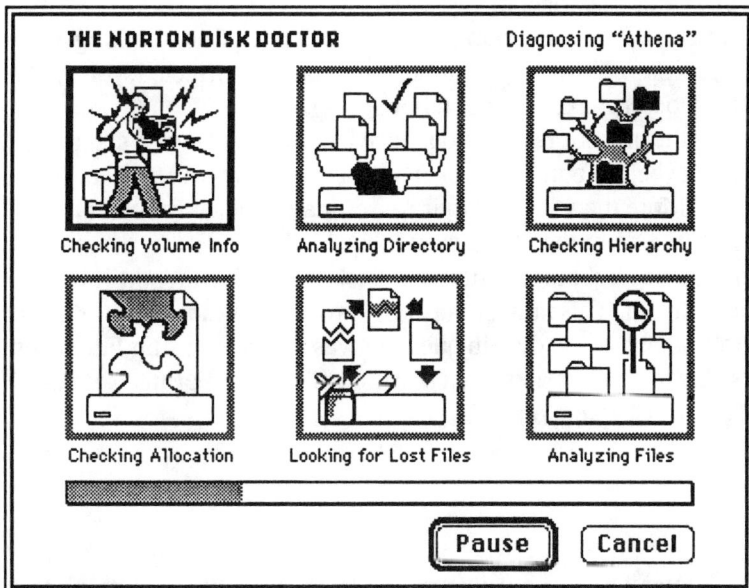

Figure 5.2 Disk Doctor Diagnosing

no harm in allowing the Doctor to try to repair it. Otherwise, you must weigh the potential benefits against the possibility, however slight, that the Disk Doctor not only will fail to repair the file, but may make things slightly worse. Thus, we would recommend that you Cancel operation of the Disk Doctor, make a duplicate of the damaged file if possible, and try again. (We say duplicate "if possible" because one symptom of bad damage to a particular file is that the file cannot be copied or moved. You might see the Finder message "The file xxxx couldn't be copied and was skipped" if you try to copy such a file from one disk volume to another.)

When the entire diagnosis and repair session has been completed, you are given the option of having a report prepared. We think it is a good idea to do so always. If, for example, you should need to call Norton Technical Support, you will be asked questions about your system the answers to which may be found in the report.

The report, once prepared, can be saved as a TeachText document. TeachText is a small application included on Apple's System disks (and included with the Norton Utilities for the Macintosh) that allows you to view and even print small text files.

When you've completely finished diagnosis and repair and have prepared and saved the report, it's a good idea to repeat the procedure at least once. Particularly in the case of very heavily damaged disks, the Disk Doctor may not find everything that's wrong the first time through. This is because certain types of damage tend to mask others. Once this kind of damage has been fixed, other problems may become apparent.

You needn't save a report if the Disk Doctor finds nothing wrong on a subsequent pass. However, if damage is found and corrected, you ought to have the Disk Doctor make another report.

Repeat the procedure until you make it entirely through a diagnosis without any damage being found. However, don't carry things on to seemingly endless extremes. More than three or four passes may indicate irreparable damage. In this case, quit from the Utilities and test the disk.

Finally, we ought to mention that Disk Doctor will report if it cannot fix a certain problem. This may or may not leave the disk unusable. You'll have to try it to find out. If the disk in question was protected using FileSaver, it may be possible to recover files from it using UnErase or Format Recover. We talk about this in Chapters 6 and 7.

Review

In this chapter we saw how even slight damage, such as may result from a few flipped bits, can render a disk unusable. We showed how to damage a floppy disk to make it unmountable by the Finder. We also showed how the Norton Disk Doctor, an important part of the Norton Utilities for the Macintosh, was able to correct the problem.

We looked at the areas on a disk that the Disk Doctor examines and discussed the kinds of damage that it can diagnose and fix.

We divided disk problems into four main types and discussed how to go about fixing each using the Norton Disk Doctor. We make a side trip through some of the intricacies of the Small Computer Systems Interface (SCSI), discussing the importance of SCSI ID numbers and proper cable termination.

At last, we discussed how to make sure that the Disk Doctor has found all problems with a disk and how to obtain a report regarding the fixed disk.

In the next chapter, we turn from volume problems and look at how to recover single files that have been deleted accidentally or otherwise. We'll start by showing how HFS manages file creation and deletion, in the process learning how it's possible to restore data that appears lost for good.

6

Recycling the Trash

Recovering Files with Norton UnErase

Introduction

Damage to entire disk volumes is, thank heaven, relatively rare. It is much more common to lose single files. And the easiest way to lose files is to delete them, accidentally or even deliberately.

There are applications (still) that erase an old copy of a file before writing a new one; if interrupted early in this process, both old and new copies can be lost. This can happen in the Finder, if you try to copy new files over existing files with the same name. If the new files are damaged or otherwise unreadable by the Finder, you'll lose the old files without having the new ones copied.

When multiple files are selected by dragging, it's also easy to pick up extra files. For many of us, selecting **Empty Trash** from the **Special** menu has become practically a reflex, to be initiated immediately upon dumping a load of files into the trashcan. An extra file unintentially swept up with the rest of the garbage usually isn't noticed until it's actually needed, and by then, of course, it's too late.

Or is it? The Macintosh trashcan is, after all, just that: a trashcan, not an incinerator. Files are not immediately destroyed when they're dropped into the trash. And as it turns out, they aren't destroyed when the trash is emptied, either.

They don't actually go anywhere. Some of their bookkeeping information is recycled, but with the right software even that can be reclaimed and the file restored to use.

This fact is of interest even to those who are methodical and careful and don't make mistakes in the Finder. After all, who hasn't deleted a file, thinking it of no more use, only to discover that it contains the only extant copy of some pressingly needed fact?

In this chapter, we're going to show you what actually happens when files are created and when they are deleted via the trashcan. Once we've gone over the process, we'll introduce the tool that can reverse it, Norton UnErase. Some call UnErase the very foundation of the Norton Utilities. First though, file creation.

How Files are Created and Destroyed

Chapters 2 and 4 have given us a reasonable understanding of how files are structured and stored on a Macintosh disk. We even know a small amount of the things that the filing system has to check before a file can be created: the volume bit map, the file allocation pointer, the new file number, and so on. What we haven't done is discuss what part of the Macintosh operating system does all the work, and how it's accomplished. We also haven't said anything at all about how files are deleted; this turns out to be critical to the operation of Norton UnErase.

The File Manager

An operating system (OS) is a collection of different programs. They are all supposed to work together to accomplish the management of a computer system. On the Macintosh, one part of the operating system is in charge of files. It's called the File Manager. Whenever an application program wants to create, open, or delete a file, the request is routed to the File Manager (FM), which does the actual work and then reports back on the results thereof. You, the user, are completely shielded from the FM, as you are from almost all aspects of the OS.

This turns out to be a good thing, because as we saw from the examples in Chapter 4, even finding a file on disk is not a simple trick; other FM operations are more difficult.

Saving New Files

Take file creation. This has to happen whenever you first choose to **Save** a document. Up to that point, the title bar of your document's window has borne the legend "Untitled," or something similar, and your document has been in dire danger; a power interruption would wipe out everything in it. You need to move it from RAM (working storage) to disk (long-term storage) so that you can be confident of having it around in the future. You choose **Save**.

At this point a number of things happen. As the file you're working on doesn't yet exist on disk, it is impossible to merely update an old version and then proceed. The application program you're using takes note of this fact, and transfers control to a special operating system routine that handles new files.

This routine is part of the so-called Macintosh Tool Box. The Tool Box routines are the foundation of the Macintosh User Interface. The particular routine we're interested in is called SFPutFile; it brings up the familiar Save File dialog box, like Figure 6.1.

You type in a name for the new file; and you decide what folder to put it in, using the scrolling list of file and folder names. (By the way, you may note that the dialog box shown above is different from what you're used to, even if you are a regular user of Microsoft Word. The dialog box has been modified, and made much more powerful, by Directory Assistance, one of the Norton Utilities for the Macintosh that we describe in a later chapter of this book.) You click **Save** and the fun begins.

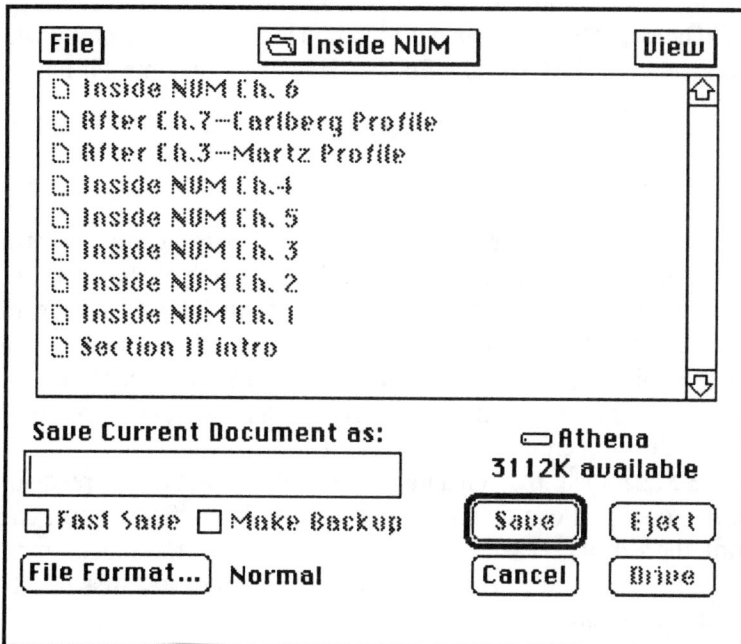

**Figure 6.1 Save File dialog box from Microsoft Word®
(modified by Norton Directory Assistance)**

Control is now transferred to the File Manager. As with the case of finding a file, the FM knows the name of the new file and the directory ID number of the folder that it'll be in. (The file itself is also assigned a number, which is picked up from the appropriate field in the Volume Info Block.) It's also told where in RAM the file's data begins, and how long it is. This last piece of information is important: the FM must locate on the target volume a space large enough to accommodate the new file.

It does this by consulting the volume bit map, which we've described before. A variable in the Volume Info Block tells the FM where to begin looking. When it finds an open space in the VBM, it notes where it is and marks it "reserved."

Now the file's data is copied from RAM to the space on disk shown up by the VBM. A simple set of calculations translates the logical block locations shown on the bit map into physical sectors on the disk. The disk drive's read/write head is positioned, and streams of magnetic pulses are directed at the appropriate sector(s) as the disk surface rotates beneath the head.

The pulses are strong enough to reverse any recorded magnetism that may already be there, changing ones to zeros and vice versa. This fact turns out to be important. It means that sectors need not be erased before new data is written to them; the process of writing new data completely destroys old data.

The disk location of the file's data is recorded in the appropriate place in the catalog b-tree, which the FM parses using the file's name and directory ID, just as we did before. The file's name is recorded in a leaf record, along with other pertinent data. The FM has now finished its work, and control is handed back to your application.

Deleting Old Files

So what happens when a file is deleted? Although there are other ways of doing it, the most common is first to drag the file's icon to the trashcan in the Finder. This action alone is not enough to delete a file; if you double-click the trashcan, for example, it will open into a window showing the icons of all files that are currently within it. Dragging an icon out of the trashcan rescues the file. It's as if you reached into the trash under your desk and retrieved a piece of paper before the cleaning crew came to empty it.

On the Macintosh, the "cleaning crew" operates at a few predetermined times. For one, you can deliberately choose to have the trashcan empty by selecting the **Empty Trash** command from the Finder's **Special** menu. The trash is empty automatically when you copy new files to a disk or when you launch an application.

However it happens, emptying the trash is a relatively simple procedure. A file in the trash is looked up in the catalog b-tree (and the extents b-tree, if necessary). Its entry is then completely erased; zeroed out, if you will. The blocks belonging to the file are located in the volume bit map, and are reset to zero, meaning they are now available for another file, new or old, to use. It may be that the new file allocation pointer in the VIB is reset, if the file's space is closer to the front of the disk than any other free space. The desktop file is adjusted to get rid of the file's icon. And that's all.

The file's data remain untouched. There's no need to do anything with it. Remember, when new data is written to that space, the old data will be completely wiped out by the magnetic fields used to write the new data. Just as you can record a new television program (say, *Twin Peaks*) over an existing one (say, *Gomer Pyle*) without first erasing the tape, any disk drive can record new data in the place of old without first erasing the old data.

So to delete a file, all the FM has to do is zero out the file's bookkeeping information, and mark its space as available in the Mac's volume bit map. You don't have to be a microcomputer expert to understand what this means.

Implications for Data Recovery—It ain't over 'til it's over

In a very real sense, a file is never deleted until another file (or two or three . . .) is written over it. Before this happens, the file is still there. Only the signposts to it have been lost. An intrepid explorer, like Coronado in the American Southwest, ought to be able to locate these Lost Data. More than that, one ought to be able to bring 'em back alive, say, using a disk exploration tool like the Norton Disk Editor.

Ought to. The task is rather difficult, actually. For one thing, file data isn't necessarily stored in a format that is easy for humans to read, even using a disk editor. Word processor files are probably the easiest to track down, as much of their data is easy to spot via ASCII translation of the hex data.

Even then, however, locating all of the file can be difficult. Recall that a file may be in several pieces spread out over a disk volume. Some files keep much of their formatting information, such as fonts, paragraph breaks, and margins, all together in a separate place within the file. If that information happens to be located in a separate part of the disk, it can be very difficult for you or me to track down. It usually isn't very easy to read and recognize.

Above all, there's the sheer drudgery of having to search upwards of 40,000 allocation blocks to find the few belonging to a file we wish to recover. There's got to be another way. And there is.

UnErasing Files

Realizing that file data aren't actually lost when a file is deleted, one of us (Norton) found a way to restore files that had been unintentionally deleted.

Although the original UnErase was written for a different machine and a different operating system, the principles behind it remain the same. Along the way, UnErase has picked up some extra features that make it easier to use and more powerful. This is particularly true of the Macintosh version, where HFS and the rest of the operating system make life a little more difficult than it is elsewhere in microcomputer land. The extra power is really needed here.

Important Notes

There are a number of things to keep in mind when you contemplate file recovery. First and foremost, you should never copy anything to a disk that has a file on it that you wish to recover. You could easily overwrite the file in so doing, rendering it lost for good. This applies to the Norton Utilities for the Macintosh. Don't install the Utilities onto a volume that has damage you wish to repair or files you want to recover. Consult the blue-bordered pages in the documentation for instructions on how to proceed in these cases.

The ability to get a file back is a limited-time offer. Should another file be written over it, it will be lost for good. The risk that a file will be overwritten in a given amount of time depends on several factors: how full the volume is, how much it is used, how close to the beginning the erased file is, and so on.

There are steps that can be taken to safeguard an erased file. The FileSaver INIT takes care of a number of things. For one thing, it moves a newly erased file's data to a contiguous location deep in the volume, if possible. This can increase the amount of time the file will be available for recovery.

Most important, however, FileSaver maintains a copy of all of a disk's housekeeping information AND of the recordkeeping data of all erased files that it has moved. There is a limit to the number of erased files that can be kept track of in this way: no more than 500, depending on the number chosen when you activated the FileSaver control panel device on the volume in question. The actual number of erased files that can be maintained at any given time depends on how large they are and how much free space is available. Even then, erased files are subject to being overwritten if the volume becomes crowded and the File Manager needs the room for real files.

Maintaining the disk addresses of erased files makes them much, much easier to recover. For this reason, as well as many others, we strongly urge you to activate FileSaver protection on all your working disk volumes; indeed, on all disks that contain valuable information, even if you never modify some of them. If nothing else, the extra copy of the catalog and extents b-tree information that FileSaver maintains will make it easy for the entire volume to be repaired, should that ever be necessary. Just having the FileSaver INIT installed and running on your startup disk is not enough; you must install FileSaver protection on every volume you wish to protect. See Chapter 3 for details on how to install and activate FileSaver.

*By the way, this file-protection feature of FileSaver's can make operation just a tad slower in certain cases. Say, if you're deleting hundreds and hundreds of files. In many cases, you may be absolutely dead certain that you don't want to recover any of the files you're trashing. If that's the case, hold down the Command key as you choose the **Empty Trash** command. This will disable FileSaver temporarily and speed up emptying the trash by a very great deal.*

And another thing: Don't install FileSaver onto a volume that has data you wish to recover. You can't protect data retroactively; you may end up erasing it for good. Recover the data before installing FileSaver. Use the red Norton Emergency disk if necessary.

Another thing to consider before you begin: You have a choice as to where you wish a recovered file to be stored. You may wish to recover files to a freshly formatted floppy disk, most especially if there are several files that you need to recover. As it stands now, UnErase does not recover files *in situ*. This means that an erased file's data is read into memory and then stored in another location on the volume you've chosen to recover to. If you choose to recover to the same volume, the new location may very well contain data that you wish to recover. This data will be lost. Thus, it's advisable to recover to another volume if you have more than one file to recover, as may be the case if an entire folder was deleted.

These considerations in mind, with a formatted floppy in hand and an erased file at risk, we're ready to begin using UnErase.

Getting Started with UnErase

Norton UnErase is accessed from the Norton Utilities for the Macintosh main menu. Double click the Norton Utilities icon to launch the main program. The Main Menu appears. (See Figure 6.2.)

Click the UnErase button to proceed. The UnErase window opens up; over it appears a dialog box, in which you must choose which volume to recover data from, and what method to use. (See Figure 6.3.)

As always, click the Drive button until the name of the volume you wish to recover from appears. If you're recovering from your startup volume, and you already have the Utilities installed thereon, the drive selection should already be correct. (By the way, you can use the Tab key to cycle through the drives available to you. Shift-Tab is the same, but goes backward.)

As you can see, three general UnErase methods are available to you. The one you choose depends on whether FileSaver was installed on the volume you're

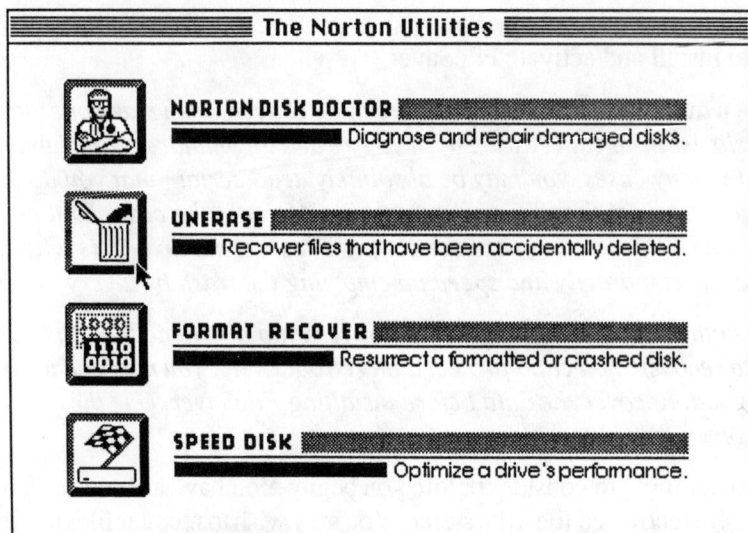

Figure 6.2 Norton Utilities Main Menu screen

recovering from. We'll talk about each method in detail as we proceed in this chapter. For now, however, we'll note that no matter which method you choose, once files have been located for recovering, they're presented in a window like the one shown in Figure 6.4.

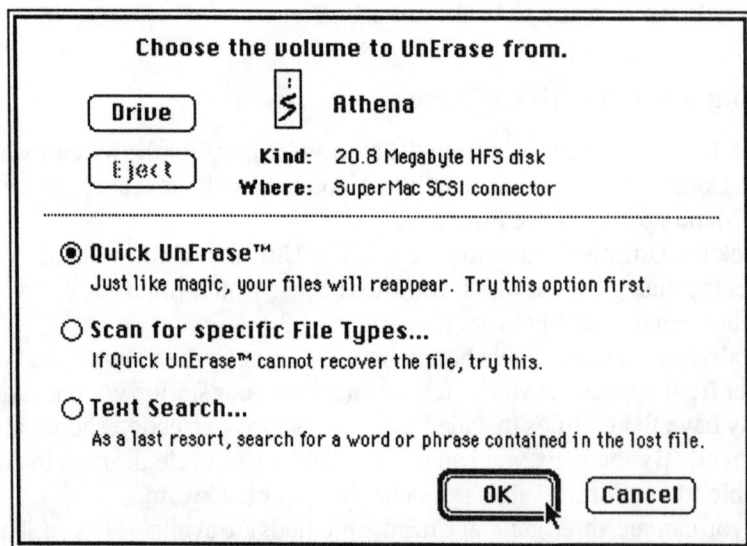

Figure 6.3 UnErase choose volume/method dialog box

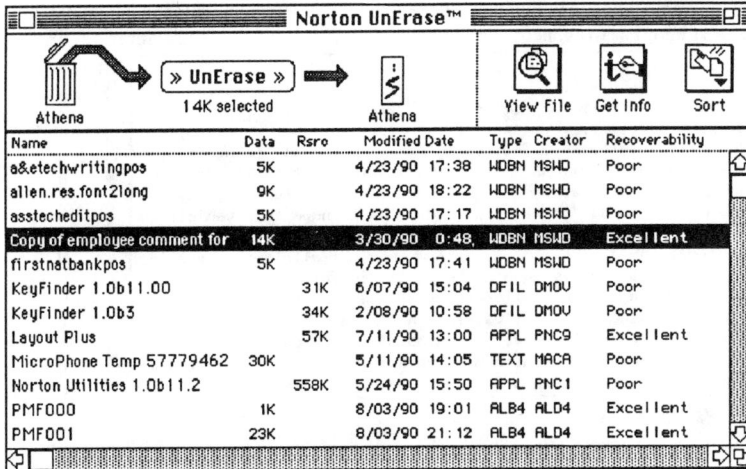

Figure 6.4 UnErase main screen

There are a number of features here. As we'll be using them throughout the rest of the chapter, it's worth pausing a bit to explain them in detail.

The screen is divided into three areas. At the upper-left corner is a graphical legend, showing which volume is being recovered from, how large the current selection is, and what volume is being UnErased to. As a default, files are recovered to the startup volume and are saved in a folder called Recovered Files. This folder is created, if necessary, and lies at root level (i.e., within the main disk window). It's possible to change this, of course. Commands to do so are contained in the menus, which we'll get to shortly.

At the center of this area is the UnErase button. Clicking this button recovers the current selection to the target folder on the target volume, as shown on the legend.

To the right of this area are three buttons that allow you to get additional information and to control what you see in the area below.

View File opens a window (Figure 6.5) displaying the ASCII contents of the current selection. In this way, you can verify whether a particular file in the scrolling list is the one you want to recover—in the case of (mainly) text files, that is. This feature isn't of much use for graphics files; they tend to look like hexadecimal salad.

You can scroll up and down in the file's data, if you need to see more. In some cases, you can adjust which fork of the file you see. (Recall that every file can have two forks: one for changeable data, the other for program resources.) Click on the appropriate radio button to change forks. If a fork is empty, its button will be grayed out. Resource Map gives you a look at the distribution of program resources. You click Done, of course, to send the window away and return control to the main UnErase window, which we'll now continue touring.

```
┌─────────────────────────────────────────────────────────┐
│ Copy of employee comment form              13,824 bytes  │
│ ┌───────────────────────────────────────────────────┐▲  │
│ │.7...........................4......#'.............│   │
│ │.............,......,.......,......,.....,...,...,O │▓  │
│ │....,:....,:.h..,¢.x.., ....-.. ..-:...-P.*..-z.o.,│   │
│ │...................................................│   │
│ │Ladies and Gentlemen,..This is my employee comment form. As my a│
│ │nswers to the questions on the form are longer than the form has│
│ │ space for, I am responding this way. I will include the questio│
│ │ns in my response for clarity. I am glad to have this vehicle to│
│ │ express my opinion about HOK. Although this is the first large │
│ │corporate place I've worked, I know that not all large companies│
│ │ give their employees such a chance to comment. I believe this k│
│ │ind of two way communication is very important to the success of│
│ │ HOK, and based on what I've read in "In Search of Excellence" t│
│ │he best run companies have this kind of communication between em│
│ │ployees and managers...Here are the questions in the employee co│
│ │mment form and my answers to them:..How do you feel about the HO▼│
│ └───────────────────────────────────────────────────┘   │
│      ⦿ Data Fork                                          │
│      ○ Resource Fork                          ┌─────────┐ │
│      ○ Resource Map                           │  Done   │ │
│                                               └─────────┘ │
└─────────────────────────────────────────────────────────┘
```

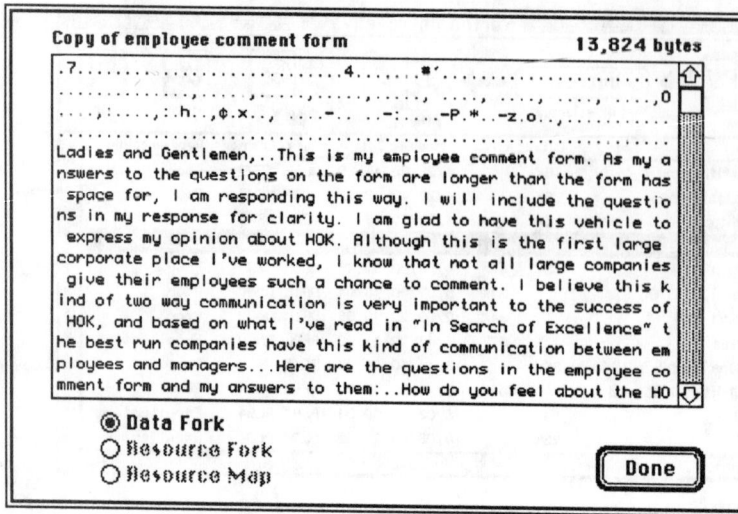

Figure 6.5 View File window from Norton UnErase

Get Info brings up a dialog box (Figure 6.6) that contains a few pertinent facts about the current selection.

You might be able to tell by looking at Figure 6.6 that this dialog box allows you not only to see facts about the selected file, but to change them as well; notice that the name field is highlighted. This lets you recover a file under a new name, if you wish. This may be wise if you have another version of the file already in existence; it will keep one from accidentally overwriting the other.

Type and Creator are interesting fields. All files have both of these attributes; they're among the data stored in the file's leaf record in the catalog b-tree. Type indicates to the Finder (and everybody else, for that matter) what kind of file this is. In the case of documents, it even indicates what sort of document. Creator indicates what program was in charge when this file was written to disk via the File Manager. In the case of documents, this means the application the file was saved by. You can change either of these values if you like (the ones shown are for Microsoft Word 4.0), but if you change them to something unknown, you may not be able to open the file by double-clicking it. The file's original application may not recognize it, either.

Also shown in this dialog box are the number of sectors in the file and how many are currently in use by another file. Zero, of course, is the optimum; anything greater than that means that some of the file's data has been overwritten, and is beyond recall. When all is said and done, you click the **OK** button to save any changes made and exit the dialog box. **Cancel** exits the dialog without making changes. And that completes our tour of this dialog box. On to the next feature in the UnErase main window (Figure 6.4).

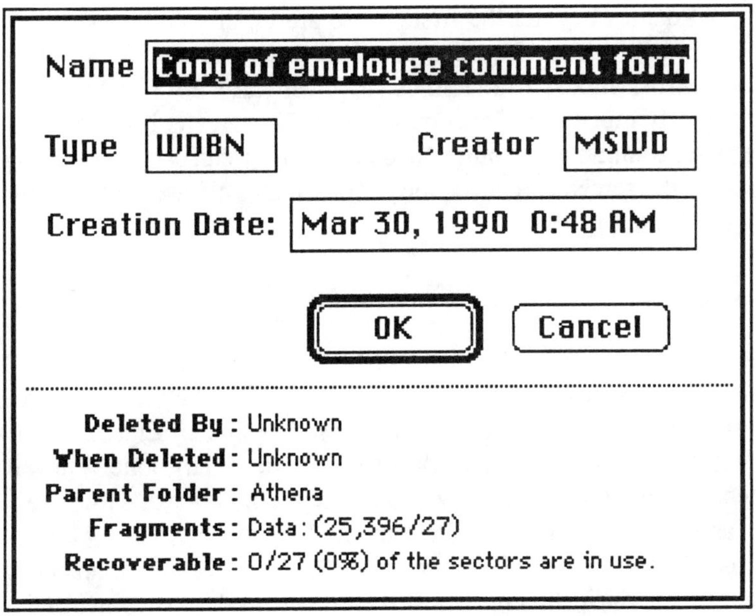

```
┌─────────────────────────────────────────────────────────────┐
│  ┌───────────────────────────────────────────────────────┐  │
│  │                                                         │  │
│  │   Name │Copy of employee comment form│                 │  │
│  │                                                         │  │
│  │   Type  │WDBN│           Creator │MSWD│                 │  │
│  │                                                         │  │
│  │   Creation Date: │Mar 30, 1990  0:48 AM│               │  │
│  │                                                         │  │
│  │              ┌──────────┐   ┌──────────┐                │  │
│  │              │    OK    │   │  Cancel  │                │  │
│  │              └──────────┘   └──────────┘                │  │
│  │  .....................................................  │  │
│  │     Deleted By : Unknown                                │  │
│  │   When Deleted : Unknown                                │  │
│  │   Parent Folder : Athena                                │  │
│  │      Fragments : Data : (25,396/27)                     │  │
│  │    Recoverable : 0/27 (0%) of the sectors are in use.   │  │
│  └───────────────────────────────────────────────────────┘  │
└─────────────────────────────────────────────────────────────┘
```

Figure 6.6 Get Info dialog box from Norton UnErase main screen

Sort lets you change the order of the files shown in the scrolling list below. You can sort by all the typical file attributes: name, date of creation/modification, size, and even by Type and Creator. Sorting by the last two lets you group together files that come from the same applications. This is especially useful if you're only concerned with documents from a particular word processor, for example.

The scrolling list below, of course, is what you see beneath the button area. There are scroll bars to let you maneuver up and down and sideways in the list. There is one line in the list for each potentially recoverable file. Shown on that line are the file's name, the size of its data and resource forks (a blank means that fork was empty in the original file), the date the file was last modified, its type and creator codes, and an assessment of its recoverability.

Recoverability is calculated from the number of sectors in the erased file and the number of sectors currently occupied by other files. "Excellent" means the file is almost entirely recoverable; "Poor" means that the majority of the file's old sectors are now taken by other, non-erased files. "Good" and "Fair" fall in between.

To select a file for recovery, you click on its line in the scrolling list. That line is then highlighted (shown in reverse video) to indicate the file is so marked. You can click and drag to select many contiguous files. To select files that aren't adjacent to each other, hold down the Shift key as you click on additional names beyond the first. These are highlighted as well, while the original name(s) remain highlighted. (This means of extending a selection is standard across almost all Macintosh applications.)

This pretty much completes our tour of this screen. There are, however, some menu commands we ought to look at, as they can be used to change what you see on the screen and hence the operation of UnErase itself. We'll do this menu by menu.

File Menu

Three of these commands are especially important; the other two are mainly for desk accessories that you may happen to want to use while in UnErase.

Start Over sends you back to the Choose Volume/UnErase method dialog box, without losing any of the work you may have already done. A new window is opened. You can use this if one UnErase method doesn't find the file you want, and you decide to try another method.

Close closes the active UnErase window. If there is more than one window present (see above), the uppermost remaining window becomes active. This command is the same as clicking the close box on the active window. Closing the last active window does not quit UnErase.

Quit closes all windows, exits UnErase, and returns you to the Finder (or wherever it is you go when you quit an application).

Edit Menu

Only one command in this menu is for use by UnErase; the others are for desk accessories.

Select All marks all files in the scrolling list for recovery.

Options Menu

We mentioned earlier that you can choose which volume to recover to and what folder on that volume to drop recovered files into. Now we show you how; the commands to do so are contained in this menu.

View File is the same as clicking the View File button described above.

Get Info is also the same as clicking the View File button.

Change Destination Volume brings up a dialog box whereby you may change which disk volume to recover to—as in Figure 6.7.

Click **Drive** until the name of the desired volume appears; click Open to make the change. Cancel sends the dialog box away without changing the destination volume.

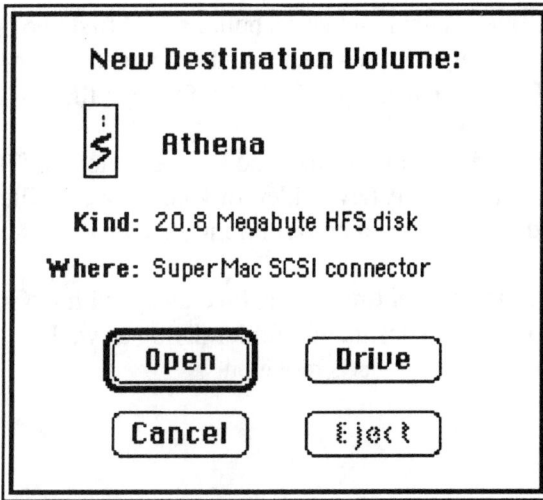

**Figure 6.7   Change Destination dialog box from
Norton UnErase Options menu**

Change Destination Folder brings up the dialog box that—you guessed
it—lets you change what folder recovered files will be stored in. It looks like
Figure 6.8.

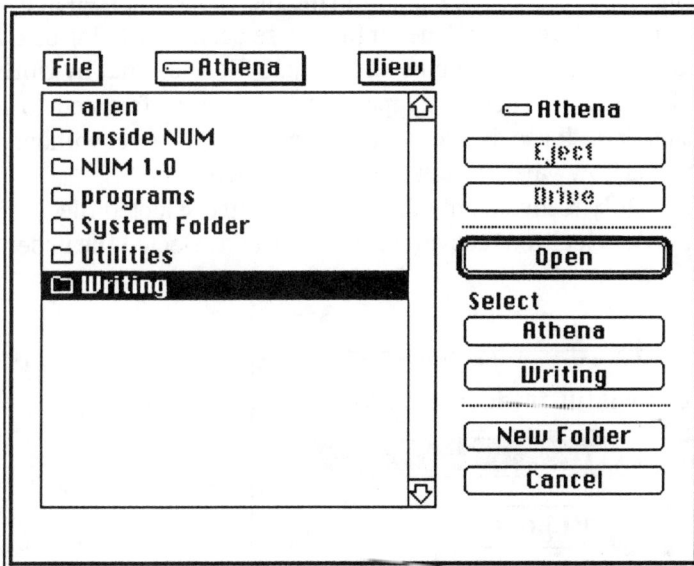

**Figure 6.8   Change Destination Folder dialog box;
Options menu; Norton UnErase**

Pertinent here are the five available selection buttons. The first two buttons show the name of the currently selected folder and its parent folder (in the opposite of that order). Clicking either one selects that folder as the new target, and sends away the dialog box.

Clicking the New Folder button brings up an additional dialog box (Figure 6.9). Here, you may create an entirely new folder for your recovered files. The new folder will be placed into whichever one is currently shown in the scrolling list on the dialog box.

Cancel, of course, sends the entire dialog box away without making changes. This applies to the main destination folder dialog as well.

We've had enough of this menu—let's move on.

UnErase Menu

This menu contains the more arcane UnErase commands, in addition to two very common ones.

UnErase is the same as clicking the UnErase button at the upper left of the UnErase main window, described above.

Save As... lets you UnErase a file under a new name. A dialog box appears into which you type the name you want the newly recovered file to have. You've seen this kind of dialog box before.

Append To also brings up a familiar dialog box, although the function of this command isn't so familiar. Data from the file you've marked in the main window is added to the end of whatever file you select in this dialog box. In this way, you can accumulate fragments into a single file. You start by UnErasing a file under a new name. Then, you append each successive fragment to it using this command. You'll use this command in text search mode, without doubt. We'll show you how when we talk about text search.

Save Text Only recovers only the data fork of the selected file.

Save Text As... lets you recover the data fork of a selected file under a new name.

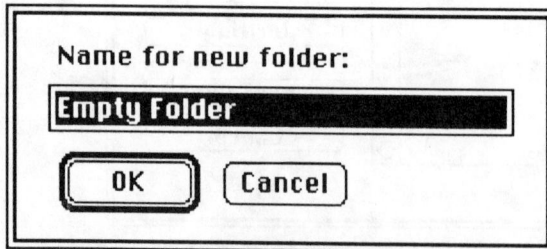

**Figure 6.9: New Folder button's dialog box;
Change Destination Folder dialog box; Options
menu; Norton UnErase**

Append Text To... lets you attach the data fork from the selected file to the end of a file you select within the Append Text To dialog box.

Utilities Menu

This menu lets you transfer from UnErase to other modules within the Norton Utilities. You'll note that UnErase itself is both checked and dimmed within this menu while you're in UnErase. Choosing another utility quits UnErase and transfers you there. (If the module you want to transfer to isn't where the Norton Utilities main program expects it to be, you may be asked to locate it via a dialog box.)

Summing Up the Main Window

Whew, that was a lot of ground to cover. To review, at this point we've seen the main areas on the UnErase window, and learned what each is for. We know about the UnErase, View File, Get Info, and Sort buttons. We know how to manipulate the scrolling list in the window to mark files for recovery. We've toured through the menus, and seen how to change where files are recovered to, and what parts of files are actually recovered, and even how they're stored.

What we don't really know yet is how to use the darn thing to actually recover files. After this whirlwind tour through the program's features, you may be a little unsure as to where to begin. Who could blame you? But it's not that hard, really. And to make it even easier, we'll start with the very easiest UnErase method, and show you how to use it with a very brief example. Let's go.

Quick UnErase

If FileSaver was installed on a volume before a needed file was actually deleted, then recovering it is easy. In this case Quick UnErase will work, and work well—presuming, of course, that not too much time has elapsed since the file was deleted. Remember, the erased file's data area is up for grabs, and can't be kept open forever, especially if the volume is crowded.

We presume you installed the Utilities in accordance with the instructions in Chapter 3, and that your Macintosh is up and running. So let's try something relatively easy. Return to the Finder, if you're not already there, and find a small text file on your startup volume. Select its icon, and then choose **Duplicate** from the **File** menu (pressing Command-D works as well). The file will be copied; the copy will bear the name "Copy of...", with the ellipses representing the name of the old file. (By the way, if the new name is longer than 36 characters, you'll be asked to shorten it via an alert box.)

Now take the duplicate file and drag it to the trashcan. Release the mouse button to drop it in. What comes next? Well, of course, you choose **Empty Trash** from the Finder's **Special** menu.

Now we're going to pretend that we didn't really want to delete this file. We already have the Norton Utilities installed on our hard disk, and we have FileSaver active. There shouldn't be any problem. So we double-click the Norton Utilities icon to launch them (Figure 6.10).

There is, we might mention, another and sometimes faster way of opening documents and launching applications contained within one of the Norton Utilities desk accessories, namely Fast Find.

We click the UnErase button on this screen to access Norton UnErase. A dialog box appears, like the one in Figure 6.11. Everything in the dialog box is set like we want it: the correct volume is shown, and the correct UnErase method is checked. So we click OK to proceed.

UnErase now proceeds to build a list of recoverable files for us to choose from. It does so by consulting the appropriate FileSaver information files. Once the list has been built, and duplicate entries have been removed, it's presented to us in the main UnErase window. It looks like Figure 6.12.

Scrolling through the list, you should see your "Copy of..." file under the C's. Ours is shown above, already selected. Notice that the recovery prognosis

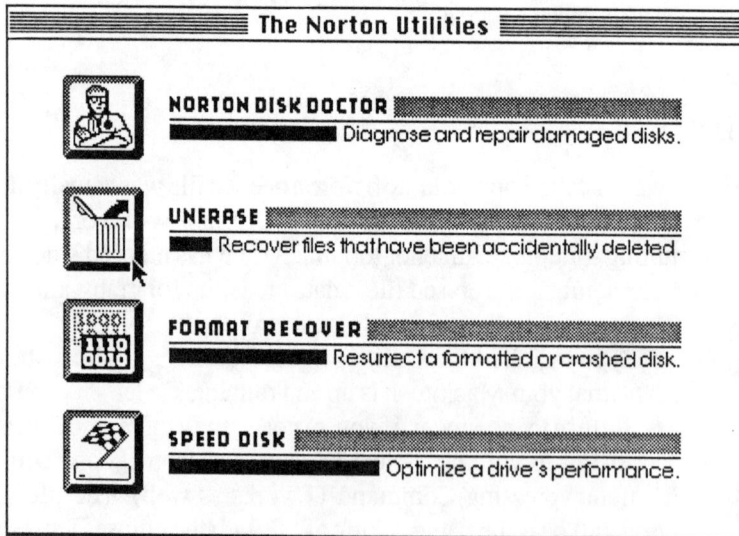

Figure 6.10 Utilities main menu

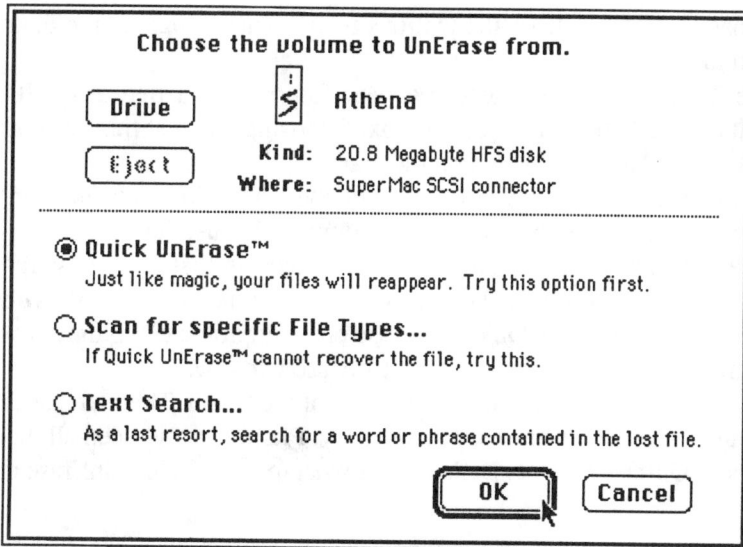

Figure 6.11 Choose UnErase method dialog box

is listed as "Excellent." We'd expect it to be, as the file was just deleted and FileSaver was active at the time.

In this instance, we're certain that this is the correct file (in the next section we'll show what to do when you're not so sure). However, we want to recover the file immediately to our startup volume. We'll insert a floppy disk and change the destination for recovery to it. We do this by choosing Change

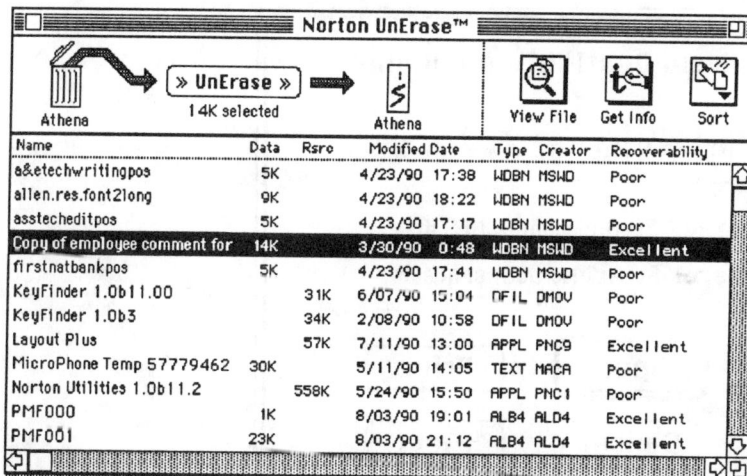

Figure 6.12 Files available for recovery on drive Athena, using Quick UnErase

Destination Volume from the Options menu. That brings up the dialog box shown in Figure 6.13.

We'll insert our designated recovery floppy into a free drive. Its name appears immediately in the dialog box. Choosing Open at this point changes destinations. This is reflected on the main window.

At this point, all we have to do is click the UnErase button, and our "Copy of..." file is recovered onto the target floppy disk. Just like that.

The only drawback to this UnErase method is that it only works when FileSaver has been activated on the recovery volume prior to a file's deletion. Indeed, if you try to use Quick UnErase on an unprotected volume, you'll get an alert (Figure 6.14) and an empty UnErase window.

This is unfortunate, but it's not the end of the world. There are, as the alert box implies, other UnErase methods to try. Plainly, we've seen all there is to see about Quick UnErase. Let's look at what to do if Quick UnErase can't be used.

File Types UnErase

When Quick UnErase is of no help, the bottom line is that you're going to have to go after a deleted file's data by a more brute force approach. This involves scanning all the free space on the recovery volume for signs of the deleted file. Fortunately, you don't have to know that much about the file to do this. And

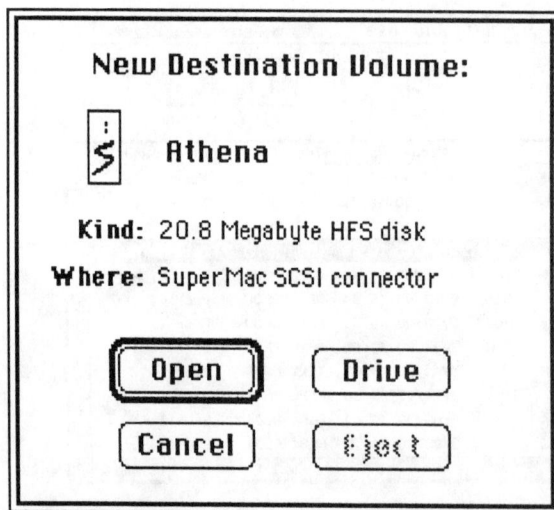

Figure 6.13 Changing the destination volume

```
┌─────────────────────────────────────────────┐
│  ┌───┐   FileSaver™ protection was not enabled for │
│  │ ✋ │   this disk, so no files could be found to    │
│  └───┘   Quick-UnErase. Try the other two UnErase   │
│  ┌───────┐  methods for better results.              │
│  │  OK   │                                           │
│  └───────┘                                           │
└─────────────────────────────────────────────┘
```

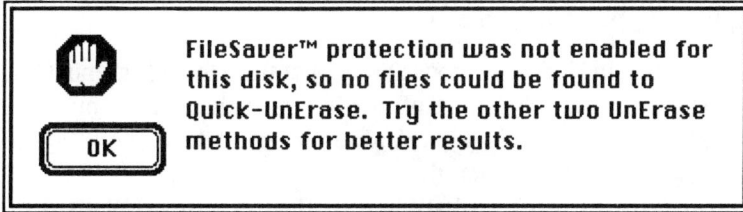

Figure 6.14 Oops! No FileSaver protection!

all the scanning is done by UnErase. There are some important file characteristics that help UnErase in its quest.

About Files

Up till now, we've mostly been concerned about external aspects of files; that is to say, how they appear to the Finder and the OS. We haven't had much to say about their actual data. Clearly, there must be some structure to, say, a document's data, if its application is going to be able to deal with it.

One important part of most (if not all) documents is the header. This is a unique area at the very beginning of the file that identifies it. Each application tends to create documents with a specific header; the very first part of the header is the same for all documents created by that application. Among other things, the header lets the application know that it's dealing with a valid document. An application may refuse to even attempt opening a file with the wrong (or a damaged) header. The header may also contain other information that is of use to the application in opening the document for modification.

This points the way toward a possible method of recovering files. We could all probably say what application we used to create a particular file. As all files created by that application will have a unique, recognizable header, we ought to be able to search all available sectors and see if they contain the header data. If so, we potentially have the correct file to recover. We'll have to check its data to make certain, however.

This is the principle behind File Types UnErase. UnErase knows the correct headers for several dozen different document types. It searches the data space on the recovery volume, looking for sectors that contain the appropriate header(s) (you can search for more than one file type at once). It compiles candidate files into a list, just as the Quick UnErase method does. Let's give it a try.

Using File Types UnErase

If you're already in UnErase, choose Start Over from the File menu. Otherwise, launch the Utilities and click the UnErase button on the main menu. Either way, you're back at the Choose Volume/UnErase method dialog box (Figure 6.15). This time, we're going to click the second radio button.

Now we have to specify what kinds of files to look for. This is done via another dialog box that appears as soon as we click **OK** on the one shown in Figure 6.15.

There are over 50 different file types to choose from. This includes those from different release versions of the same software: Microsoft Word 3.0 and 4.0, for example. Different program versions frequently use different file headers and other structural aspects; those new features have to be encoded in new ways. Because File Types UnErase is looking for exact matches to the given file headers, we must specify exactly which version of a particular application was used to create the file(s) we wish to recover.

In this example, we're going to limit ourselves to searching for Microsoft Word 4.0 files. As you can see from the dialog box in Figure 6.16, however, you can choose to look for all file types simply by clicking the Select All button. This will slow down operation considerably, to be sure, as UnErase has to check each sector in the erased data space for upwards of 50 different file headers.

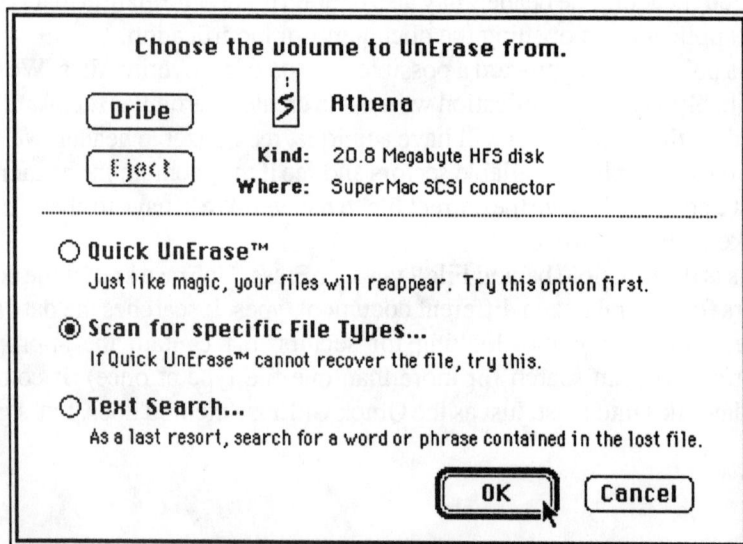

Figure 6.15 Choosing File Types UnErase

Choose which file types you wish to search for:

```
MacPaint 2.0 file            ⬆
MacProject II file
MacServe volume                      ┌──────────────┐
MacSqz! file                         │ Select All ⌘A │
MacWrite 5.0 file                    └──────────────┘
MacWrite file                        ┌──────────────┐
Microsoft Excel chart                │  Options...   │
Microsoft Excel file                 └──────────────┘
Microsoft Word 3.0 file              ..................
Microsoft Word 4.0 file              ┌──────────────┐
Microsoft Works 2.0 (DB) file ⬇      │     Do It     │
                                     └──────────────┘
                                     ┌──────────────┐
                                     │    Cancel     │
                                     └──────────────┘
```

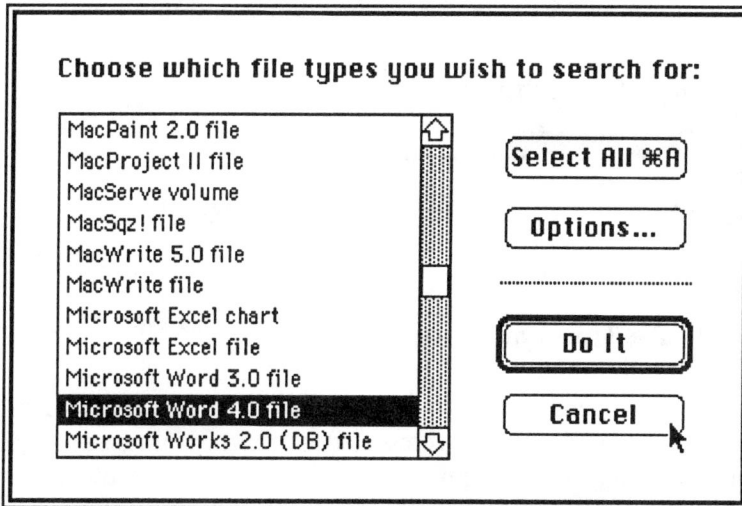

Figure 6.16 Choosing which types of files to search for

Limiting your selection of file types to the ones you actually use and/or wish to recover is wisest. You can extend your selections in this dialog box in all the typical Macintosh ways: by clicking and dragging to select multiple file types, and by holding down the Shift key to add newly clicked-on names to the existing selections. Clicking a second time on a selected item, with the Shift key down, toggles its selection "off" without affecting others. Clicking an item by itself without the Shift key down toggles everyone else off and selects only that item.)

We keep mentioning the "erased data space." Actually, you can have File Types UnErase search other areas on the disk than just the sectors currently not in use by any file. This is done via a dialog that is accessed by clicking the Options... button in the dialog shown in Figure 6.16. We'll show you this dialog and discuss the options available at the end of this section. For now, we're going to continue to limit ourselves to searching the free space on the volume. Having clicked the name "Microsoft Word 4.0 file" to select that file type, as shown in the illustration, we now click **Do It**. (A rather atypical command name that, it is staunchly maintained, was in no way inspired by Bo Jackson.)

UnErase now proceeds to scan the sectors on the target volume for possible matches. It informs us of progress via a small alert box that features a progress bar (Figure 6.17).

Clicking the **Cancel** button, by the way, stops UnErase dead in its tracks at this point. Any files found to that point will be shown to you in the UnErase window. This lets you interrupt a long search if you believe that UnErase has already found the correct file.

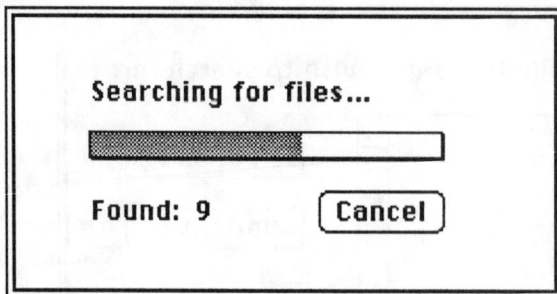

Figure 6.17 File Types UnErase reports progress

However it happens to finish, whether we tell it to stop or it runs out of places to search, the list of files found is presented to us in the UnErase main window.

In the case shown in Figure 6.18, we seem to have hit the jackpot. Unfortunately, you will note that none of the files has a name. Files frequently don't know their own names; they rely on the operating system to take care of that kind of detail. Thus, when the OS's bookkeeping information is lost, as it usually is when operating under File Types UnErase, we have to rely on other cues to find the right file.

In this case shown here, the search is complicated somewhat by the fact that Microsoft Word tends to create quite a number of working files; files that are erased in the course of ordinary operation and usually contain absolutely nothing of interest. Because they contain the correct signature information, there is no way to tell UnErase not to list them.

Figure 6.18 Result of searching volume Athena for Microsoft Word 4.0 files

The only way out of this situation is to examine all likely candidates using the **View File** button. You can narrow down the number of files you examine by a good amount, though. If you have a general notion of the size of the file in kilobytes, you can only look at files close to that size. In any event, View File doesn't take that long; it's possible to go through a fairly sizable list in just a few minutes.

Once we've located the file(s) we wish to recover, we proceed as before. We adjust the Volume to Recover To via the command in the Options menu, choose a destination folder via the next command in that menu (**Change Destination Folder**), make certain the desired file's name has been selected in the scrolling list, and click the **UnErase** button.

If we experience difficulties in finding the type of file we want to recover, it may be that we need to expand the area in which we're searching. As we implied earlier, this is done via the Options dialog box, accessed from the File Types Choice dialog box shown earlier. To bring it up now, choose Start Over from the UnErase File menu. Click the File Types radio button and press the Return key. The file types dialog box appears. Now click the Options button. This dialog shows up (Figure 6.19).

Thus, we can choose to search just the erased (unoccupied) area (the default choice), just the area currently occupied by files (strange but explicable), or the entire disk. Searching the entire disk, of course, can be very time consuming, but potentially worth the trouble.

Why would you ever want to search the occupied data areas? We've said that File Types UnErase looks for headers, but actually there is other signature information in a file that can give it away; not all of it is necessarily located at the very beginning. It turns out that when new information is recorded to a particular sector, not all of the old information is necessarily destroyed if that

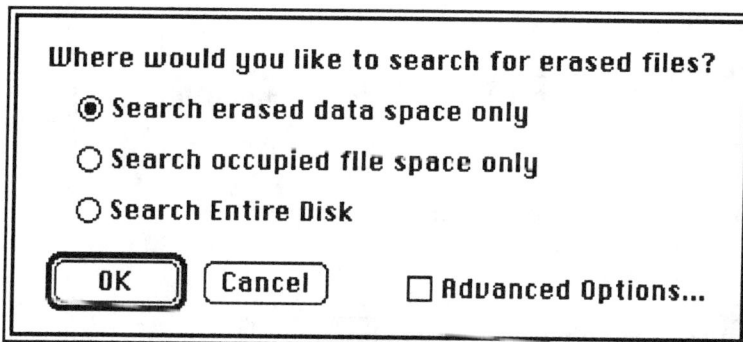

Figure 6.19 Options dialog box in File Types UnErase: Searching areas other than just the unoccupied data space

sector happens to be the last one in the new file. The new file may not need all of the sector; it may only need a few bytes of it.

Only the few bytes containing the new data are changed; the others are left alone. Any remaining old data is left intact. If it happens to contain legible file signature information, perhaps because it used to be the first sector in a file we want to recover, UnErase can scan it and determine that it is a candidate for recovery. Again, this process can be very time consuming, and results are variable.

Additional options are available through this dialog box; they appear when we click the Advanced Options checkbox. Doing so expands the dialog box so that it looks like Figure 6.20.

Four additional options become available at this point. We can choose to recover unknown file fragments; these are small pieces of files that match part of the search criteria, but not all. They may contain valuable data; they may not. The exhaustive search looks at every byte on the disk. This increases the likelihood of finding data, but is very time consuming.

To narrow the search down, we can specify a maximum upper bound to the size of a file. If you never create files larger than, say, 50K, it makes no sense to let UnErase recover 500K fragments, which it could do. (With 512-byte sectors, 9999 sectors as shown in Figure 6.20 is four megabytes. Setting the value to 99 gives an upper limit of 50K.) Finally, we can set the number of sectors per allocation block. This will limit the number of sectors examined if

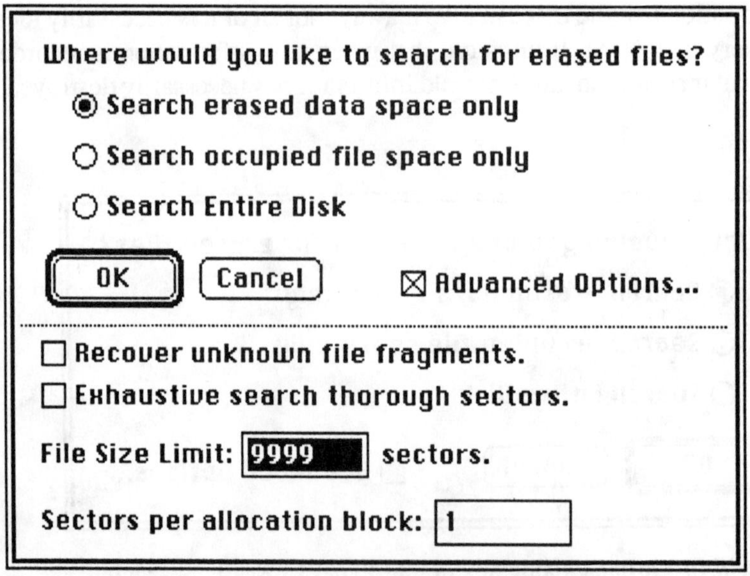

```
┌─────────────────────────────────────────────────────┐
│                                                       │
│   Where would you like to search for erased files?    │
│                                                       │
│      ◉ Search erased data space only                  │
│                                                       │
│      ○ Search occupied file space only                │
│                                                       │
│      ○ Search Entire Disk                             │
│                                                       │
│   ╔═══════════╗  ┌──────────┐                         │
│   ║    OK     ║  │  Cancel  │    ⊠ Advanced Options... │
│   ╚═══════════╝  └──────────┘                         │
│   ┄┄┄┄┄┄┄┄┄┄┄┄┄┄┄┄┄┄┄┄┄┄┄┄┄┄┄┄┄┄┄┄┄┄┄┄┄┄┄┄┄┄┄┄        │
│   ☐ Recover unknown file fragments.                   │
│   ☐ Exhaustive search thorough sectors.               │
│                                                       │
│   File Size Limit: ▐9999    ▌ sectors.                │
│                                                       │
│   Sectors per allocation block: │1         │          │
│                                                       │
└─────────────────────────────────────────────────────┘
```

Figure 6.20 Advanced options available to users of File Types UnErase

it's set to any value other than one. Setting it to two, for example, restricts UnErase to examining every other sector. (Only whole blocks are assigned to files; it makes no sense to look in the middle of a block for a file header, although other information may be present there.)

Clicking **OK** accepts the new options and sends us on our merry way. After what may be a lengthy search, we are again confronted with the UnErase main window and a chance to examine the files found to see if any are right one(s).

It may happen that this method will fail also, most especially if the exact file(s) we want to recover have been partially written over by new files. Think about it. Suppose just the first sector of an old file has been completely overwritten by new data. In that case, the file's header is lost. If there is no other signature information in the file, then File Types UnErase will pass over the rest of the file, failing to find its header. What then?

All is not lost. There is a last UnErase method available, one that relies on you to supply the hidden keys that will help to unlock the file and bring it into the light of day once more. The process is not simple, but it is not difficult. It can take a little time and be somewhat tedious, but it requires no great wit. And it helps immensely to have a printed copy of the file in hand. Interested? Let's give it a look.

Text Search UnErase

It turns out to be a very lucky thing for us that a given sector on a disk (or a block on a volume, if you will) can belong to one and only one file at a time. If only a small part of the data in that sector can be determined to belong to a file, then it follows that all the rest of the data does too (unless, of course, part of it has been subsequently overwritten. This happens, but is not necessarily fatal.) This points us toward another way of recovering erased files: looking for the specific data they happened to contain. We don't have to supply all of it; just a few words or a small sentence will do.

You may rightfully ask, what good is this, especially if I happen to have the print copy of the file that you mentioned a couple of paragraphs back. Fair question. We'll ask you one: How fast do you type? A 40 words per minute touch-typist can input 512 characters of data in about two and one-half minutes. (By convention, a typist's word consists of five characters, spaces and punctuation included. 40 wpm is thus 200 characters/minute.) UnErase is faster than retyping the old data, and you don't have to type: You can go for coffee, in fact.

The advantage is not necessarily large if you find yourself recovering single sectors and having to reassemble them into a whole file. (We'll show you how and why to do this.) However, you can recover entire blocks of sectors; this is done in roughly the same amount of time as it takes to recover a single sector with valid data. The advantage increases immensely, then. And if you don't type as fast as 40 wpm, or you don't have a print copy of the file, well . . . .

▼ Optical Character Recognition

There's a new method of inputting data into a microcomputer, one that doesn't rely on typing, although it does rely on an existing print copy of the desired data. The method is called Optical Character Recognition (OCR). It involves using a scanner to convert a document into a picture file that a computer can handle, and then using sophisticated—well, relatively sophisticated—pattern-recognition software to examine the picture and convert the graphics into ASCII characters. The result is a text file which can then be read and formatted via any word processor or page processing software (e.g., Microsoft Word and PageMaker).

How well does it work? Not very. Not yet. Not long after we got our scanner at PNC, we were literally deluged with requests to scan in documents, so that harried co-workers wouldn't have to re-type them. (Lawyers and other professionals don't usually send actual files on disks so that copy can be modifed with retyping.) And, we will admit, at times or two we have lost important working documents and found ourselves without a reliable backup. However, we had print copies of the documents. (Since then, we've learned to keep two or three disk copies of working files in various places around the office and at home.)

Eventually we broke down, tired of disappointing co-workers and having to re-type things ourselves, and bought an OCR software package. Or two. We will not name names. We tried using them. We gave up. Here's why:

First of all, it takes time to scan a document, and to scan it correctly. You can count on one or two minutes per page, and each page has to be scanned individually and saved as a picture. (By the way, do you know how large those pictures are, and how much RAM they take up? Lots. Don't even think about it if you have less than 4 megabytes of RAM in your Mac. Some OCR packages claim to work in less, but you still need wads and wads of disk space.)

After you've scanned a page, you then submit it to the OCR software for evaluation. This also takes a number of minutes. Then you get the results. An OCR application can rate its performance as "excellent" even when it has missed two or three characters in every line, if not actually in every word. It also doesn't handle proportional spacing very well, and can insert spaces in bizarre locations. Watch out for right-justified margins! So anyway, the file you get out can have enough errors that, although the software thinks it deserves an "A", any typing instuctor would give it an "F." And there will be no formatting.

Say it takes 15 minutes just to scan, intrepret, export, and then correct and format one page. (Not counting overhead—the time it takes setting up the equipment to read a particular kind of document). With 1-1/2" top and bottom margins, and 1" side margins, a page occupies 6-1/2 by 8 inches. That's about 48 lines of 75 picas (or characters) per line. 48 x 75 = 3600 characters = 720 words. Well, that's a rate of 48 words per minute, which is not bad for most of us. But 48 wpm is not very good for a typist, and if you have one available, he or she will be faster and much better.

It's also worth noting that the figures estimated above represent, in our experience, the absolutely optimum amount of output you can get—and one we never succeeded in achieving. A number of factors can slow you down: if the document is not highly legible—if it's a fax, forget it; if the characters are too close together; if the font is unusual; if you've a limited amount of memory; if you've a slow scanner, etc., etc. No matter what, you're going to be stuck at your Macintosh scanning, correcting, and formatting for a longer time than you thought it would take. OCR is not highly automated, and it is trickier than just typing.

In our experience, OCR is still too much in its infancy to be of very great use. Maybe next year . . .

The exact method of recovering files we're talking about here is Text Search UnErase, of course. With Text Search, you supply UnErase with a few words that you know the lost file contains. UnErase scans the disk looking for exact matches to that sequence of ASCII characters. Sectors that contain an exact match are presented to you as candidates for recovery. If UnErase believes that such a sector represents just the beginning of a block of data belonging to a single file, it will present all the sectors in such a block as a single candidate.

Notes   We use this method as a last resort, for volumes without FileSaver protection and upon whom File Types UnErase was not successful. If a file is in many fragments across a disk, (or sometimes even if it is not), it may be necessary to recover it in pieces and then assemble these pieces into a whole. UnErase has tools to let us do that. You'll have to search for each fragment one at a time, using a new search for data likely to be in the desired fragment. Again, a print copy of the file is a big help. Without one, you'll have to rely on your own memory, or that of someone else who knew the file well. Also note that the recovered file will almost certainly lack formatting information, and may be incomplete. Its own application may not recognize it; you'll have to open and save it in an application that reads ASCII files (Microsoft Word can be made to open any file as an ASCII file; hold down the Option key while dragging down the **File** menu to **Open**.) Still, it's better than nothing.

Remember back in Chapter 4, when we found an unoccupied space on the volume Athena and left a small message in it? Let's go back and see if we can find it. We'll use Text Search UnErase, and in the process introduce its operation.

Finding the Fragment from Chapter 4

As before, we access Norton UnErase from the Norton Utilities main menu. This time, we click the third radio button on the screen in Figure 6.21.

Clicking OK at this point brings up (you guessed it) a dialog box (Figure 6.22) into which we type the text we want to search for. In this case, it's the "Hi There!" that we left in absolute sector number 10,452 on volume Athena, back in Chapter 4.

You don't need to worry about the hex data shown here; UnErase automatically translates the ASCII you type into hexadecimal, which of course is what it really looks for on your disk—in this case, nine consecutive bytes with the value \$486920546865726521. The converse is true, by the way; you can type hex into the hex field and see the ASCII come out on top. Rare is the person who can do this. Probably doesn't need this book, either.

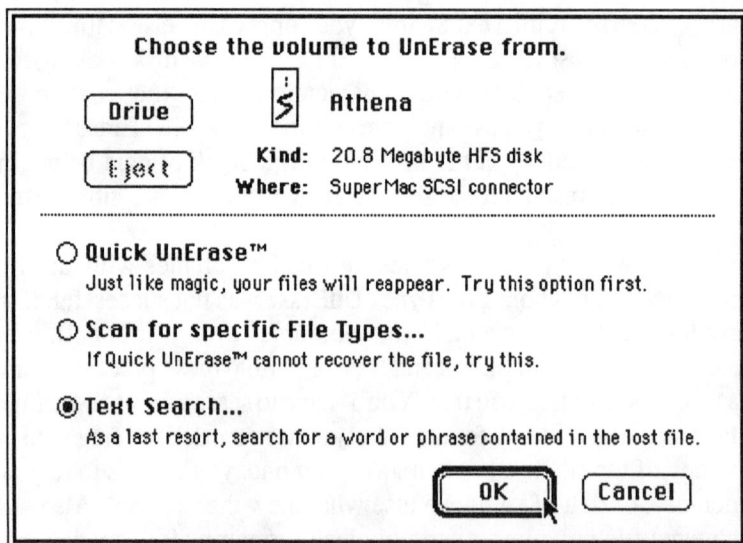

Choose the volume to UnErase from.

Drive

Eject

Athena

Kind: 20.8 Megabyte HFS disk
Where: SuperMac SCSI connector

○ **Quick UnErase™**
Just like magic, your files will reappear. Try this option first.

○ **Scan for specific File Types...**
If Quick UnErase™ cannot recover the file, try this.

◉ **Text Search...**
As a last resort, search for a word or phrase contained in the lost file.

OK   Cancel

Figure 6.21 Now we search for text

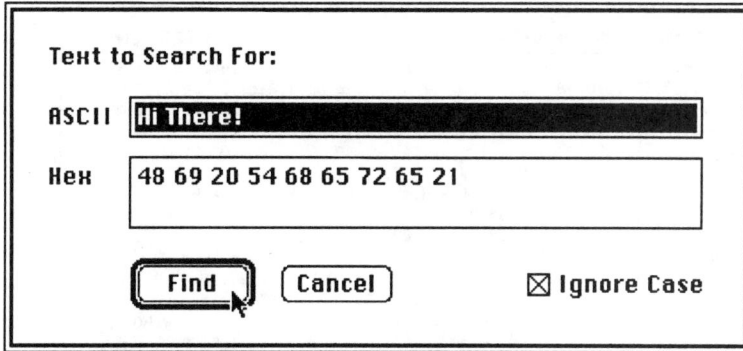

Figure 6.22 Typing in the text to search for

One more thing: As a default, Text Search UnErase will ignore case as it proceeds, unless you click on and uncheck the box in the lower right corner of the dialog box. There are times when case (capital vs. small letters) may make a difference. Usually it isn't significant.

Once we've typed in the text we wish to find, we click Find. UnErase now scans the disk looking for an exact match to the text string we typed (possibly ignoring uppercase vs. lowercase letters, to be sure). Progress is reported via an alert box, as ever. Once UnErase finishes, candidates for recovery are shown in the main UnErase window (Figure 6.23).

When using Text Search UnErase, it's a good idea to examine all candidate fragments using the View File command. Doing so with the single fragment above selected shows a screen like Figure 6.24.

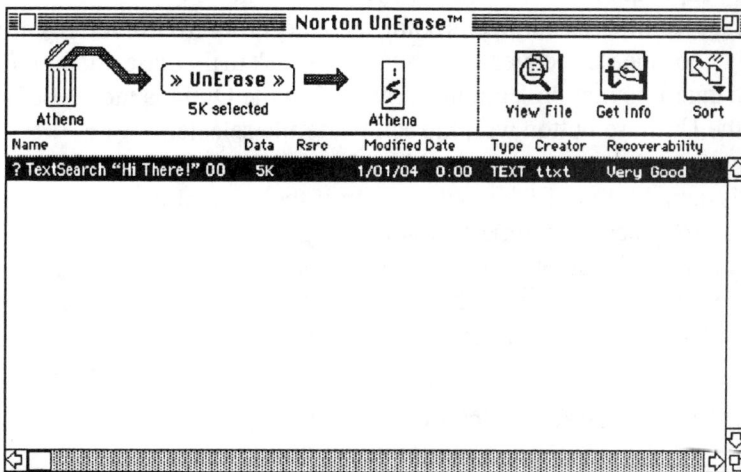

Figure 6.23 A fragment found; file features "Hi There!"

```
? TextSearch "Hi There!" 00                          5,120 bytes
Hi There!.+......ò..ô.±ôÃ∆c..ô.ì0.3.8a........+.......-....±..ô
..ôÃ∆c..ô.É0>.3.0a•®.........;...®.H/......ò.ô..lôÃ∆c..ô..ôÉ.3?33
0a.®........?..è.®.H/....ò.ôÃÃ.ôÃ∆c..ôôÃôÉ.30330'.®........?..è
.®.H......ò.ëââ±ôÃ∆c..ô.ââì.31330'........?......./.....ò....ôè
Ã∆aè.ò..ò..3.>.00.D........?.......*......Ã......0...D........?
.......$......Ã......0..D......-.?...............
™.?...........®C.....'.?...¿.®.H.....®C....Đ.?...p.®.H.....
®C.....T.?.....®.H......8*.?.........™.ƒ...p..?...x<......
.U.D......Ã?...√Ã.......™.ƒ....®?.....d.......U......Ã?..
... û.......™.¿G..¿.`?...®..¿.®.H.....¿L...√.†?...®..0.®.H...
...®N/.....P...ü..€.®.H.......ã...............D:".....
.........d........D<ã....¿.............D?"....®.....
..Ã.........ãe.................®."?...........®.HO
....>.®¬.®.........Ã..®.ãè.........®.H1....!.®®.®.....
`.....Ã..®.b'....Ã........¿®®H4 ...!"xF.Xp.<D.£á..a.ãû\.%áÃ.
....ã....B.............2 ...!"DB"dâ."D.$HÃ.í$L"a.&HÃ..E.b....%..
```

○ Data Fork
○ Resource Fork
○ Resource Map   [Done]

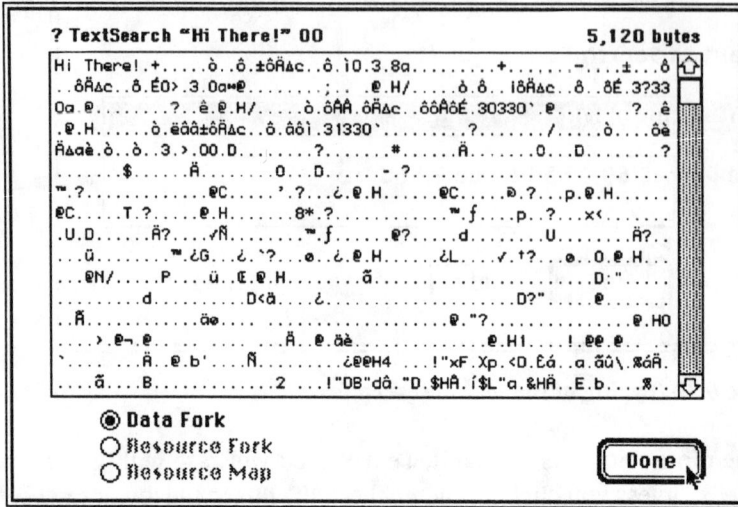

Figure 6.24 There it is; "Hi There!"

This example points up something to deal with. All we did, after all, was record a measly nine bytes of data at the beginning of one sector. Text Search UnErase, on the other hand, seems to believe that this file is over 10 sectors long. What gives?

Well, it turns out that the next several sectors after the one we modified contained ASCII data as well and were not currently part of any existing file. As an operating rule, UnErase will group all such data into a single recovery candidate, whether the subsequent data actually belongs to the file or not. If extraneous data is included, you will have to cut it out using your ASCII-reading application, after you've recovered the file.

Well, that's not so bad. At this point, recovery proceeds as ever. It's probably a really good idea to recover to a spare floppy disk in this case, though. Just use the Change Destination Volume command in the Options menu, before you click the UnErase button with the candidate file selected.

Now, in real life, you may try this method, only to discover that but part of a file is actually found. This will happen if the original file was fragmented, with parts of other (existing) files intervening. In that case, you're going to have to assemble all the pieces, and you absolutely must recover to another volume to be certain of getting everything back that can be got back. We've said all along we would show you how to do this. Now's the time.

Assembling Files from Scratch

It should go without saying, but it won't, that you have no hope of recovering executable files (applications, system files, etc.) this way. As for documents, you'll get back data, but formatting is virtually certain to be lost. With those caveats, we proceed.

Oh, one or two more things before we forget. When you go to recover a file using Text Search UnErase, choose a few words, a phrase or a sentence from the very beginning of the file. Do this for each subsequent section as well. If you go too far into a section (past 512 characters, say) you risk not picking up one or more sectors at the beginning of that fragment. OK, now we're really ready.

Suppose we examine our "Hi There!" fragment using View File, and discover it to be incomplete. Not to worry; we just have to find and amalgamate the other pieces.

First though, we save "Hi There!" in a safe place. We choose Save As... from the UnErase menu, change volumes, type in the name "Our File," and press Return.

From here on out, we are going to append additional fragments of the file to "Our File," which now contains the original "Hi There!" data on a separate volume. Let's say that, in examining "Hi There," we discover that it ended just before "As I was saying..."

At this point, we choose **Start Over** from the UnErase File menu. Again, we click the Text Search radio button and press Return. Now, when the text search dialog box appears, we type in "As I was saying..." and press Return again. UnErase now scans the disk for a text passage beginning with this phrase.

When (and if) UnErase finds a candidate fragment, it shows up in the scrolling list. We click on it and select View File to make sure it belongs; sure enough, it does. So with the fragment's name still selected, we choose Append To from the UnErase menu. The standard Open File dialog box appears. It should actually be set to the correct volume (a floppy would be best, as we say) and to the correct directory on that floppy, if we didn't save "Our File" at root level. In any event, we find "Our File," click on its name to select it, and press Return.

Now, the data from the second fragment, beginning with "As I was saying..." is added to the end of the data from the first fragment. At the end of the procedure, both fragments have been incorporated in order into a single file called "Our File." Pretty nifty, huh? You can keep going like this for fragment after fragment, always looking for text at the beginning of the next fragment, and appending fragments found to a single file that you accumulate on a floppy disk.

You may want to use the "text only" versions of the two commands, Save As... and Append to... These are also found in the UnErase menu. They will, among other things previously mentioned, strip out all ASCII control codes, which are likely wrong anyway.

Well, well. Now you know how to use all three parts of Norton UnErase. That should be enough to cover virtually every contingency. But what if . . . .

If All Else Fails

There will be times when UnErase can't get files back for you. This does not necessarily mean that they are absolutely gone for good. Now if only a few files are missing, alas, they're probably goners. Overwritten by new files, never to be seen again.

However, if massive numbers of files are missing; files that you never deleted, this could be a symptom of something else altogether. Your disk may have suffered some sort of formatting catastrophe, with all its bookkeeping information rewritten in a way so as to hide perfectly legitimate, recoverable files. Only the erased data space is checked by Quick UnErase, after all. If some of a file's sectors are shown as occupied by another file (even if that isn't really true), then that file will be partially or totally unrecoverable. At least by UnErase.

There is something you can do in the case of such a massive failure. It happens to be the subject of the next chapter.

Review

We've seen how the File Manager creates and deletes files on and from a disk. In particular, we've noted that a file's data is not erased when a file is deleted; it is merely made available for use for new or expanding files. If it can be got to before someone else claims its space, the data can be recovered. Norton UnErase can do the job.

We examined UnErase in general, checking out its window and looking at the commands in its menus. We've looked at the three UnErase methods: Quick UnErase, which uses the FileSaver INIT's data files to reconstruct files; Files Types, which examines disk space for special signatures left by different types of files; and Text Search UnErase, which searches the text for words or phrases belonging to a file. We've seen how to use Text Seach UnErase to accumulate fragments of a file into a single place.

Now we're ready to examine what to do in the case of truly massive damage to a hard disk. The kind of damage that can result from accidentally formatting the disk, or from virtually complete disturbance of its vital bookkeeping info. With a little foresight, it's possible to render such damage merely transitory. Format Recover is the key to setting things back to rights.

7

Reshuffling
the Deck

Setting Things to Rights
with Format Recover

Introduction

Since PC time began,* the apotheosis of disaster has been the accidentally formatted hard disk. Oh, how easy, how dreadfully easy, it used to be to do! Format C: <Enter> <Enter>—that was all it took. And everything, everything on that hard disk was lost.

Thankfully, we Macintosh users have always been shielded from the naked horror of the command line, where typing such innocent little commands can get one into such amazing difficulties. However, 'tis said that no system can be made foolproof, for fools are far too ingenious. So true. And even the wisest among us (indeed, sometimes it seems *especially* the wisest) do foolish things. Like format a hard disk. Even on a Macintosh.

Well, if you followed along carefully this far, it will not surprise you to learn that all data is *not* necessarily lost when a hard disk is formatted. It's true of PC-clone types, and it's true of Macintoshes as well. With a little ingenuity, the data

---

* Said by many to be January 1, 1980, which is the time that an IBM PC's system clock defaults to—Apple II owners may dispute this figure.

can be recovered. Fortunately, that ingenuity happens to be packaged in a module of the Norton Utilities for the Macintosh called Format Recover.

Format Recover can be used to fix more than just accidental formatting. At times, the bookkeeping information on a disk can become so severely damaged that it needs to be completely redone. Format Recover can accomplish this, as well. In addition, Format Recover can restore all the comments that you've attached to your files using the Get Info command in the Finder's File menu. These comments are lost when you rebuild the desktop. ("The disk xxx needs minor repairs. Do you want to repair it?") Format Recover gets them back.

We're going to learn how to use Format Recover in this chapter. But first, we're going to review some fundamental formatting concepts, just so we know what we're up against.

Formatting Review

As we've said elsewhere, formatting is the process of making a disk ready for use by a particular computer's operating system. It involves dividing the disk into small, discrete areas into which data may be written. It also involves creating the bookkeeping structures that will keep track of the disk's data. These two processes are separate, and represent the two different kinds of formatting: hard, or physical formatting versus soft, or logical formatting. The differences are very important and are crucial to the operation of Format Recover.

Hard versus Soft Formatting

When first manufactured, the surface of a disk is relatively smooth and undifferentiated. A computer system, however, needs more organization to be able to store and locate data; think of a mass of papers on your desk in contrast with a filing cabinet with drawers, hanging files, and folders. The physical aspects of disk organization have to come first: the file drawers, folders, etc. (or at least, their disk equivalents) have to be constructed.

The exact details of this construction depend on the disk drive hardware and on the disk media. When we say media, by the way, we're referring the surface of a disk as a medium for carrrying information. It consists of very small particles of metal oxide bound to a plastic substrate. The size of the oxide particles is important; it sets an upper limit on the amount of data that can be stored on a disk.

You see, the first thing that happens is that tracks are laid down. These are concentric circles around the center of the disk. Each has the same width. A small amount of empty space is left between tracks to eliminate cross-talk. We don't want data from one track interfering with data from another. So the size of the data-carrying metal oxide particles on the disk surface dictates how small tracks can be. The disks used with the 1.4-meg drives on the new Mac II series can support twice the number of tracks per inch that the older 800K drives can. (800K disks have the same density as the very oldest 400K disks sold with the original Mac; they happen to have data recorded on both sides, whereas the 400K disks were single-sided.)

Tracks aren't enough. We've seen how an error of just one bit can totally throw off the interpretation of data. So clearly we need, at least, a way to tell where the data on a track begins. Indeed, it turns out that quite a lot of data can be stored in one track; more than we need in many cases. The optimum solution would be to divide up the track and allow separate pieces of data to be stored within each division.

The dual problems of dividing a track and identifying its beginning are solved by creating marked segments on it. These segments are the sectors that we've introduced earlier; they usually contain 512 bytes of data, plus a small header that identifies the sector. This sector address is given in terms of the disk side number, the track number on that side, and the sector number within that track. Numbering begins with zero. Sectors also contain a small amount of data at the very end that are used to verify that no destructive changes have occurred since the sector was last written to. These data are compared with the sector's actual contents via a mathematical function; if the two values do not agree, the sector has become damaged somehow and its data are suspect.

The process of creating all these physical structures on the disk media (composed as they are of magnetized regions in an unmagnetized background) is what we refer to when we speak of physical formatting, or hard formatting. It's a darned shame, but there is a complete lack of consistency here in the use of terminology. Hard formatting is sometimes just called "formatting;" sometimes it's called "initializing;" and sometimes it's even called "set up" (as in Apple's HD Setup utility, which is used to physically format Apple hard disks.)

The worst of this is that sometimes these same terms are used to refer to soft, or logical formatting, which is an entirely different process. Soft formatting on a Macintosh disk is simply the creation of the bookkeeping structures that we examined in Chapter 4: the boot blocks, the volume info block, the volume bit map, and the catalog and extents b-trees. On a given disk type, these structures are always going to go in the same sectors (once the sectors themselves and their ordering have been established via hard formatting).

The critical difference is this: Soft formatting merely creates new bookkeeping records; the data area on the disk is not affected *per se*. Hard formatting, on the other hand, creates new tracks and sectors; because the beginnings of sectors must be clearly marked for the drive mechanism to be able to locate them, any trace of old sector boundaries on a disk must be eliminated. So there it is: Hard formatting *completely destroys any data that happened to be stored on a disk.*

Beyond this point (and it is a critical one), hard disks and floppies are treated differently. It's worth summarizing how.

Hard Disks

One thing we ought to mention about hard disks right off the bat is that a hard disk drive may have more than one disk within it. Each disk is called a platter. There is a separate read/write head for each side of each platter. The collection of tracks along the same location on each platter is called a cylinder.

Physical formatting of a hard disk is usually done via a utility program that the manufacturer places on a diskette included with the drive. You may never have launched this utility; almost all hard drives these days come from the factory already formatted. Indeed, most have already been soft-formatted as well, and include Macintosh system software and possibly other software that the disk manufacturer has licensed from its developers. In any case, it's worth noting again that running your hard disk setup utility, whatever it's called, will likely destroy all the data on your disk. Nothing on earth can get it back at this point. Not Format Recover, not anything.

The more common way for you or us to format a hard disk is to choose the **Erase Disk** command in the Finder's **Special** menu. In the case of hard disks, this command performs a soft format; new bookkeeping information is laid down. (You can't erase your current system—mostly likely your startup—disk, by the way.) Another way this might happen is if the disk suffers some sort of damage to the boot blocks, the VIB, or the b-trees. You might get a message from the Finder via an alert box like "This disk is damaged. Do you want to initialize it?" If you click **Yes,** a soft format will be done.

Wait. Didn't we say a while back that "to initialize" usually meant "to perform a hard format? Yes we did. In the case of floppy disks, it means just that.

Floppies

Floppies are formatted in the same way as hard disks; they simply have fewer tracks. The Macintosh OS handles floppy formatting; when you insert a fresh floppy into the drive, you get a message like "This is not a Macintosh disk. Do you want to initialize it?" If you click Yes, the Mac performs a hard format on the disk, followed by a soft format.

See the difference? In the case of hard disks, "initialize" means "soft format only;" in the case of floppy disks, it means both. Thus, initializing a floppy disk completely destroys all data on it, beyond recall.

The same holds true for using the Erase Disk command. Doing so on a floppy performs both kinds of formatting, and effectively wipes the disk clean of any old data. See where we're going with this? If you want to erase a floppy disk, we recommend that you simple open its window, choose Select All from the Finder's Edit menu, and drag the entire contents to the trashcan. As we said in the last chapter, trashing a file or folder simply erases its bookkeeping information, not the data, as the Erase Disk command does.

Only floppies whose files have been deleted in this way can be restored using Format Recover. A floppy that has been initialized or erased via the Finder has been, to be quite blunt, lobotomized. It also bears repeating that you must activate FileSaver protection on each and every floppy that you would like to protect from massive file deletion. This is done by clicking the FileSaver icon in the Control Panel (Finder's Apple menu), inserting the floppy and making sure its name and icon show up, using the **Drive** button if necessary, clicking all the radio button options to **On**, and then clicking **Save**. The same is true of all hard disks you wish to protect.

Undoing the Damage

Hard formatting is a lost cause; we know that. Fortunately, it is rare in the case of hard disks. With regard to floppy disks, we can make it equally rare with a little behavior modification—not using **Erase Disk** to delete all files on a disk, for example. Soft formatting, on the other hand, is a different story. Since soft formatting merely rewrites the bookkeeping information, shouldn't we be able to re-record the old bookkeeping data, restoring all files on the disk to accessibility? And shouldn't we be able to do this when the bookkeeping data has been severely damaged, rather than actually rewritten? Well, we can. Provided we've had the foresight to install FileSaver on the disk in question. And sometimes, even when we haven't . . . .

Using Format Recover

Format Recover uses the FileSaver data files to recreate the bookkeeping information on a disk volume as it was when those FileSaver data files were last modified. If there have not been substantial changes to the data on the disk since this bookkeeping data was recorded, the disk will be restored to the same condition is was in at the time. It is worth noting, however, than any files stored on it since the last FileSaver update will be lost. It might be possible to recover them using File Types UnErase.

In the case of FileSaver, we can easily introduce you to its operation via an example. You need to do a little advance preparation. Get hold of a clean diskette; one that doesn't have anything on it at all, or at least has nothing but obsolete files (you aren't going to get them back in this example). Format it (if needed) or delete all the files on it (if any), and use it to make a copy of your Norton Utilities for the Macintosh Installation diskette. Put the original away.

Now we launch the Norton Utilities for the Macintosh, double-clicking its icon as ever. This time, when the main menu screen (Figure 7.1) appears, we click the Format Recover button; it's the third one down the list. (If you already have the Utilities running, choose Format Recover from the Utilities menu of whatever module you happen to be in; most likely UnErase if you're following along in order.)

After we click the Format Recover button, the main Format Recover dialog box appears (Figure 7.2), presenting us with a number of choices.

As it turns out, you don't have to use the FileSaver control panel device to install protection on a disk; you can do it directly from Format Recover, as we see from the second radio button option shown in Figure 7.2. In fact, that's just what we're going to do. Click the second radio button and then click OK (or press the Return key). What we see next is shown in Figure 7.3.

When the dialog box first appears, we have to insert the Installation Disk copy and possible click **Drive** before the dialog box looks very much like the

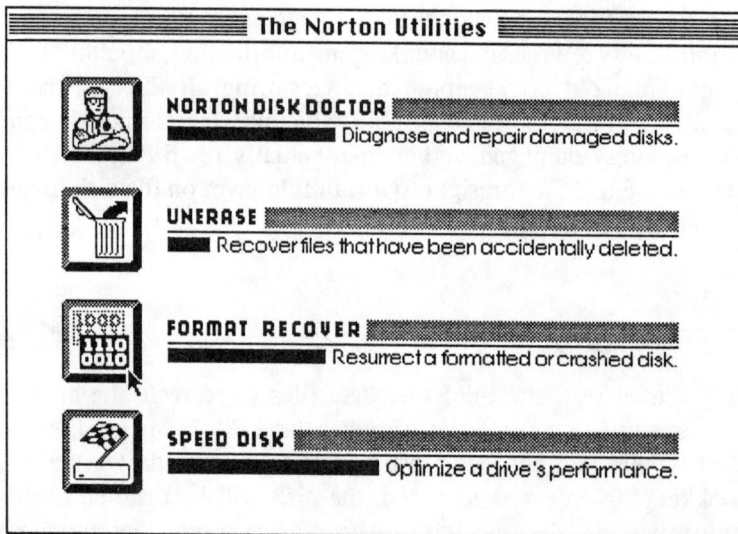

Figure 7.1 Back to the main menu again; this time for Format Recover

```
 ┌─────────────────────────────────────────────┐
 │ What do you want to do?                       │
 │                                               │
 │  ● Restore Formatted or Crashed Disk          │
 │    Attempt to recover your lost folders and files. │
 │                                               │
 │  ○ Install Disk Protection                    │
 │    Create a new FileSaver information file for a particular disk. │
 │                                               │
 │  ○ Update Disk Information                    │
 │    Manually update the FileSaver info.        │
 │                                               │
 │  ○ Restore Finder Comments                    │
 │    Restore Finder's Get Info comments after a desktop rebuild. │
 │                                               │
 │  [  OK  ]   [ Cancel ]                        │
 └─────────────────────────────────────────────┘
```

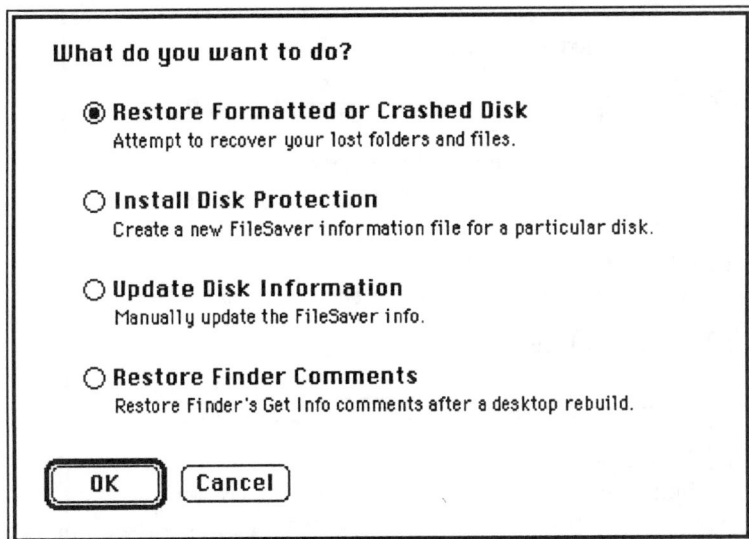

Figure 7.2 The main Format Recover dialog box

one in Figure 7.3. To finish installing, we check all three boxes by clicking them, set the number of files to protect to some low number (there are less than 10 files on the disk, after all), and then click **OK**.

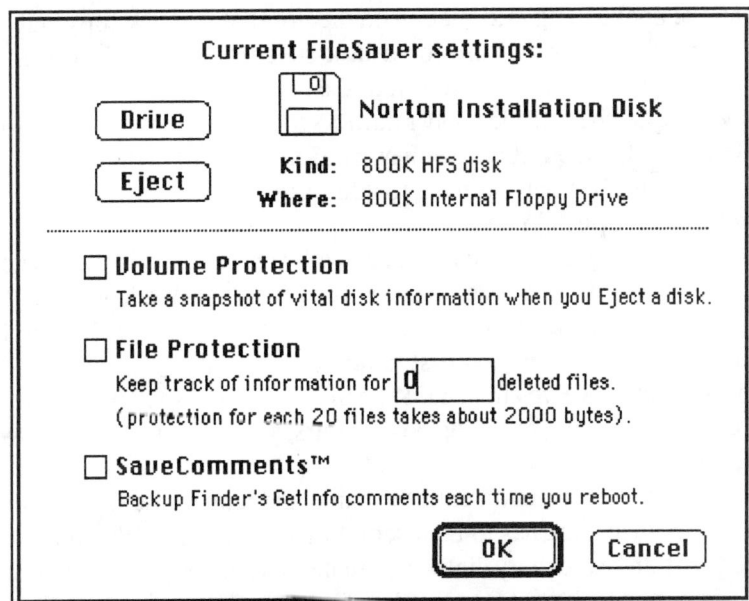

```
 ┌─────────────────────────────────────────────┐
 │           Current FileSaver settings:         │
 │                                               │
 │   [ Drive ]      ▢  Norton Installation Disk  │
 │                                               │
 │   [ Eject ]    Kind:  800K HFS disk           │
 │               Where:  800K Internal Floppy Drive │
 │ ········································· │
 │  □ Volume Protection                          │
 │    Take a snapshot of vital disk information when you Eject a disk. │
 │                                               │
 │  □ File Protection                            │
 │    Keep track of information for [ 0 ] deleted files. │
 │    (protection for each 20 files takes about 2000 bytes). │
 │                                               │
 │  □ SaveComments™                              │
 │    Backup Finder's GetInfo comments each time you reboot. │
 │                   [  OK  ]   [ Cancel ]       │
 └─────────────────────────────────────────────┘
```

Figure 7.3 Within Format Recover, installing FileSaver protection on the Norton Installation Disk copy

```
┌──────────────────────────────────────────────────┐
│              Current FileSaver settings:           │
│                                                    │
│                      ┌──┐                           │
│         ┌─────────┐  │ □│   Norton Installation Disk│
│         │  Drive  │  └──┘                           │
│         └─────────┘                                 │
│                       Kind:  800K HFS disk          │
│         ┌─────────┐  Where:  800K Internal Floppy Drive│
│         │  Eject  │                                 │
│         └─────────┘                                 │
│ ·················································· │
│   ⊠ Volume Protection                              │
│     Take a snapshot of vital disk information when you Eject a disk.│
│                                                    │
│   ⊠ File Protection                                │
│     Keep track of information for │ 20│ deleted files.│
│     (protection for each 20 files takes about 2000 bytes).│
│                                                    │
│   ⊠ SaveComments™                                  │
│     Backup Finder's GetInfo comments each time you reboot.│
│                                                    │
│                       ┌──────────┐  ┌──────────┐   │
│                       │    OK    │  │  Cancel  │   │
│                       └──────────┘  └──────────┘   │
└──────────────────────────────────────────────────┘
```

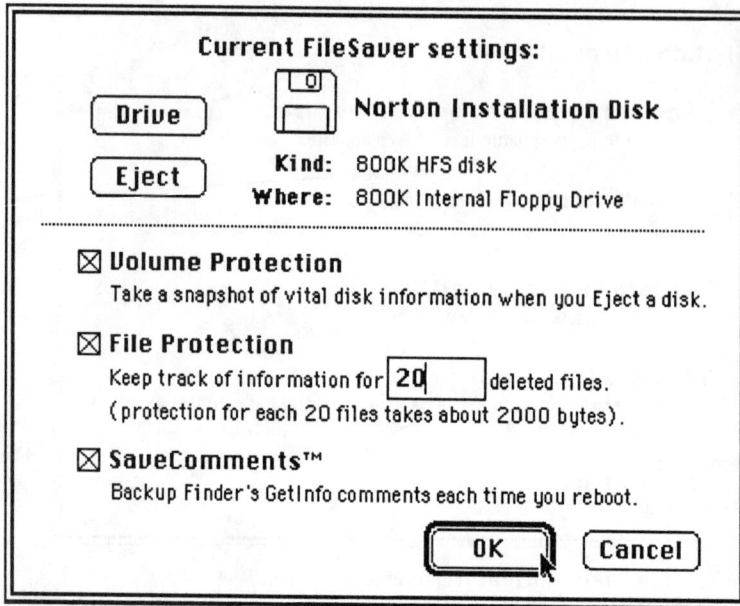

**Figure 7.4 FileSaver installation within Format Recover;
all settings the way we want them**

Once we click **OK** on the dialog box shown in Figure 7.4, Format Recover reads all the bookeeping information on the Installation Disk copy and creates a new copy thereof, which is stored in a specific, easy-to-find format and location. When it finishes, we return to the main menu.

Now we quit the Utilities and return to the Finder. We double-click the Installation Disk's icon, choose **Select All** from the **Edit** menu, and drag all of its contents into the trashcan. And to add insult to injury, we choose **Empty Trash** from the **Special** menu.

Now, we could get all those files back with UnErase, but in the case of total disk erasure like this, it's easier to use Format Recover. We launch the Norton Utilities for the Macintosh again and click the Format Recover button (Figure 7.5). This time, we choose the first radio button option.

This time, once we've clicked OK on the dialog box shown in Figure 7.5, a small choose-volume type dialog box appears, asking us what disk we want to recover (Figure 7.6).

We click the **Drive** button until the name and icon of the Installation Disk copy appear. (The disk has to be inserted in a drive first.) We click **Open** to proceed. The drive recovery dialog box makes an appearance, as in Figure 7.7.

As you can see, Format Recover has found the FileSaver data file that we created not long ago. Let's click the Restore button and see what happens.

What do you want to do?

◉ **Restore Formatted or Crashed Disk**
Attempt to recover your lost folders and files.

○ **Install Disk Protection**
Create a new FileSaver information file for a particular disk.

○ **Update Disk Information**
Manually update the FileSaver info.

○ **Restore Finder Comments**
Restore Finder's Get Info comments after a desktop rebuild.

[OK] [Cancel]

Figure 7.5 **Let's get those files back!**

Well, as it turns out, an alert box appears, informing us that Format Recover was able to restore the volume successfully. We click OK and find ourselves back at the Norton Utilities main menu. We quit the Utilities and return the Finder. A quick peek inside the disk window of the Installation Disk copy reveals that, yes, all the icons are back. You might want to open one of the Read

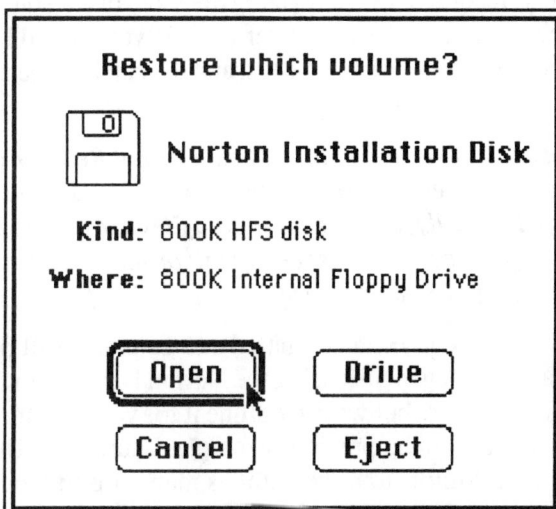

Restore which volume?

Norton Installation Disk

Kind: 800K HFS disk
Where: 800K Internal Floppy Drive

[Open] [Drive]
[Cancel] [Eject]

Figure 7.6 **Choosing which volume to recover**

```
┌─────────────────────────────────────────────────────────────┐
│ ┌───────────────────────────────────────────────────────────┐ │
│ │  ⊗  FileSaver information has been found for "Norton Installation │ │
│ │     Last updated: Sep 13, 1990  2:08 PM.                  │ │
│ │  Do you want to completely restore the disk using this information? │ │
│ │ ············································································· │ │
│ │  ┌───────────┐                                            │ │
│ │  │  Restore  │▷  Restore this volume.                    │ │
│ │  └───────────┘                                            │ │
│ │  ┌───────────────┐                                        │ │
│ │  │  Keep looking │  Search for more recent FileSaver information. │ │
│ │  └───────────────┘                                        │ │
│ │  ┌───────────────┐                                        │ │
│ │  │  Reconstruct  │  Recover the disk without using FileSaver information. │ │
│ │  └───────────────┘                                        │ │
│ │  ┌───────────┐                                            │ │
│ │  │  Cancel   │  Do not restore this volume.              │ │
│ │  └───────────┘                                            │ │
│ └───────────────────────────────────────────────────────────┘ │
└─────────────────────────────────────────────────────────────┘
```

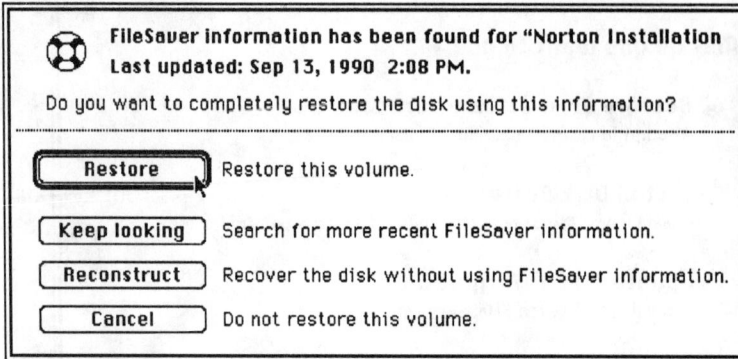

Figure 7.7 This volume can be restored!

Me files (such as the Installer notes) just to satisfy yourself that, yes, the data are all there.

So now we've seen that Format Recover can restore a disk whose files have been deleted from the disk's bookkeeping record. That's what happens when you drag files to the trash and empty it, after all. The same thing happens whenever a disk is soft-formatted.

We mentioned that Format Recover can also be used to restore disks that have been severely damaged, rather than formatted. How about that?

There are a number of ways in which such damage can occur. Some software, for example, plays fast and loose with the catalog and extents trees. This is particularly true when you're using Multifinder. File changes are not necessarily immediately recorded to the catalog tree on disk; sometimes they're buffered in memory and written at a later time. If you should happen to suffer a power outage, those changes will be lost and the catalog tree may be left in a bad way.

By the way, as you can see from its main dialog box, Format Recover can be used to occasionally update protection to a disk; this is a good idea if you rarely turn your Macintosh off. Normally, the FileSaver data files are updated when you shut down or restart; if you don't do this very often, you may want to update the data files manually using Format Recover.

Just as we can simulate a recently soft-formatted disk by erasing all files on a floppy, we can simulate a damaged disk using the Norton Disk Editor. We'll leave the procedure as an exercise, but we can outline it for you. Use the same Installation Disk copy we used in the previous example. Launch the Utilities and choose the Norton Disk Editor from the Utilities menu. Insert the Installation Disk copy and press the Return key.

Now choose Catalog B-Tree from the Objects menu. This switches you to a view of the root node of the tree. What you're going to do is find the leaf node that contains the Installer Notes file leaf record, and completely zero the record out. Click the Down button and then the Right button until the leaf node containing the Installer Notes comes into view. (This won't take long; there are only a few nodes in the tree on this disk, which has but a dozen or so files to take care of, all told.) Now switch to View In Hex. When the window changes to a hexadecimal view of the data, hold down the zero key on your keyboard until all the data in the entire sector has been wiped out; this may take a few minutes. Then click the window's close box. You'll be asked to save changes; do so. Then quit the Disk Editor.

Now you have to get the disk past FileSaver, which is going to want to update it as is—which is not what we want to do!* Hold down the Command, Shift, and number 1 keys to eject the disk. You may get a message asking you to reinsert it. Hold down the Command and period (.) keys to make that message go away.

If you reinsert the disk at this point, there's no telling what you'll see. When we tried this experiment, all the file icons were gone except for the Accessories Notes. We ran Format Recover on it, following the instructions above, and got everything back.

Another trick we tried, by the way, was zeroing out the root node of the catalog tree on the Installation Disk copy. This created a lovely problem: The Finder refused to mount the disk. Not only that, but the drive kept spitting it back out at us when we tried to insert it while running Format Recover. Turns out, we were running under Multifinder. Multifinder, in some ways, sits between a disk and an application, like a guard at a drawbridge. It simply wouldn't let the "damaged" disk past. So we switched to running under just the Finder (Set Startup). That time, Format Recover worked like a charm.

Well, all-in-all, this has been a good tour through the basic workings of Format Recover to this point. In real life, you're going to face two possible situations. Here's how to deal with each.

FileSaver Installed—Yeah!

We've covered this case. In both examples above, we made sure that FileSaver protection was installed. If you followed along at your Macintosh, you saw how

---

* This does point out something you should know about FileSaver. When you eject a disk in the normal way, or shut down your Mac, FileSaver will update its data files based on the current state of the catalog and extents trees. If these have been subtly damaged, that damage will be copied into the FileSaver data files. If you suspect such damage, hold down the Command key before ejecting the disk; this keeps FileSaver from updating the data files. Run Norton Disk Doctor immediately on the suspect disk.

easy and quick it was to restore these disks to health. It doesn't take that much longer to restore a damaged hard disk.

It's worth repeating (again)—be sure to install FileSaver protection on all your important disk volumes. Remember, you have to manually do it for each; it isn't enough to just have FileSaver running on your startup disk.

Well, what happens if you need to recover data from a disk that you don't have FileSaver protection for?

FileSaver Not Installed—Don't Give Up the Ship!

It's possible to recover data from such a disk using Format Recover. The process is not nearly so easy, straightforward, or even certain as when FileSaver has been activated, but it can be done.

When you run Format Recover on such a disk, it will look for (and not find) the FileSaver data files. Failing to find them, it will present you with a dialog box informing you of this fact (Figure 7.8) and ask how to proceed.

If you click Reconstruct at this point, Format Recover will take you someplace quite familiar; namely, to UnErase (although the window will bear the title "Format Recover"). From this point on, it becomes a matter of UnErasing everything on the disk. Format Recover will have already chosen its UnErase method (File Types, all kinds selected). You will need to recover all of the files onto other volumes; you can't (and more important, shouldn't) recover onto the damaged volume. Remember that you can choose **Select All** from the **Edit** menu to mark all the files at once.

Note that if the damaged disk was very badly fragmented, then it is likely that you'll have to reassemble files. You may even end up missing a few pieces. Let us not underestimate the value of having FileSaver installed. (By the way, we're going to show you how to deal with all that messy file fragmentation in the very next chapter, which starts a whole new section.)

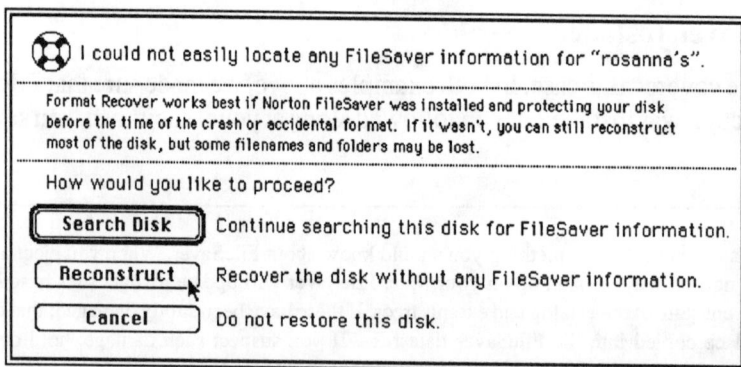

Figure 7.8 Recovering a disk that was not protected with FileSaver

Oh, and one more thing before we go; Format Recover has a last trick up its sleeve. Remember we said it had to do with restoring Finder comments.

Restoring the Desktop

To help it manage the location of all your icons (and the icons themselves, for that matter), the Finder maintains an invisible file called the Desktop. We say invisible, because the Desktop doesn't have an icon of its own, and normally can't be seen in a disk's window. It's there, though. The Desktop file remembers what windows are open, where they've been positioned on screen, and how they're stacked up.

All of this information is updated whenever a disk is ejected in the usual ways. (The Desktop is not updated when you eject a disk with Command-Shift-1 or Command-Shift-2, or when you eject it via an Eject button in an Open or Save dialog box.) The Finder checks the Desktop against what it knows about file icons from the catalog b-tree (remember, a file's icon position is recorded as part of its leaf record in the catalog tree) whenever a disk is first inserted, and makes any necessary changes.

Now, if the Finder discovers discrepancies between the catalog tree and the Desktop file, it will decide that the Desktop is damaged and needs to be rebuilt from scratch. When you first insert such a disk, you'll get a message via an alert box like Figure 7.9.

There's nothing in the world wrong with clicking OK at this point and allowing the Finder to recontruct the Desktop from the catalog tree leaf records, except . . . .

It turns out, the Desktop file is where the Finder stores the comments you may have attached to files via the Get Info command in the Finder's file menu—like Figure 7.10.

Some people like to use this little window to jot down notes about particular documents and stuff; that way, at least, they can tell what the file is in the future. Sometimes the name alone isn't enough. Having a little bit more information

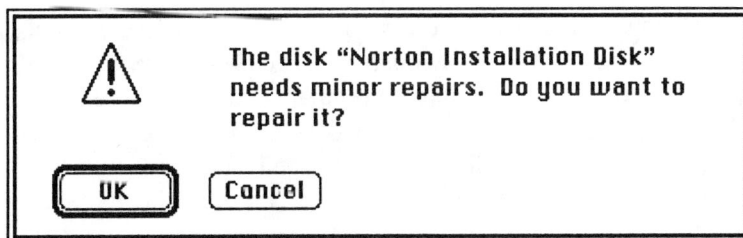

The disk "Norton Installation Disk" needs minor repairs. Do you want to repair it?

OK   Cancel

Figure 7.9 What you see when the Desktop file on a disk is damaged

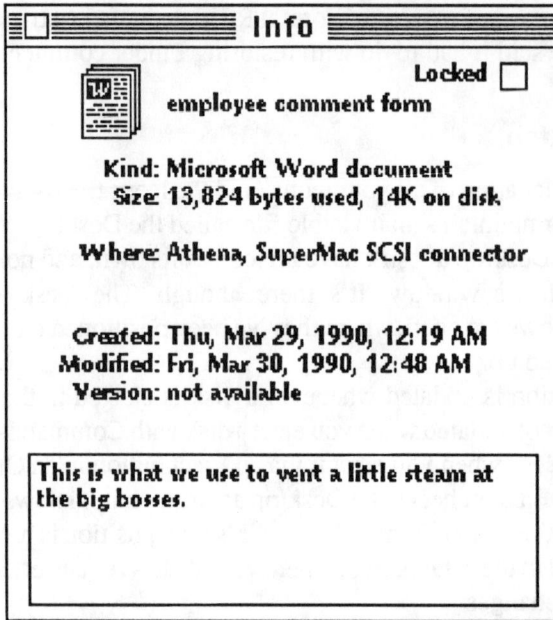

Figure 7.10 Finder comments for a Word document

available from the Finder is better than having to open the document to see what it is.

Well, as you may have guessed, rebuilding the Desktop file completely destroys these comments; wipes 'em out for good. Unless the disk they were on happened to be protected with FileSaver.

That's the reason for the "Save Finder Comments" option in FileSaver, by the by. It includes any and all "Get Info" comments in the data it saves about a disk. This data can be used to restore the comments after a desktop rebuild.

There's another way to rebuild the Desktop: You can do so deliberately. Holding down the Command and Option keys while you insert a disk—or as you first start your Macintosh—indicates to the Finder that you want the desktop rebuilt. You'll get a dialog box asking if that's what you want to do.

The last option in Format Recover is used to restore comments to the Desktop file of a disk that was previously protected with FileSaver. (Before you begin, you'll need to restart under the regular Finder if you've been running under Multifinder. Multifinder keeps the desktop file on all disks open all the time; open files can't be modified by other applications.)

Clicking OK with the last option checked (Figure 7.11) then brings up a choose volume dialog box, like Figure 7.12.

```
┌─────────────────────────────────────────────────────┐
│ What do you want to do?                               │
│                                                       │
│   ◉ Restore Formatted or Crashed Disk                 │
│      Attempt to recover your lost folders and files.  │
│                                                       │
│   ○ Install Disk Protection                           │
│      Create a new FileSaver information file for a particular disk. │
│                                                       │
│   ○ Update Disk Information                            │
│      Manually update the FileSaver info.              │
│                                                       │
│   ○ Restore Finder Comments                           │
│      Restore Finder's Get Info comments after a desktop rebuild. │
│                                                       │
│  ┌──────────┐  ┌──────────┐                           │
│  │    OK    │  │  Cancel  │                           │
│  └──────────┘  └──────────┘                           │
└─────────────────────────────────────────────────────┘
```

Figure 7.11 The last option is for restoring Get Info comments

When you've found the right volume, and have clicked Open, Format Recover will search for its Finder Comments backup data. A small alert box appears informing you of progress, like Figure 7.13.

```
┌──────────────────────────────────────┐
│ Restore Desktop Comments on:          │
│                                       │
│  ┌────┐                               │
│  │ ▢  │   Norton Installation Disk    │
│  │    │                               │
│  └────┘                               │
│                                       │
│  Kind: 800K HFS disk                  │
│  Where: 800K Internal Floppy Drive    │
│                                       │
│   ┌──────────┐   ┌──────────┐         │
│   │   Open   │   │  Drive   │         │
│   └──────────┘   └──────────┘         │
│   ┌──────────┐   ┌──────────┐         │
│   │  Cancel  │   │  Eject   │         │
│   └──────────┘   └──────────┘         │
└──────────────────────────────────────┘
```

Figure 7.12 Choosing which volume to
restore comments for

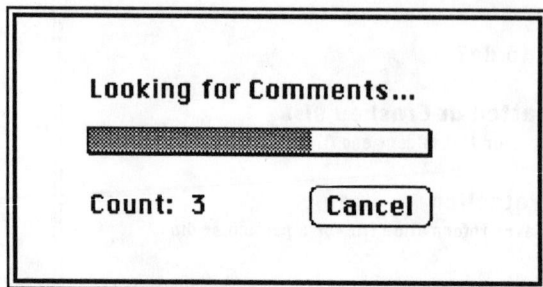

Figure 7.13 Format Recover is restoring Finder comments

You can click the Cancel button to stop the process, if you're quick enough. It doesn't take long to restore comments on a floppy.

And that, dear friends, sums up Format Recover. Time for a doughnut and a cup of joe...

Review

We reviewed the difference between hard and soft formatting, showing how hard formatting is completely destructive, but soft formatting can be reversed. We discussed problems with inconsistant terminology. We discussed the importance of the FileSaver INIT and its data files; they should be installed on all your disks.

We saw how to use Format Recover to restore all files to a floppy disk that had had its file dumped into the trashcan. We also saw how to use the Norton Disk Editor to simulate damage to a disk's directory information, and how to use Format Recover to restore it. We also discussed how Format Recover can be used to recover data from disks that were not previously protected with FileSaver.

Finally, we introduced the Desktop file, indicated why it is important, showed how it might be damaged so that the Finder wants to rebuild it, and discussed the implications of such a rebuild. We saw how Format Recover can be used to restore Get Info comments to a disk that was previously protected with FileSaver.

That concludes this section of the book. These Utilities tend to be used under somewhat harrowing circumstances. The rest of the Norton Utilities are for everyday use, and can make computing a lot easier and more fun.

Meeting the Makers

Introduction

The Norton Utilities for the Macintosh are the result of more than 10 person-years of development effort. That's an interesting figure, but somewhat of an abstraction. In an effort to flesh out that abstraction, we thought you might like to know more about the persons who spent all those years slaving away at their keyboards, working until two, three, four, and even five a.m. to bring you what is arguably the finest and easiest-to-use set of disk and data repair utilities ever. Now, as we've just used the Installer to bring the Utilities to a hard disk near you, it seemed to us logical to begin with the young man who conceived and perfected it.

Michael Martz

Although the Macintosh Utilities development team at Peter Norton Computing put in a lot of hard hours, not all the hours spent at the firm's Santa Monica, California offices were what you might characterize as "hard time." They couldn't be, in an office suite complete with a ping pong table and a view of the Pacific Coast Highway and the ocean beyond it. So the work was punctuated with well-earned opportunities to relax and blow off steam. And whenever there was a hot ping pong match going, or a pineapple and ham pizza being devoured at midnight, or a new high-score set playing *Solarian II*, Michael Martz was sure to be at hand, because during his on-duty hours no one worked harder on his part of the utilities package.

A 1988 graduate of Case Western Reserve University, Michael came to work for Peter Norton Computing early in 1989. He started as Quality Assurance Engineer—testing software for bugs—and as network administrator, "doing a little bit of everything," as he puts it. However, he had his heart set on developing software for the Macintosh. Other members of the Macintosh development team supported him in this ambition, and although it meant a lot of extra hours, he began to take on development work in addition to his other duties. Because—as the deadline for releasing drew nearer and nearer—the team was in dire need of development resources, it wasn't long before he'd moved almost exclusively into product development.

Although Michael is proud of earning his developer's stripes, other aspects of the Norton Utilities for the Macintosh project brought more satisfaction. "Proving myself was an underlying concern, but best of all was working with the others, learning, and helping to perfect the total user interface, like we all did with the Norton Disk Doctor," he says.

A devotee of progressive music, whose current favorites include The Jam ("the public gets what the public wants") and The House Martins, Michael is also an avid rollerblader. (For those who don't know, rollerblades are skates in which all the wheels lie in a single line and are quite narrow, not much wider than the blade of an ice skate. They are very fast and maneuverable.) He's into physical exercise of all kinds, and of course, is fond of computer games. Though the ping-pong table has given way to cubicles as PNC has expanded, you can still find Michael at his screen from time to time, trying out the newest game software, when he's not busy with the rest of the development team charting the course and laying the groundwork for the next version of the Norton Utilities for the Macintosh.

Marvin Carlberg

"My name is Marvin,
The Mac's my game
When I get through with the Utilities,
They won't look the same!"

This line from the 1987 Peter Norton Computing staff Christmas recording project, *The Norton Rap*, belonged to an optimistic Marvin Carlberg, newly hired Macintosh software developer and architect of the effort to bring to the Macintosh world the functionality of the acclaimed Norton Utilities for the IBM PC. He little realized at the time how difficult that effort would prove.

"I graduated in June, took a nice long vacation, and came to work in September. That was the last real vacation I've had." We spoke with Marvin in his office in September, 1990, a few short weeks after the Norton Utilities for the Macintosh had, at long last, been released to highly favorable reviews and stronger than expected initial sales. In addition to photocopies of some of these reviews, his office was strewn with disks, disk drives, and their innards, testimony to the recent hard effort to bring the Utilities, and in particular the Norton Disk Doctor, to life.

A 1987 graduate of the University of California at Santa Barbara, Marvin Carlberg worked on initial versions of the Macintosh Utilities for over a year before their debut. (Although a few generalized algorithms were borrowed from the developers of the PC Utilities, the vast differences between the Mac and PC filing systems, combined with the profound user-interface differences between the two machines, meant that much of the effort had to proceed from ground zero.) A few select corporate clients got the first look at the Mac Utilities at '88 Fall Comdex in Las Vegas. Because the Mac II containing the Utilities was kept in a closely guarded bedroom of the Norton hospitality suite at the Sahara Hotel, some present took to calling the Mac Utilities "Sleeping

Beauty." By all accounts, early viewers were pleased with what they saw of the slumbering software.

"I try to put myself in the place of the user, not the programmer. When I write something, I don't just code it and hand it off. I try to write stuff that I enjoy using, and I *do* use it." This attention to needs of the user has paid off handsomely.

When he's not writing software, Marvin enjoys a variety of other pursuits. During the blockbuster movie season of Summer 1989, for example, he was usually in charge of the premier parties put together by PNC research and development staff, buying tickets and holding places in line on opening day for other members of the group. That year's favorite PNC flick? Why, *Batman*, to be sure.

Marvin is quite active on local bulletin boards and enjoys socializing in person with other bbs'ers. Indeed, many of his pursuits revolve around computers, which is not surprising in someone so focused. (There are those who maintain that he is similar in many respects to the character Bryce Lynch in TV's *Max Headroom*.) For example, he's currently working with a 1970s-vintage PDP 11/70 minicomputer, trying to bring it back to fully operational status. "Some people restore classic cars; I restore classic computers," he says. We're confident that if anyone can do the job, Marvin Carlberg can.

III

Day-to-Day Operations

Data disasters such as crashed floppies, formatted hard disks, and lost files are not an everyday occurrence. At least, we hope that such problems aren't that common for you; otherwise, you must be laboring under a particularly evil star. (That, by the way, is the literal Latin translation of disaster—*dis aster*.) Presuming then, that your luck is no worse than anybody else's, you won't find yourself needing the tools we covered in the last section too often.

Nice as it is to know that the Norton Utilities' data recovery tools are there when you need them, you may find yourself wanting other kinds of help on a regular basis. Additional help, as it were, with the thousand little concerns and annoyances that are part of everyday computing. Wouldn't it be nice if . . . .

Trust us to take better care of you than that. We, too, have used our Macs practically every day (and many nights) for years now, and both prior to as well as during the development of the Norton Utilities for the Macintosh, hardly a day (or night) went by that we didn't say "Wouldn't it be nice if . . ." Wouldn't it be nice if you could tune up your hard disk drive for maximum performance and increased data safety? Wouldn't it be nice if the Find File desk accessory was much faster, and would let you peek into files and maybe even open them directly within the DA itself? Wouldn't it be nice if you could find out where the å and the ï and the Æ characters were without having to guess at what modifier key(s) to hold down? Wouldn't it be nice if you could change the font the Finder uses to show file names, to something easier to look at (or just plain different, for a change), and if you could customize the spacing of icons within windows? Wouldn't it be nice if, while saving a file for the first time, you could actually create a new folder to put it in, without quitting your application or even leaving the **Save** dialog box, or could find another file you want to put the new file next to *fast* just by typing the old file's name, and without having to spelunk through your directory structure? Wouldn't it be nice if you could hide file icons from prying eyes, or could surgically remove bad spots in a file that make its application refuse to have anything to do with it? Wouldn't it be nice?

Guess what. It *is* nice. Because, dear friends, the Norton Utilities for the Macintosh can do all these things, and more. In this section, we're going to find out how. We're going to finish our tour of the Utilities by looking at the last two program modules: Speed Disk, which optimizes hard disks; and Layout Plus, which lets you customize your Finder. We'll learn how to use the two Norton DAs, Fast Find and KeyFinder, to quickly locate (and even open) files and to easily find out how to get fancy characters in all your installed fonts. We'll see how the Directory Assistance INIT customizes the **Save, Save As,** and **Open** dialog boxes to let you create folders, find and delete files, and more. And finally, we'll take that long promised closer look at the Norton Disk Editor, seeing how it can be used to alter file attributes and even file data, in particular, to make damaged files readable again.

First up is Speed Disk and the vexing question of file fragmentation.

8

Setting Things Right with Speed Disk

Introduction

At one point in an earlier section, while we were touring the intricacies of the Macintosh Hierarchical Filing System (HFS) and its associated data structures, we recall remarking how nice it was that the operating system keeps us shielded from it all—we don't have to know anything about how files are stored on disk in order to work with them. That's true enough, but it's also true that what we don't know can hurt us.

You see, one consequence of the way HFS handles files is that, in time, things on a disk are apt to get a little messy. Now that you've had a peek at the directory data structures on a disk—the catalog and extents b-trees—you ought to be able to guess why: pieces of files here and there and everywhere, with the OS having to bounce around from place to place to put it all together and make it look like it's all smooth and continuous. All this bouncing around is well enough, at least in the nice effect it produces, but it all takes time and microprocessor resources, which could be better spent elsewhere.

Which is why PNC invented Speed Disk. This remarkable part of the Norton Utilities for the Macintosh hunts down all the pieces of all your files and assembles them into contiguous chunks, so that each file's data is all in one

147

place and not scattered all over Heck and Half of Georgia. Speed Disk also organizes your disks, so that frequently needed system files are easier for your Mac to get at, and so that files which expand and shrink quite often are put toward the end of the occupied data area, where the spare room is. Speaking of the spare room, Speed Disk also squeezes it all into the back of the disk, so that new files have every chance of coming into the world in one piece. And it does it all quickly and safely.

In this chapter we're going to look at the problems Speed Disk was created to help solve, and we'll see how to use it to fix them. First, back to HFS and, in particular, the question of extents and fragmentation.

The Thousand Natural Shocks

Some people work in a ferment of activity—copying new files from other folks and working with them, deleting old files to open up space on a too-crowded disk, trying out new software, always dragging icons hither and thither and making that dear old disk light blink like a telegraph sending an urgent SOS. Other folks are more methodical and modest—working with but few files and fewer applications, maintaining an organized desktop that rarely changes. However, both types of users—and everyone in between, which means you and me of course—will eventually face operating problems, because the mere act of using a disk, hard disk or floppy disk, eventually causes its performance to deteriorate. True, with more use it happens faster, but it happens to all of us sooner or later.

Fragmentation

We introduced the concept of fragmentation back in Chapter 4 to explain what the extents b-tree was for. Recall that the extents tree is there to hold four or more file pieces in each fork. Such pieces are called extents; if a file has more than three extents in either fork, the overflow must be accounted for in the extents tree, which records the beginning location and length of each such extent.

How does a file wind up in so many pieces? Well, suppose you worked each day with three files, call them documents A, B, and C. We'll say that you usually work with them in that order, and that you tend to add data to each file every day.

Well, when A, B, and C are first created, they follow each other sequentially on the disk. Like this:

AAABBBCCC

Immediately after A's data is B's, and immediately after B's data is C's. So that when it comes time to add data to file A, there is no place for it to go except after C; there's no free space before then, since files B and C come right after A.

AAABBBCCCA

So what happens when you add something to file B? You guess it, B's new data has to go after the new piece from A.

AAABBBCCCAB

And a new piece of file C? Goes right after the piece from A.

AAABBBCCCABC

Suppose you started out with three blocks in each file and added a block per day, in order, to each file. At the end of one working week, your disk's data area would look something like:

AAABBBCCCABCABCABCABC

We've highlighted all the pieces of file B, so you could see them more clearly. In this case, file B has five extents. As we're talking about documents here, all these extents are in B's data fork (its resource fork is empty; no extents), so that two of them will have to be referenced in the extents b-tree, in addition to the three that the catalog b-tree can handle.

What would happen if you deleted file A? Designating free space by zeros, you get:

000BBBCCC0BC0BC0BC0BC

Now add four new sectors to file C:

*CCC*BBBCCC*C*BC0BC0BC0BC

Now file C has seven extents, the first of which actually comes before any of file B's data. What a mess!

We could go on and on like this. But, so a disk gets a little messy; the operating system hides all that mess from us, and shows us files in order, without our having to go looking for all the pieces. What's the big deal?

What Fragmentation Does to Performance

Whether you have a hard disk drive or you're limited to floppies, you're undoubtedly familiar with two drive noises; the high pitched whirr of the motor that spins the disk platter, and the buzzing sound that occurs when data is read from or written to the disk. That sound is associated with the read/write head; it represents the head being slewed across the surface of the disk.

It takes time to do that. In computer terms, it takes significant amounts of time, because the mechanical parts that move the drive head are much slower than the electrons that do the work inside your computer's CPU and RAM circuitry. The more the drive head has to be moved, the slower your system operates. The CPU ends up cooling its heels, waiting for data to arrive from the disk.

When the File Manager requests a chunk of data from the disk drive, it specifies the sector at which to begin reading and how many sectors to read. The drive head has to seek to the correct position. This may involve reading sector addresses along the way, like a delivery service courier checking the Thomas Guide for the location of a particular street. The drive head, once positioned over the correct track, has to wait for the beginning sector to come spinning by. Then data can be read. This may take more than one revolution of the disk platter, depending on how sectors are actually laid out on the track and on how fast the drive circuitry can read and buffer (temporarily store) data. (The critical concept here is the interleave factor; it is explained in the *Disk Companion*.)

This process has to be repeated for every extent in the file being read. And if there are extents beyond three that are referenced in the extents b-tree, then a few extra overhead steps are added, since the extents tree is on an area of the disk separate from the catalog tree, and thus requiring additional drive-action to seek the sectors that reference the additional extents.

What's more, this kind of slowdown affects more than just the opening and saving of files. As applications have gotten larger and larger (PageMaker is now so big it is shipped in chunks on two different diskettes; its installer then assembles the chunks into one application), it has become impossible for all of their program data to be kept in RAM on a typical Macintosh. (Multi-meg machines are typically running Multifinder, and their users—like us—don't like to devote all the RAM needed to keep an entire application in memory, preferring to reserve space for other applications to run simultaneously.) Thus, different parts of an application are kept on disk and only read into RAM when needed—for example, dialog boxes and other results of menu commands. Clearly, having an application spread out all over a disk can slow down performance, when it comes time to read in all those pieces.

Having something scattered all over a disk is fairly easy even if the entire file is copied at once and never subsequently modified, as is the case with almost all applications. As you erase files, the space they used to occupy is freed up for new files. Over time (and not very much time at that), this can result in a patchwork of small extents of free space across the disk. A large new file, copied to the disk, will probably find itself fragmented across all of this free space if there isn't enough room at the end of the disk to hold the whole thing (and sometimes even then)—doomed from the start, as it were, to involve the OS in unnecessary wear and tear on the drive head.

The effect is perhaps most critical on the OS itself. What do you suppose happens when you update your System file (say, from version 6.0.2 to 6.0.4) using Apple's utility? The new parts of the system are separate pieces, and will be copied to wherever there's room for them. This can leave you with a fragmented System, and as much as that thing is used, the slowdown can be quite significant. The same is true of any new fonts or DAs you install using Font/DA Mover. (Or, in the case of the KeyFinder and Fast Find DAs, that you installed directly into the system using the Norton Installer.)

Finally, there are effects on files you never see, such as the Desktop that we briefly talked about in Chapter 7 in the context of restoring Finder comments. The Desktop file, since it manages all your icons, windows, and such, is constantly growing and shrinking. On a crowded disk, it is easy for the Desktop to fragment very quickly, and to fragment into a large number of pieces. This slows down the Finder to a very great degree.

Can anything be done about all this fragmentation? Yes. It can be fixed, and, what's more, it's even possible to arrange things on a disk so that future fragmentation is kept to a minimum. That's what Norton Speed Disk was created to do.

Using Speed Disk

Speed Disk is a stand-alone application (i.e., you can launch it without launching the other Norton Utilities for the Macintosh) that assembles files into single extents for both resource and data forks. It also places files in a predetermined order on the disk. Files that almost never change are placed toward the front. This includes System files and applications. Another advantage of this placement is that these files are slightly quicker to locate in this position. Documents are placed toward the end of the disk. The Desktop file is placed last of all, right next to the disk's free space, which is squeezed out from between all the other files and put at the end of the volume, where it belongs.

How does it do this? The basic principle is easy to grasp. Let's go back, briefly, to the last extents example we had a few paragraphs back. It looked like this:

CCCBBBCCCCBC0BC0BC0BC

Let's just suppose that this situation represents the entire volume. Our goal is to organize files B and C so that all their data is contiguous, so that B comes before C (as it does in the alphabet), and so that all three free blocks are at the end of the disk.

If we had a large amount of RAM, we could just copy the whole thing, work it all out via the CPU, and write the entire new disk. But what would happen if the power failed while the new data was being written? If such a failure happened after the first three new sectors were written, but before any others, we'd get

BBBBBBCCCCBC0BC0BC0BC

and you just have to count and compare this configuration with the other to know that three sectors of C's data are now lost for good, and that the first three sectors of B are repeated. In effect, the whole disk is trashed.

That's no good. An application that's supposed to improve performance can't run a significant risk of destroying everything. Since relying on RAM is risky, we'll use disk space instead; there are, after all, three free sectors on the disk. Going back to the beginning:

CCCBBBCCCCBC0BC0BC0BC

It would be nice to get all the free space together; then we could copy bigger chunks into it and save moves. Let's copy the last sector into the first free space, like this:

CCCBBBCCCCBCCBC0BC0BC

Once we have a clean copy of that sector, we can erase the old one without risk to the data. That leaves us with

CCCBBBCCCCBCCBC0BC0B0

Now we move that last piece of file B, again, into the first free sector. (What used to be the first free sector is now taken by a piece of file C.) That move gives

CCCBBBCCCCBCCBCBBC0B0

Now we erase the old sector, giving

CCCBBBCCCCBCCBCBBC000

and our goal of organizing all the free space at the end is complete. (By the way, sectors aren't actually erased, of course: they're simply marked "free.")

It shouldn't be to hard to figure out how to organize B and C now, so that B is first and both are in but one extent. You could probably work it all out in your head (although it's important to remember what order the extents of each file were in before we did all that moving to consolidate the free space.) We'll leave the exact details as an exercise for you. The important thing is, it can be done, and it can be done safely. Although the exact operating details are much more complicated (and are proprietary, to boot), this is, in a nutshell, how Speed Disk goes about its work.

Things to Keep in Mind Before You Begin

Notice that we said Speed Disk is "safe." That is to say, it's much safer than anyone else's disk optimizer (the generic term for software that defragments files and consolidates free space). In fact, based on the way it operates, we can claim that Speed Disk is more than 99% safe even in the case of a catastrophic hardware failure, such as total loss of power during execution. But 99% is not 100%.

Even at 99.9% safety, it's a cinch that one time in a thousand, Speed Disk will fail if its operation is interrupted, say by a power loss. The odds of such a power interruption have to be figured into the equation, to be sure. How often has it happened to you, out of all the times you've launched and run applications? The odds may seem vanishingly small, making it over 10,000 to one that you'll ever suffer a severe Speed Disk failure.

The consequences of failure vary in intensity and cannot be predicted. But they range from the loss of a single file to the loss of the entire volume. That's what you have on the line.

Surely you see where all this is leading. We don't want to see anybody lose data. So even though the odds of its happening to you in particular are very remote, we must insist that you completely back up any drive that you intend to optimize using Speed Disk. This takes time but so does buying health insurance. Just one payback makes it all worth it. Accidents happen.

Rule One: Back up your disk before you optimize it.

Another thing you should know is Speed Disk cannot optimize the current System disk. The easiest way around this problem is to start up your Mac using the Norton Applications diskette. Starting your Mac with this diskette boots you directly into Speed Disk.

Rule Two: Run Speed Disk from the Applications Disk.

Finally, all files on the volume you wish to optimize must be closed. This includes the Desktop file. However, Multifinder keeps open the Desktop on all mounted disks. The bottom line: Don't run Speed Disk under Multifinder, unless the disk(s) you wish to optimize aren't yet mounted. (This is really only possible with floppies.)

Rule Three: Run Speed Disk under the Finder, not MultiFinder.

If you follow these three rules, you should have no trouble at all.

Now that we've slogged through the tedious preliminaries, we can get back to the good stuff. Supposing you start up your Macintosh using the good old Norton Applications diskette. You'll see Speed Disk appear in short order. Let's take a look at it.

Touring the Speed Disk Interface

However you happen to launch Speed Disk, the screen shown in Figure 8.1 appears when you do so.

The large area at the top, shown mostly in solid black in Figure 8.1, is a map of the currently selected volume. Dark areas are occupied and white areas are free. Below this, in the center, are two buttons that control Speed Disk: **Optimize** initiates optimization of the selected drive; **Check Drive** examines certain characteristics of that volume—including its degree of fragmentation—and reports it all back to you. To the right of these buttons is a panel showing the current volume selection; click on the arrows to cycle among available volumes. In the far right bottom corner is a panel giving facts about the current volume. Above it, an assessment of that volume's condition (after **Check Drive** is selected) is given.

Looks pretty easy, huh? That's actually literally true, because this is the screen as it appears in Speed Disk's **Easy** mode. Checking out the **Options** menu, you'll see the command **Go to Expert**. This switches to Speed Disk's other mode, which has more features. The other command in the **Options** menu, by the way (**Show Pencil**), activates an animated pencil graphic that appears during optimization. It shows you when Speed Disk is writing data, and when it is erasing it. It's kind of fun to watch but it slows down operation.

Not to complicate things too much right off the bat, but if you choose **Go to Expert**, the entire screen (and the menu bar) changes as shown in Figure 8.2.

In addition to an extra menu (Explore), we have some new areas on the screen to talk about. These take the place of the Speed Disk logo from the Easy mode screen. In the far bottom left corner is a magnified view of the area of the

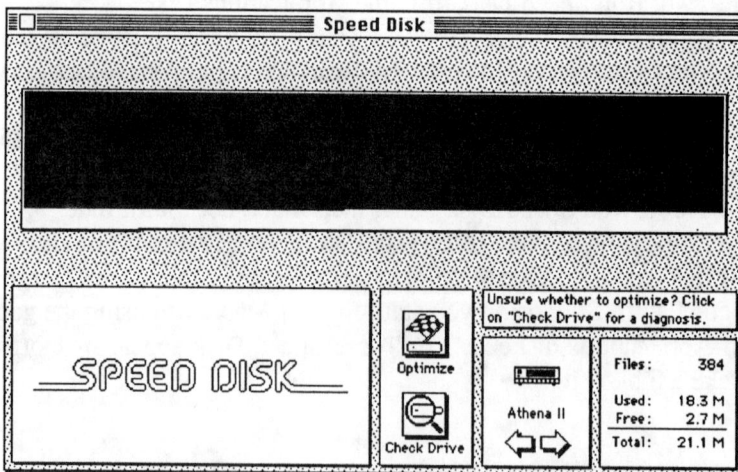

Figure 8.1 The Speed Disk screen

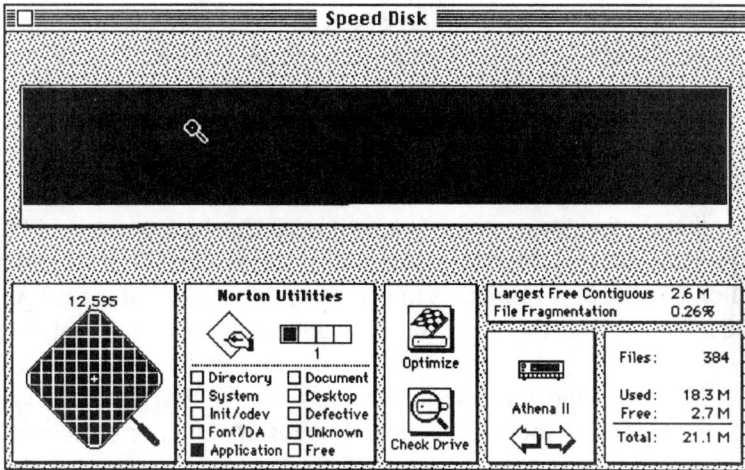

Figure 8.2 The Speed Disk window in Expert mode

volume map currently under the pointer. The pointer changes, by the way, to a small graphic of a magnifying glass when it's over the map. The name and type of the file to which the exact block under the magnifying glass belongs is shown in the panel next to the magnifying glass.

All of this shows up best in color (and isn't half bad in gray scale, either), because different file types have been assigned different colors. (You can change color assignments by double-clicking on the small color squares next to each file type name; the Macintosh color wheel then appears.) When you click Check Drive, Speed Disk examines the disk, determines where files are stored, and then colors in all the blocks in the appropriate colors.

One more thing is shown by the rightmost of the two new panels: how many fragments the currently shown file is in.

Expert Mode Menus

The menu commands in Expert mode aren't that difficult to grasp. They mainly consist of options that let you specify exactly what Speed Disk does, or that let you perform individual operations without resorting to a full optimization.

Options Menu   **Go to Easy** switches back to Easy mode. **Show Pencil**, again, animates the pencil during optimization.

The next three options are all checked as a default. **Prioritize Files**, when checked, puts all System files at the front of the volume, puts applications next, documents following them, and finally the Desktop file. Unchecked, files will be left pretty much in their current order after an optimization (optimizing will be faster.) **Verify Media** checks that all sectors on the volume are in good shape. Bad sectors (ones in which Speed Disk determines that data cannot reliably be stored) are marked and taken out of service. This is important: Leaving bad sectors available may cause a crash, if data can't be moved into them or out of them. Finally **Verify Data,** when checked during an optimization, makes sure each file's data can be read successfully. Data from bad sectors is lifted out and moved.

Note that these three commands are options; checking any one of them has no immediate effect; it merely changes what steps Speed Disk will take when you click **Optimize.** Commands to actually perform two of these operations individually, outside the context of an optimization, are contained in the **Explore** menu.

One last command remains in **Options: Turbocharge.** This command disables the graphics routines. Though this results in a boring screen during optimization, it speeds things up. The CPU is allowed to devote all its resources to moving files, and doesn't have to worry about drawing neat pictures on the screen.

Explore Menu   The first command in the menu, **Check Drive,** has the same effect as clicking the **Check Drive** button. **Check Media** performs a diagnosis of the sectors on the disk. **Check Files** checks all files on the disk to make sure their data is good. Finally, **Largest Free Contiguous** looks for the biggest uninterruped area of free space currently available on the selected volume.

Well, that's what it all looks like, and what it all does. How do you use it, and when? That's easy.

Optimizing a Disk: An Example

As it turns out, FileSaver has a few tricks built into it, tricks that let it determine when a disk is becoming badly fragmented. If it notices this happening, it'll tell you about it (Figure 8.3).

In this case, FileSaver has noticed that the diskette on which we've been keeping copies of the files for this very book has become very fragmented.

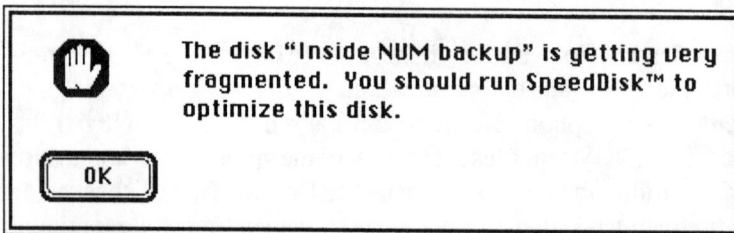

The disk "Inside NUM backup" is getting very fragmented. You should run SpeedDisk™ to optimize this disk.

OK

Figure 8.3 Time to optimize our backup disk

That's because we're always erasing old, incomplete versions of chapters and writing new ones. FileSaver will do the same for you whenever you eject a disk or attempt to **Shut Down** or **Restart**.

In the absence of such a message, you could just launch Speed Disk and test a suspect volume; you can do so without optimizing. You may find out the disk is fine. Depending on how much work you do, you might want to check a disk out every month or so. (If you want to follow along at your Mac, use an old floppy disk that is relatively full and contains files you don't care that much about.)

Well, we know that this backup disk is fragmented; FileSaver told us so. Let's run Speed Disk on it, and see what happens. First, we launch the program. A screen appears as shown in Figure 8.4.

The very astute among you will notice that we have started Speed Disk from our startup drive. That's okay; we're going to be optimizing another volume. (By the way, since last we spoke, our old, reliable hard drive, Athena, has passed on to its reward, although not, happily, before confiding all its secrets to our new drive—a removable-cartridge model that we have named Athena II.) Speaking of which, we now insert the fragmented floppy into a drive. The screen now looks like Figure 8.5.

Do we believe FileSaver? Maybe we should check this disk out before proceeding; no use optimizing if the disk isn't badly fragmented. (And after all, you might be at this point not at the bidding of FileSaver, but just out of curiosity and a desire to speed things up. Worthwhile seeing if an optimization will make much difference.) Let's click the **Check Drive** button.

Speed Disk performs a few checks and comes back with the diagnosis (Figure 8.6). The Disk is pretty badly fragmented. (One more thing—set your

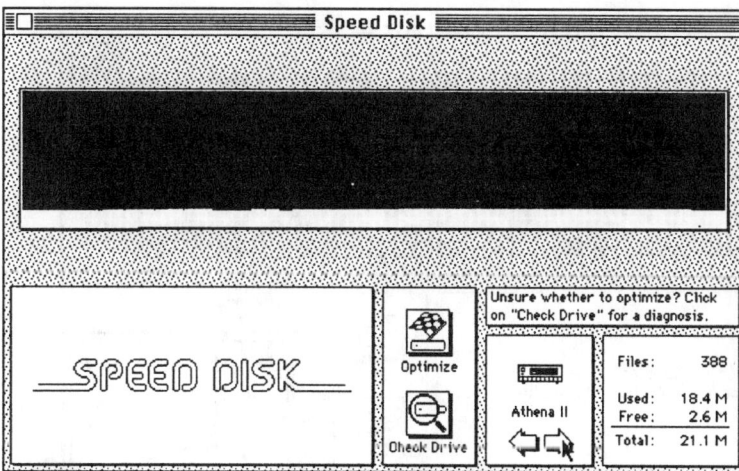

Figure 8.4 Getting ready to optimize

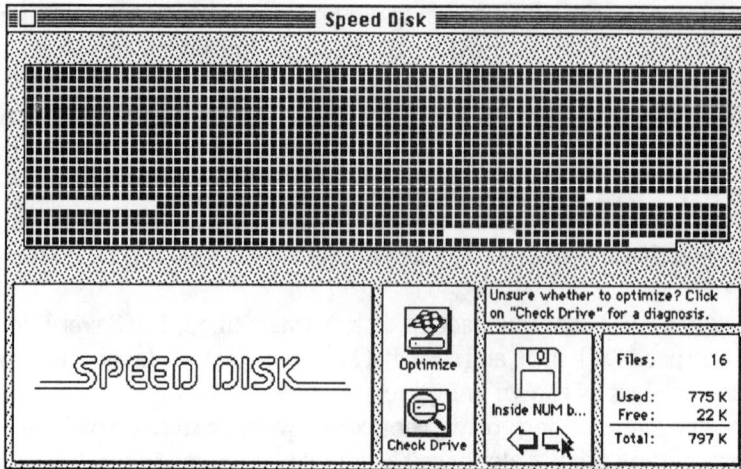

Figure 8.5 Now preparing to optimize our backup floppy disk

monitor for two-color black and white, and choose **Show Pencil** from the **Options** menu; it's worth seeing just once.) Now we click the **Optimize** button.

Speed Disk examines the files on the disk, checks to see if all the sectors are in good shape, and then begins moving files around. In any case, when the pencil is animated, as it is now in our example, you see Speed Disk read sectors, write them to new locations, erase the old data, and move new data into its place.

The process is actually quite fast. You can count on about 10 minutes to optimize a 20-megabyte hard drive partition. Floppy disks take about 5 minutes themselves; that's because floppy drives are so much slower than hard disk

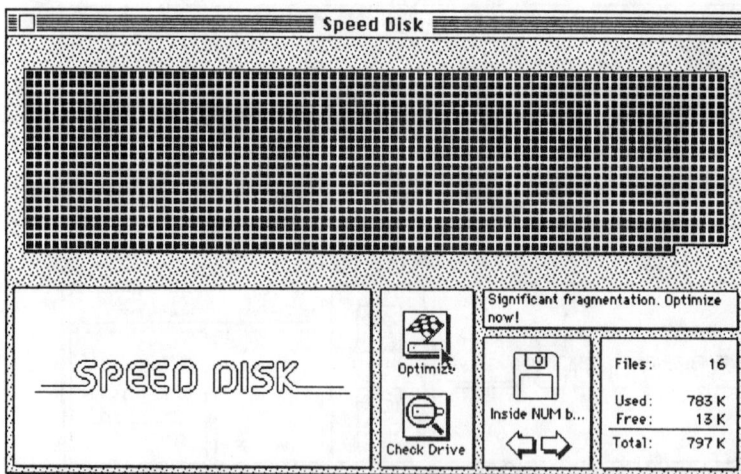

Figure 8.6 Yep, this disk is fragmented

drives. When the process has been completed, you'll see a message. That's all there is to it.

You can, by the way, interrupt an optimization. While Speed Disk is working, the **Optimize** button changes to **Stop**. Clicking it makes Speed Disk cease working at the first safe opportunity. You can even quit the program at this point without damaging the volume you were working with.

If you are running Speed Disk from the Applications diskette, then there is no Finder to quit to. Instead, when you quit you will be confronted with a dialog box asking whether you care to Restart or Shutdown your Macintosh. You can then restart with your usual startup disk.

The above procedure can be followed in either Easy or Expert mode. Expert, really, just gives you more information about your disks and gives you more choices on how exactly to optimize them. Speed Disk will work faster if you uncheck Prioritize Files, although at the sacrifice of later performance. (It really is better to have those system files up front. Having all the control panel documents together, for instance, makes the Control Panel appear quicker.) And although it is true that the program will work faster if you uncheck the **Verify Media** and **Verify Data** options, we strongly recommend against doing so. If Speed Disk should encounter bad sectors while optimizing, sectors that were not identified because the diagnostics were skipped, it will refuse to continue. This could result in significant damage to the single file in question, or to the entire volume.

If you're simply curious about the condition of your disk, you can use the three commands in the Expert mode Explore menu **Check Drive**, **Check Media**, and **Check Files**. If Speed Disk finds problems that need fixing, it will offer to do so.

Finally, after you've watched the pencil-and-map optimization show for a few times, you may decide you've other things to do while your disk is being optimized. In that case, you may want to select the option **Turbocharge** in the Expert mode **Options** menu. This devotes all your computer resources to optimizing. The graphics are great but they take a lot of computing power. You can direct all that power to the task at hand if you don't need the graphic feedback.

After you've optimized a disk, once a month or so in the future should keep it in top shape. As we said, you can always check a disk out if you suspect it might need work. And if files get very badly fragmented, FileSaver will let you know.

Time once again to look back over what we've learned—and then to plot our course for the next Utility.

Review

We've seen how normal operation will leave a Macintosh disk in increasingly fragmented condition over time, with much-modified files stored in many extents across the disk. We've shown, through a simple example, how easy it is for this to occur. We explored the effects of such fragmentation: slower opening of documents, slower launching of applications, and just general system lethargy. We considered how such fragmentation might be simply and safely fixed.

We introduced Speed Disk, the Norton Utilities for the Macintosh application that de-fragments files, prioritizes their arrangment, verifies the condition of a volume's media, and even consolidates all free space. We showed how to use Speed Disk to optimize a badly fragmented floppy disk. And we briefly discussed the options available in Speed Disk's advanced mode.

In the next chapter, we'll see how the appearance and functionality of the Finder can be customized. Not simply a matter of aesthetics, customizing the Finder can make it run like you want it to, and make it show you data in a way that's easier to read.

Meet the Makers

John Blackburn

The summer of 1989 was a critical time in the Norton Utilities for the Macintosh effort. It had been determined that Speed Disk was going to be vitally important to the success of the whole package. Yet there was no one available to work on it.

Enter John Blackburn. Within just a few weeks of his joining the PNC Macintosh development team, he demonstrated the kind of technical savvy and artistic flair that would be needed to complete a module such as Speed Disk. He was on the case.

On the face, of it, John would seem to be an unlikely candidate for the title "Ace Software Designer." A 1984 graduate of California State University at Northridge (in the beautiful San Fernando valley about which you have undoubtedly heard so much), he majored in music, even taking an M.A. in music in 1986. His thesis piece, *Variations for Orchestra*, was publicly performed in Los Angeles, with John at the keys of the piano.

Still, it isn't that great a leap from a piano's keys to those of a Macintosh, especially in these days where computers and music are drawing closer all the time via the MIDI standard. (MIDI, for those who don't know, stands for

Musical Instrument Digital Interface. It's a networking standard that allows keyboards, computers, drum machines, tape recorders, and much more to be linked together in harmony.) John wrote his own MIDI application for the Macintosh; it impressed the other members of the Mac team enough that he soon got a job with them.

The job was tough. John remarked to us regarding the "agony of having thousands of ideas and being forced by time constraints to choose only a few." Still, the excitement of the project kept him going, even through the stressful times. He says "We were coming out with something new, something that had been eagerly anticipated and was going to be worth the wait. It was clearly going to make a stir."

In addition to his interest in computers and in the arts, John enjoys motorcycling. When the Macintosh Utilities debuted in the summer of 1990, he at last got the chance to take his new bike on a tour of the Southwest, making it as far as Santa Fe, New Mexico and Shiprock, Arizona. He plans a more extensive tour of the country later on.

Asked about his development philosophy, John replied that he is interested in creating not just tools, but elegant tools. "Do it right, and make it beautiful," he says. We think he succeeded.

9

Fixing Up
the Finder

Layout Plus

Introduction

When people are going to live someplace for a very long time, they're apt to want to fix it up. This applies to apartment dwellers as well as home owners, especially in areas like New York and Los Angeles, where there's rent control and folks tend to find residences and stay put. From painting the walls, hanging new drapes, and buying new furniture to refinishing floors and replumbing bathrooms, people are always doing things to customize their environment.

The same might be said about the Macintosh. Since the machine appeared on the market in 1984, there have been any number of ways to customize its operation. Desk accessories, utilities, applications—you name it, somebody's done it.

Although there have been a lot of ways to customize operation, there haven't necessarily been that many ways to customize the appearance of the Mac. By that, we mean the Mac interface, not the machine itself; and we will pass over in silence the fuzzy mouse covers (with ears yet) and faux marble finishes that some have offered to the market to increase the Mac's external appeal. No, we're thinking of the Desktop, actually, and the central Macintosh application, the Finder.

163

You spend a lot of time in the Finder. The same old surroundings tend to get stale and boring. What's worse, if aspects of those surroundings are not to one's liking, the sojourn can be even staler. But the Finder is not carved out of stone. It's made of resources, and you may recall our saying that resources exist to be changed. In particular, we refer to things like fonts and text strings—the latter have to be changed in order to localize software for international markets, if for no other reason.

There have always been tools with which to alter Macintosh resources. The most commonly used is still the application called ResEdit. You may never have seen it. Apple Computer doesn't like for it to get into the hands of folks like you and me; it's "too technical" and "too dangerous." Still, folks like you and me have been using ResEdit for years, to change text strings in the Finder to friendly messages, to alter command keys and menu command names, etc.

ResEdit is difficult to use, though, and it's limited. There's only so much amusement one can get out of inserting frivolities into dialog boxes. There are other aspects of the Finder that can be changed, and doing so can make the thing easier to use; but actually making the modifications has been tricky—until now.

One application within the Norton Utilities for the Macintosh is designed to make it easy and intuitive to change visual and operational aspects of the Finder. You can change the font used to display file and window names. You can increase the width of text columns and the size of default Finder windows. You can alter the spacing of Finder icons, staggering them so that even long names don't overlap. You can even change the amount of time that elapses before the watch pointer appears, and you can choose to skip forever that annoying message that appears whenever you try to delete an application.

In this chapter, we're going to look more closely at the Finder itself than we have done before. Then, we'll introduce you to the main features of Layout Plus. We'll show you how to use it to make certain interesting modifications in the Finder. We hope these changes will make your environment more interesting, and even more functional.

About the Finder . . .

Well for one thing, why is it called "the Finder?" We don't know for certain, but we can guess, especially given what we know about how it works, and about how files are organized on a Macintosh disk.

The Finder does just that, it finds files and opens them. As we said in Chapter 2, it presents files to the user through the central metaphor of the desktop, with small pictures that correspond to individual files and to the folders in which files (and other folders) are kept and organized. This organization has some manifestations within the computer itself, at least in terms of how files are referenced in the directory structures of a disk. However, it really says nothing about how files are actually laid out across a disk.

We don't need to know. The Finder, via the File Manager, uses the catalog and extents b-trees to locate all the pieces of a file, once we've indicated that we're interested in seeing it. If the file is a document, the Finder knows how to find out what application the document was created in, and how to launch that application and load the document's data into it.

The Finder knows a lot about a disk, really. It knows the contents of each and every folder. It knows how to draw them whenever they're opened, remembering where each icon was placed or whether the window was set to show only text. It knows how to respace all the icons (via the Clean Up command in the Special menu) to make a disk or folder window appear more neat and organized.

What it doesn't know is how to allow enough room for files to be distinguishable by name, and that has been a source of considerable consternation to many. Even when you change to View by Name, or one of the other text-type view options, space may be given to one field in a file's entry and denied to another. There isn't enough room in the name field to distinguish files with really long names; this can be a problem when you have a file-naming convention that results in names similar up to the very end.

Then there's the question of text itself. The Finder uses the font Geneva for text inside windows. Aside from being among the least easy to read of all fonts, it happens to be ugly. Thin and spidery and undistinguished. On a machine that is renowned for its font possibilities, among many other things to be sure, it is hardly fitting that an important part of the display be given over to such a mediocre brand of text.

All of this, thank Heaven, can now be cured.

Layout Plus

Layout Plus is an application program within the Norton Utilities that is used to modify certain display and operating characteristics of the Finder. It does so by presenting a replica of the Finder's Desktop interface, one equipped with controls whereby the interface may be manipulated and changed. There are also menu commands and associated dialog boxes for effecting other changes to the Finder.

A very nice thing about Layout Plus is that it can be used to work with the currently active Finder; that is, the one on the system disk. If you are simply using the Finder, any changes you make will take effect as soon as you quit Layout Plus. If you're running under MultiFinder, then changes won't take effect until you restart your Macintosh. You can also choose to work with Finders on disks other than the current system volume.

When you launch Layout Plus, it opens into a window like the one in Figure 9.1. Notice the file with the really long name, on the top line of icons in the window. This gives you an idea of how to make names avoid each other, by changing the distance between icons. You do this by dragging the two icons that have arrows on them. Dragging the topmost staggers the icon offset; every other row will be lower than the others, allowing names more room without opening up any additional space between icons. Dragging the lower icon increases the actual amount of space between them.

This, in general, is how Layout Plus works. When you choose to change a certain kind of window, you are presented with a typical version of that window. Dragging any of the controls, including the grow box and even the title bar to move the window itself, changes the default attributes for that window type. When you then create a new window for a folder within the Finder, it will look like the one you designed in Layout Plus.

Commands to dictate which window view type to manipulate, among other things, are contained in Layout Plus's menus, which we had better look at before we do anything else.

File Menu

Open: Brings up the standard open file dialog box. This lets you pick which Finder to open. Use the **Drive** button and the scrolling list to navigate to the exact place where that Finder is stored.

Save: Saves all changes from the current Layout Plus session.

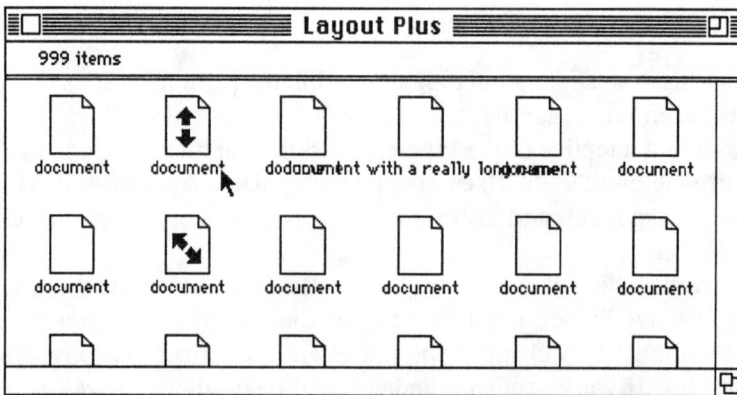

Figure 9.1 Layout Plus starts up into a View-by-Icon window

Revert: Throws out all changes and returns the Finder to the way it was when you started the current Layout Plus session.

Restore All Defaults: Throws out all changes you have ever made to the current Finder, returning it to "shipped from the factory" condition.

Copy From: Brings up an Open dialog box. Copies the settings from whatever Finder you specify to the currently open Finder. You could use this to return all your chosen settings to a new version of the Finder, if you happen to upgrade Systems (make a backup copy of that Finder before running the new System installation; installation otherwise destroys the old Finder copy); also can be used to bring settings from the Finder on one volume to the Finder on another.

Quit: Exits Layout Plus.

Edit Menu

As is typical with the Edit menu, this menu in Layout Plus is for the convenience of Desk Accessories that you may happen to want to run while Layout Plus is active.

View Menu

This menu controls what window view type you're working with. The current selection is checked.

by Small Icon: Apple has included a small icon view in the Finder; this lets the Finder jam more icons into the same space, but preserves more of the graphic quality of the Finder than the text view does. Choosing this option changes the Layout Plus window to look like Figure 9.2. Dragging the small icon with the arrows changes the amount of space between rows of small icons.

by Icon: This is the view shown in Figure 9.1, which we described earlier. We'll give an example of its use a little later.

by Text: Changes the Layout Plus window to a text-only view of a typical folder's contents, as shown in Figure 9.3.

This window type has more controls than the others. If you look toward the top of the graphic, between and just under the words Size and Kind, you see that the pointer has changed to another shape. When positioned over one of the small triangles above and between two columns, the pointer changes to show that you can now drag the triangle to change the width of the column. The arrows at the bottom of each column show how text is currently aligned

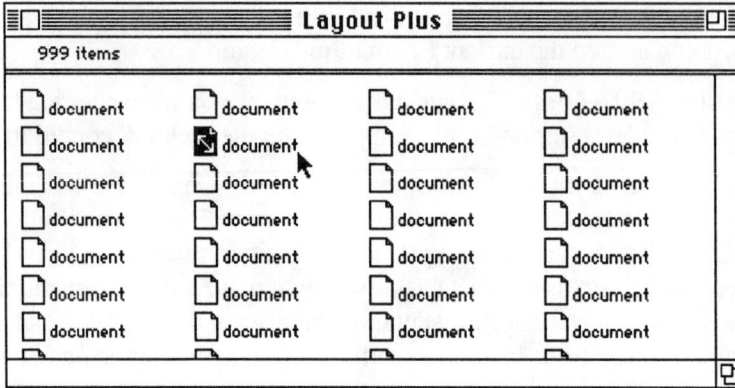

Figure 9.2 by-Small-Icon view of Layout Plus window

within each column. If the arrow faces left, then text is aligned with the left of the column; if the arrow faces right, the column is right-justified. Click on an arrow to toggle between the two options. We'll give an example of how to manipulate this view in order to get more room for a file's title without losing any other information, even without changing the default window size.

Change Window Size: Changes to a blank window (Figure 9.4). Dragging the grow box to size the window changes the size that any newly created window will have.

Default View...: This command brings up a dialog box (Figure 9.5) in which you may indicate what type you want newly created windows to be. As shipped by Apple, all new Finder windows come up in **by Icon** view. This command lets you change that.

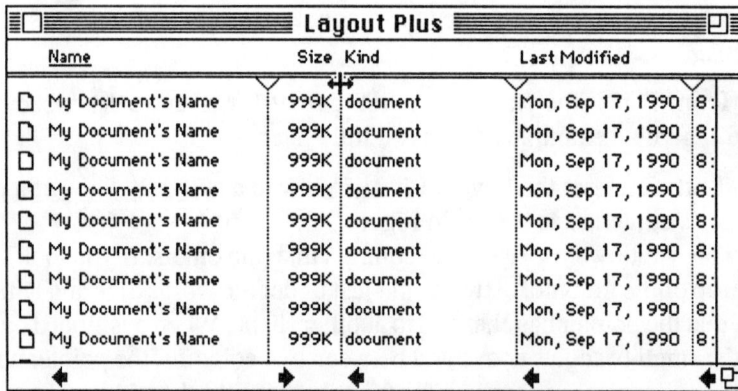

Figure 9.3 Layout Plus window in by-Text view

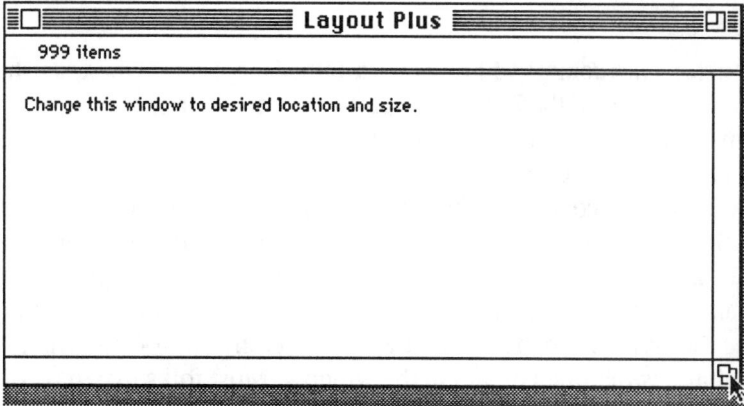

Figure 9.4 Layout Plus window set to change default window size

The last four radio button options, by the way, are all Text View options. The difference is, each organizes files by a different field in the text view window.

Use Default Tabs: When working with the by-Text window, this option switches all changes to the columns back to the factory-shipped condition.

Lock to Grid: This option, when checked, lets you make changes in discrete intervals only. When you drag an item, it will spring over and lock to the nearest available grid line. The grid itself is invisible.

Date Format: This item brings up a submenu just to its right. There are three date display options. One is the full date, the second is an abbreviated version thereof, and the third is a by-numbers-only version. This last option saves the most space.

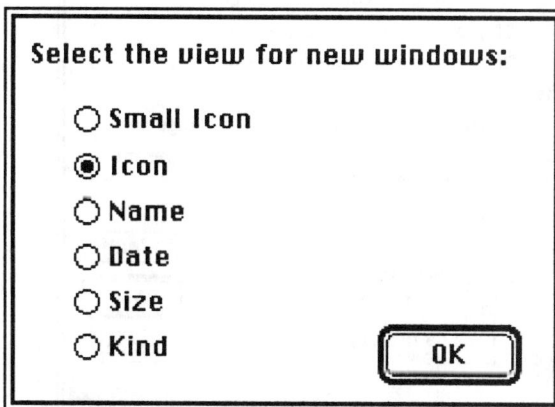

Figure 9.5 Default View... dialog box

Special Menu

Options...: This command brings up a rather large dialog box, as shown in Figure 9.6. Some of the Finder's operational characteristics may be changed thereby. There is a whole smorgasbord of options available here. We'll explain them all in a later section.

The three final commands in the **Special** menu let you change the font used to display text in a Finder window. As we said, 9-point plain Geneva is the default. Each of these commands has a submenu out of which you may choose from among all your installed fonts in all the available sizes. You may even choose the style to use to indicate the sort column in a **by-Text** window. The sort column is the first column in the window. Most folks like to sort files by name. Anyway, you get to choose the style of the label at the top of the column.

Now that we've toured the Layout Plus interface, we'll consider how to use it through a few brief examples. You can follow along at your Macintosh without making any actual changes, if you wish. After we're done, just choose **Revert** from the **File** menu.

Doing the Windows

First, let's adjust the appearance of the Finder's windows. We'll take each view in turn. With Layout Plus up and running (it is listed in the Utilities menu of the Main Menu screen), we choose **by Small Icon** from the **View** menu. A screen like Figure 9.7 appears.

That isn't enough space to show a really long filename. So we position the pointer over the icon with the arrows, hold down the mouse button, and drag

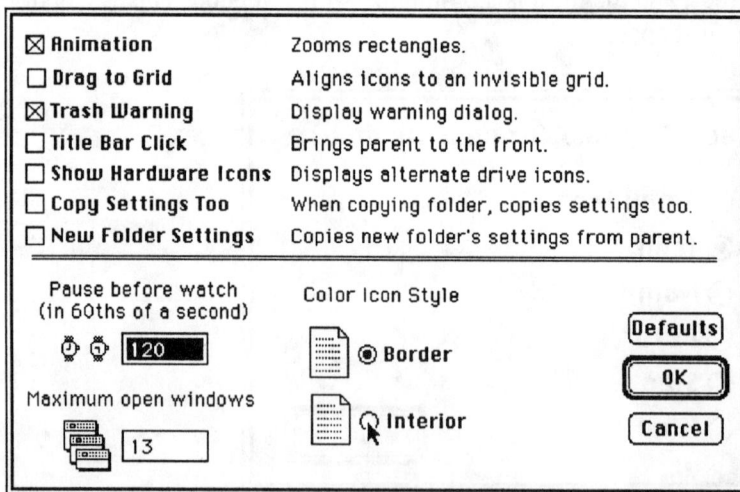

Figure 9.6 Options... dialog box; Layout Plus Special menu

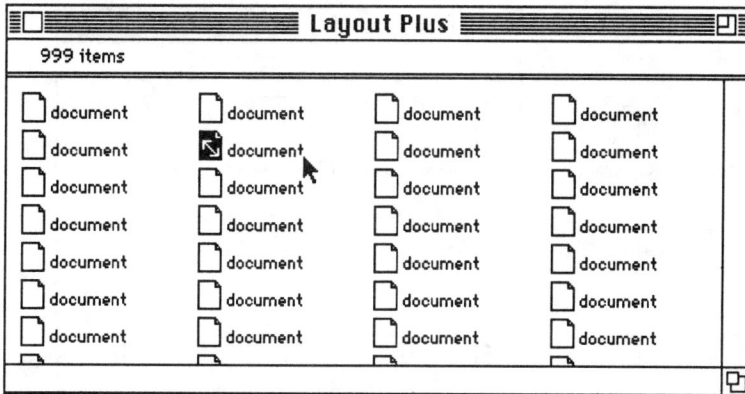

Figure 9.7 Changing the icon spacing in by-Small-Icon view

to the right. Then we release the mouse button. All the small icons move, as shown in Figure 9.8. This should be enough space.

Now to the regular icon view. We choose **by Icon** from the **View** menu; the window changes to look like Figure 9.9.

Really, that's not enough space for documents with long names. But if we drag the columns farther apart, we won't get to see as many icons. The trick here is to stagger the icons. We move the pointer over the icon with the vertical, as opposed to diagonal, arrows, and then drag down. Now every other line is lower. We can also grab the grow box and make the window bigger, so that we can see all of that last line of icons. The results are shown in Figure 9.10.

That's much better. Now on to the most challenging view of all: the text view window. We choose **by Text** from the **View** menu. A screen like Figure 9.11 appears.

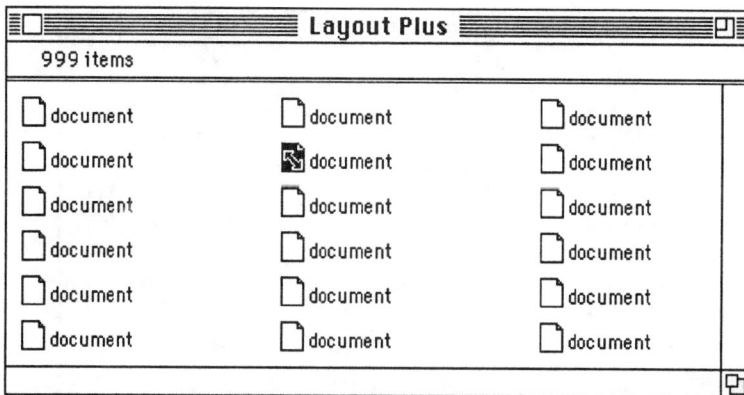

Figure 9.8 More space for small icons

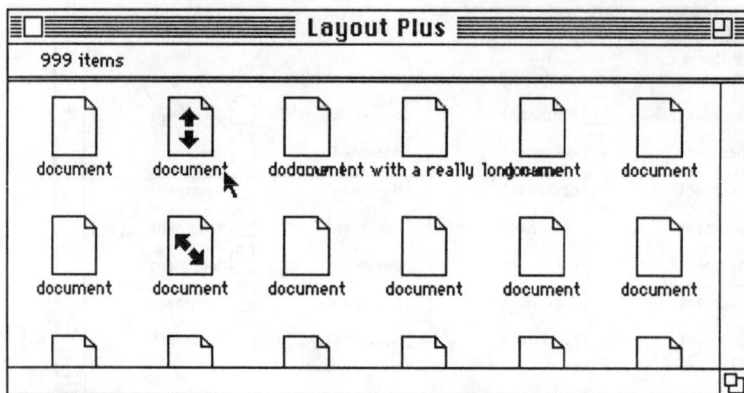

Figure 9.9 Default setup for by-Icon view in Finder window

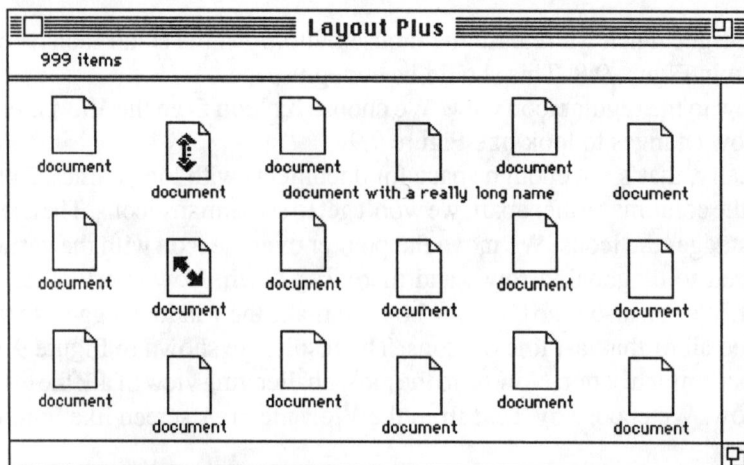

Figure 9.10 More room for big icons

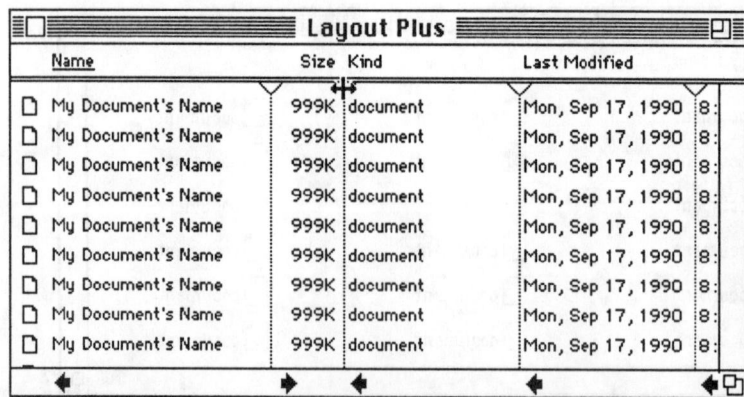

Figure 9.11 Changing the spacing of fields in a text view Finder window

Our goal here is to get more room for document names without necessarily altering the size of the window, or taking so much room away from another column that data can't be displayed in it.

Well, we talked about Date Format earlier. There's an option within it that lets us change dates from the format shown above to a shorter one, like 9/17/90. Let's choose it. The date format changes, opening up more space in that column. Now to make a column narrower, we drag on the triangle opposite the margin it's aligned with (the one the arrow at the bottom is pointing away from). This closes up the free space in the column. Dragging the other triangle moves that column and all others to the right of it. (If you think about it, dragging one column's left margin is the same as dragging the preceding column's right margin. (Like sharing armrests on an airplane.) So we drag the triangle above the right margin of the date column over to the left, remembering to leave enough space for double-digit months and days. Finally, we drag the right margin of the name column over to the right. The results look like this Figure 9.12.

There's just one last thing. We really hate 9-pt Geneva type. For one thing, it's too small. For another, it doesn't show up very well: it's too light. And, can we talk about ugly? With everything else the same, we choose, say, B Optima Bold from the Fonts submenu and 10 pt from the Size submenu. Now the screen looks like Figure 9.13.

Want to see the results? Since we worked so much with the text window type, we'll make it the default for new windows, using the **Default View...** command. Then we quit Layout Plus. (In our case, we have to restart the computer to see changes; we're running under MultiFinder.) When we're back, we create a new folder, and drag a few files into it. We open it up to see a screen like Figure 9.14.

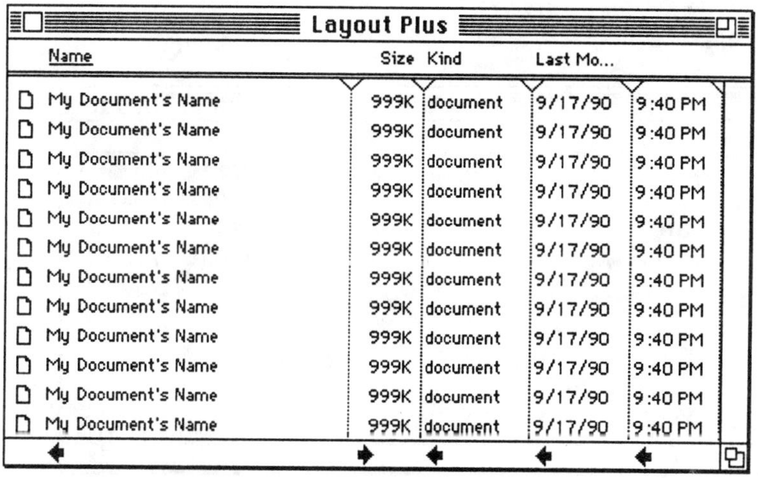

Name	Size	Kind	Last Mo...	
My Document's Name	999K	document	9/17/90	9:40 PM
My Document's Name	999K	document	9/17/90	9:40 PM
My Document's Name	999K	document	9/17/90	9:40 PM
My Document's Name	999K	document	9/17/90	9:40 PM
My Document's Name	999K	document	9/17/90	9:40 PM
My Document's Name	999K	document	9/17/90	9:40 PM
My Document's Name	999K	document	9/17/90	9:40 PM
My Document's Name	999K	document	9/17/90	9:40 PM
My Document's Name	999K	document	9/17/90	9:40 PM
My Document's Name	999K	document	9/17/90	9:40 PM
My Document's Name	999K	document	9/17/90	9:40 PM
My Document's Name	999K	document	9/17/90	9:40 PM

Figure 9.12 An improved by-Text view window

Name	Size	Kind	Last Mo...	
🗋 My Document's Name	999K	document	9/17/90	9:51 PM
🗋 My Document's Name	999K	document	9/17/90	9:51 PM
🗋 My Document's Name	999K	document	9/17/90	9:51 PM
🗋 My Document's Name	999K	document	9/17/90	9:51 PM
🗋 My Document's Name	999K	document	9/17/90	9:51 PM
🗋 My Document's Name	999K	document	9/17/90	9:51 PM
🗋 My Document's Name	999K	document	9/17/90	9:51 PM
🗋 My Document's Name	999K	document	9/17/90	9:51 PM
🗋 My Document's Name	999K	document	9/17/90	9:51 PM
🗋 My Document's Name	999K	document	9/17/90	9:51 PM
🗋 My Document's Name	999K	document	9/17/90	9:51 PM
🗋 My Document's Name	999K	document	9/17/90	9:51 PM

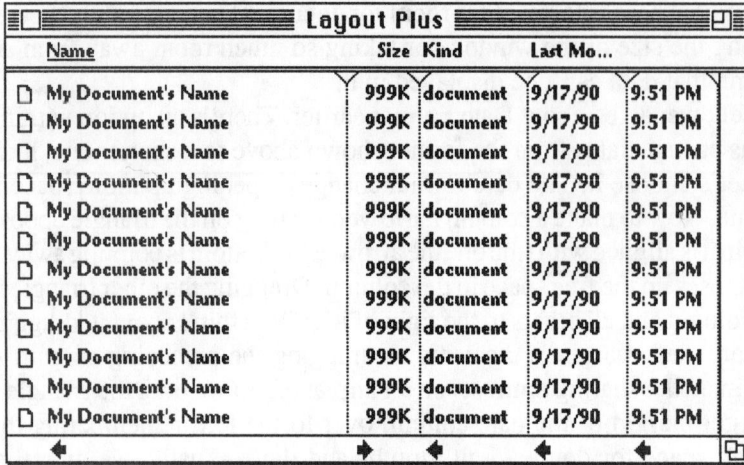

Figure 9.13 A more aesthetically appealing by-Text view

The default icon view of this window now looks like Figure 9.15.

And the small icon view looks like Figure 9.16. Note that the small icon view picked up the staggered offset from the regular icon view, and that all these windows have the font and size we chose while working with the text window.

Well, we've dressed up the Finder's windows pretty well and made them easier to read (and, we hope, to use) in the process. But our work isn't done. As we keep saying, Layout Plus can be used to change not just the Finder's appearance, but some of its operational characteristics as well. To see what that means, let's take that previously promised look at the items available in the Options... dialog box.

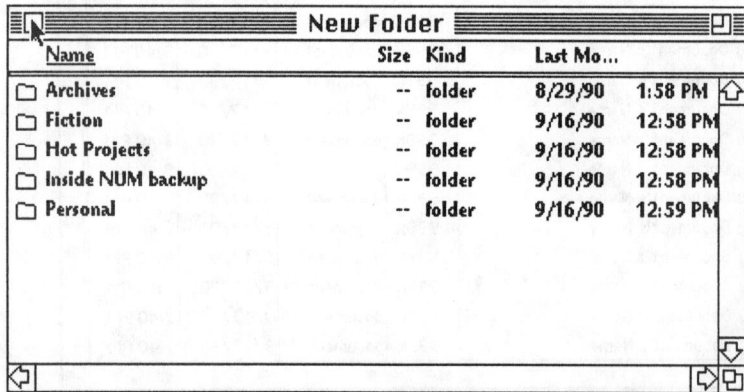

Name	Size	Kind	Last Mo...	
🗁 Archives	--	folder	8/29/90	1:58 PM
🗁 Fiction	--	folder	9/16/90	12:58 PM
🗁 Hot Projects	--	folder	9/16/90	12:58 PM
🗁 Inside NUM backup	--	folder	9/16/90	12:58 PM
🗁 Personal	--	folder	9/16/90	12:59 PM

Figure 9.14 Showing off our newly redecorated Finder windows

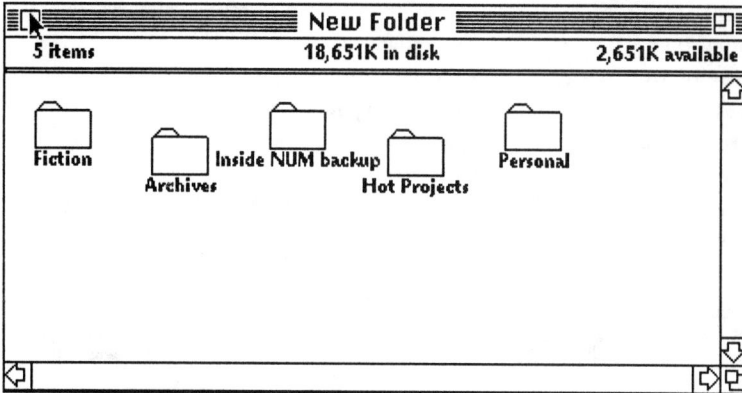

Figure 9.15 A better icon view

Operational Options

The Finder has its own way of doing things. Ever consider what happens when you open a folder? When you copy several files? When you drag an application to the trashcan? You can change what the Finder does in these cases, and more. The place to go is the **Options...** dialog box in Layout Plus's **Special** menu.

Rather than try to take you through an example of its use, we're going to limit ourselves to explaining the various options available. The settings you'd like to have are probably not the ones we'd want, and we wouldn't want to force anything on you.

Returning to Layout Plus, though, we choose **Options...** from the **Special** menu, to see the dialog box in Figure 9.17.

First, let's consider the checkbox options at the left.

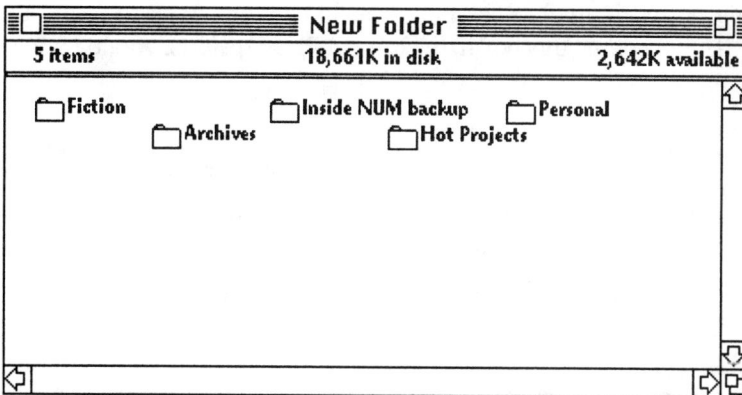

Figure 9.16 A better small icon view

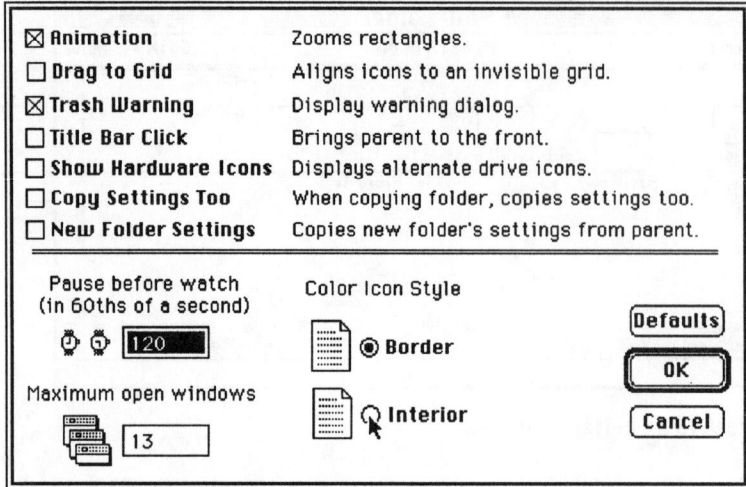

Figure 9.17 Changing aspects of how the Finder works

Animation: When you double-click an icon to open it, the Finder doesn't just pop up a window. Instead, it sort of explodes the icon into a window via animation. If you uncheck this option, the Finder will open windows without animating. This saves just the least little bit of time.

Drag to Grid: When you drag icons around on the desktop or inside a window, the Finder lets you put them just about anywhere. With this option checked, however, icons will snap over to the nearest grid point when you release the mouse button. This keeps things lined up; you don't have to choose **Clean Up** all the time.

Trash Warning: Ordinarily, when you drag a system file or an application to the trash, you get a warning dialog asking if that's really what you want to do, as in Figure 9.18. Not all of us like being kept safe from ourselves. Well, unchecking this box in the Layout Plus **Options...** dialog will skip the warning. You're on your own, kid.

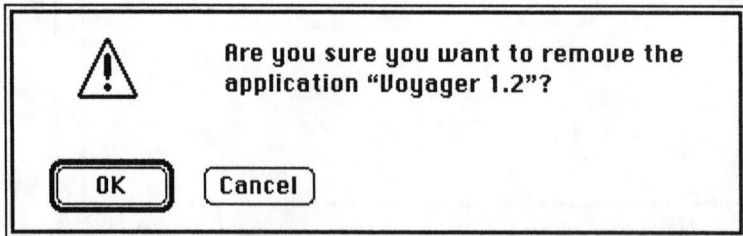

Figure 9.18 The Finder watches over you

Title Bar Click: This has an interesting effect. When the option has been unchecked, double-clicking on the title bar of a window (the window's very top) brings that window's parent to the front. "Parent" simply means the window that something is contained in. In this example, Figure 9.19 shows that Athena II is the parent of Utilities, and Utilities is the parent of Norton Utilities. Double clicking on the title bar of Utilities would bring Athena II to the front, unless the appropriate box were checked in the Layout Plus **Options...** dialog.

Show Hardware Icons: Many hard disk drives feature their own special icons. Like the one in Figure 9.20 for the MicroNet removable cartridge drive that we had to buy on an emergency basis one Sunday. The hardware icons are frequently boring, but some people prefer them. They show up when you check this option.

The next two options concern AppleShare, the AppleTalk file-server software. Those of you who deal with this little gem may know that you can

Athena II				
Name	Size	Kind	Last Mo...	
☐ Applications	--	folder	9/16/90	12:52 PM
☐ NUM 1.0	--	folder	9/16/90	1:06 PM
☐ System Folder	--	folder	9/17/90	10:28 PM
▦ Utilities	--	folder	9/16/90	1:00 PM

Utilities				
Name	Size	Kind	Last Mo...	
◈ FKEY Installer	19K	application	2/8/86	9:10 AM
☐ Micronet Utils	--	folder	9/16/90	1:00 PM
▦ Norton Utilities	--	folder	9/16/90	12:58 PM

Norton Utilities				
Name	Size	Kind	Last Mo...	
◈ Layout Plus	57K	application	7/11/90	1:00 PM
◈ Norton Utilities	578K	application	9/11/90	10:48 PM
☐ Norton Utilities Help	300K	Norton U...	7/11/90	1:00 PM
◈ Speed Disk	157K	application	9/17/90	3:08 PM

Figure 9.19 A window, its parent, and its grandparent

Figure 9.20 Micronet drive icon (not a paid announcement)

control who gets access to files that you create on the file server. This is done via a command in the Finder's **File** menu, namely **Get Privileges**. People are always creating new files and folders, and then forgetting to set the privileges on them so that their co-workers can use them.

Copy Settings Too: With this option checked, when you copy a folder, the new folder has the same access privileges as the old folder, not the default settings that don't let anybody else see it.

New Folder Settings: With this option checked, a new folder will be created with the same settings as its parent folder.

That takes care of all the checkbox options. There are only three more things to consider in this dialog box.

Pause before watch: When you undertake a lengthy operation (such as copying a whole bunch of files from one volume to another), the Finder changes the pointer to an animated watch, just to let you know that it's still working and it's apt to be a while at it. The number in this little field controls how long the Finder waits before switching to the watch. The unit used is ticks; there are 60 Macintosh ticks in a second. (Sixty times a second, a *raster* paints the Macintosh screen. During the time that the raster is being pulled back up to the top to start again, the System generates a phenomenon called the *vertical retrace interrupt*. Operation is halted to let certain system housekeeping tasks be accomplished, and this includes updating the watch cursor.) Thus, setting the number in the field to "30" means a pause of only a half second. Setting this number to a very small value will be extremely annoying, because the pointer is going to switch back and forth from arrow to watch in a flickering manner.

Maximum open windows: You can't keep on opening windows forever. For one thing, the Finder has a limited amount of memory to work with; you'll run out eventually, since every new window has to be stored in RAM somehow. Still, the default Apple limit is less than you probably have memory for. This field lets you set how many windows you'd like to be able to have open. Just because you set it to a number doesn't mean you'll have the RAM to open that many windows; if you don't have the space, you may crash in the attempt. Be conservative.

Color Icon Style: Of interest only to those with color and gray scale monitors. Those of you who do may know that you can set the color of an icon via the Color menu. These two radio buttons control whether the border or the interior of the icon is painted in the color chosen. Purely an aesthetic concern, although color interiors are easier to see, when there are any interiors. (The default document icon is blank, but the default icon is only used when the Finder doesn't know what application a document belongs too, perhaps because it isn't there.)

Now then, to the buttons on the dialog box. Clicking Defaults, of course, returns all the settings to the ones Apple set the Finder to originally. Clicking Cancel throws out all the work you just did and returns you to the main Layout Plus window. And clicking OK accepts all changes. Remember, if you're running Multifinder, you won't notice any changes until you restart.

So now you see how the Finder can be customized. Go out there and give it what for. A little varnish, some new curtains, fresh paint . . . .

Review

We've talked about the Finder and the Desktop in this chapter. We talked a little bit about what the Finder does, and how it presents things, indicating that Apple's choices in that regard are not necessarily the ones that you or I would make. We looked back at a little history, that is to say, the use of ResEdit to alter things like menu command names.

Then we introduced an alternative to using ResEdit to alter the Finder. We saw how Layout Plus can be used to change the appearance of all types of Finder windows: Small Icon view, Icon view, and Text view. We even changed the font used to show names on the Desktop. Finally, we discussed some of the operational parameters that can be changed using Layout Plus.

These are the kinds of changes that you won't need to make very often. Indeed, the two applications we talked about in this section—Speed Disk and Layout Plus—are things you don't need all the time. Maybe once a month at most, and that only in the case of Speed Disk. But the Norton Utilities for the Macintosh contains tools that you'll want to use every day. In the next chapter, we look at two of them: the Norton Desk Accessories Key Finder and Fast Find.

10

Everyday Power

Using the Norton Desk Accessories

Introduction

Well, data recovery utilities are nice to have around when you need them, which may be almost never. And disk optimizers and Finder improvers are great, but they aren't called for constantly, either. But PNC has included several nifty tools that you'll be using every day.

In this chapter, we look at two of the three everyday Norton tools: the desk accessories KeyFinder and Fast Find. Designed to replace the equivalent Apple desk accessories Key Caps and Find File, the Norton DAs offer additional power and flexibility. And, especially in the case of Fast Find, they are **fast**.

What a Character!

Think of a few things that have set the Macintosh apart from every other personal computer, right from the beginning. Surely you thought of the graphics. One of the nicest aspects of Macintosh graphics has always been the variety of text fonts that are available. Even at the beginning, the Macintosh was shipped with Geneva, Chicago, London, and more. It wasn't long before there were scores of fonts available. Now there are hundreds, if not thousands.

There has always been even more to Macintosh text than nice fonts. Remember the first time you discovered that, at long last, you could print accent marks directly over characters? It quickly became chic to head up one's job history with Résumé, which looks so much nicer than just Resume.

▼ **Fonts**

In our continuing quest to bring you fascinating information that you may not know, may not care to know, and may never need to know, but still ought to know, we have decided to say a few words about fonts.

First, the word *font* itself is misused in the Macintosh world. The correct term for a coherent set of letters, numbers, and other characters is a *typeface*. A font,* strictly speaking, is a complete set of letters and characters in one size of one typeface.

Type was invented in the fifteenth century A.D. Prior to that time, all text was either written or engraved by hand. Johannes Gutenberg of Germany is usually credited with perfecting the first movable type. Rather than write the same letters over and over, the early printers learned to cut them into blocks of wood. With enough of these letters, one could assemble within a rectangular frame enough type to form an entire page, which could then be rolled with ink and pressed onto paper, leaving behind an inked impression of a page. More important, such pages could be mass produced. The explosion in knowledge among common people, who heretofore had no access to books, dates from that time.

The first typefaces were modeled closely on the handwriting of the time, a heavy, brushed style called Blackletter. Later, Italian printers revolted against this "barbaric" style, modeling type on the letter forms that the ancient Romans chiseled into their monuments. Thus, the *Roman* family of typefaces was born.

In the early sixteenth century, Aldus Manutius (for whom Aldus Corporation, the makers of PageMaker, is named), in an effort to squeeze more type onto a page, developed a typeface modeled after a style of cursive handwriting that could be quickly written. Later, Italian designers perfected this slanted style of typeface; it came to be known as *Italic*. Soon, companion Italic typefaces were developed for the more common Roman typefaces.

---

* The term dates back to the days of foundry type; letters cut onto metal blocks that were then assembled in forms to compose a page of text. The words foundry, font, and even fondue all came into English from the same ultimate root—the Latin word *fundere*: to melt.

As the Industrial era dawned and progressed, type came to be cast in metal. This so-called foundry type was more durable than wood-cut letters. A complete font of foundry type contained many of each letter, including obviously a large number of E's and lesser numbers of Q's. The type was stored within drawers in large cases. Capital letters were kept in the top drawers, small letters in the drawers beneath. This was the origin of the terms *upper case* and *lower case* for capital and minuscule letters.

By the late nineteenth century, a machine had been invented that could cast entire lines of type based on keys pressed by an operator. This Linotype machine (Samuel Clemens, a.k.a. Mark Twain, was an early investor) contained several fonts in two typefaces, usually a Roman and its companion Italic. The machine assembled the letters from the font into a line, which was then filled with hot lead to create a *slug*. The descendant of Merganthaler Linotype, Allied Corporation, is currently known for its laser imagesetter, the Linotron.

Slugs were composed into pages by hand. To create an appropriate amount of space between lines, the compositor sometimes inserted small sheets of lead in between the slugs. The term *leading* still refers to the amount of space between lines.

Many of the terms used to refer to type date from the days of cold metal. The basic unit of measurement is still the *point*: roughly, but not exactly, equal to 1/72 of an inch. There are 12 points in a *pica*. The pica is the basic unit of horizontal measurement; the point, of vertical measurement. Thus, the total height of a font (measured from the baseline, on which all characters sit, to the top of the capital letters) is measured in points. Twelve-point type is about 1/6th of an inch tall. It's usually best to include about two points of leading with such a font. This is indicated via the shorthand notation 12/14, meaning 12-point type on 14-point leading. The width of a line is measured in picas; the optimum line width is about 43 picas, which is why newspapers are printed in columns, and not all the way across the page. Long lines are too hard to read.

A font also includes nonprinting "characters," the spaces. There are two standard spaces: the *em-space* and the *en-space*. Roughly equal to the width of a capital M and a capital N, the two are defined in terms of the font's height. An em is equal in width to the font's height; an en is 1/2 em. Thus, a 12-point em is one pica wide.

Actually, because the Macintosh lets you vary the parameters of type freely, it makes sense to use the term "font" to refer only to the typeface. In past times, you had complete sets of letters with all characteristics already determined. Now, you can virtually create your own fonts. With the right software, you can even create typefaces. We've come a long way since Gutenberg!

Is it possible to have too much of a good thing? The revolution in available characters gave us lots of things we could never type before: the signs for British pounds and Japanese yen, strange letters squashed together like in the British spelling of hæmmoraghe—so many characters and symbols, in fact, that it became impossible to fit them onto a standard typewriter-style keyboard, even using the shift key.

Apple knew this was coming and included a second shift key on the Macintosh keyboard; they called it *Option*. This effectively doubled the number of combinations. Since only the letters and numbers are printed on the keys themselves (the special characters available with Option change from font to font sometimes), how on earth could a person tell how to get those fancy characters?

Apple knew that was coming, too, and shipped a desk accessory called Key Caps. You could select the font to view, although not all fonts fit nicely into the spaces (London didn't). And it didn't show all the characters at once; you still had to hold down the shift and or Option keys to see what characters were available. If you didn't know the typewriter keyboard like the back of your hand, you had to revert back to the standard view and see what keycap the desired character was on.

All of that is a thing of the past.

Norton KeyFinder

KeyFinder is a Norton Utilities desk accessory* that simultaneously displays all the characters available within a font. It also indicates what keystrokes are needed to obtain any selected character. It will show the characters available in all the fonts installed on your system, using actually available point sizes. It also can be configured to show the ASCII control codes and the ASCII value associated with each character.

When you select KeyFinder from the Apple menu, a screen like Figure 10.1 appears.

There are three areas on the screen: the character matrix to the left; the keystroke indicator to the upper right, which shows you what to type to get the character currently selected on the matrix (the Apple symbol on the graphic above); and a font list. Scroll in the font list to find the typeface you want to know about; click on its name to switch KeyFinder to a view of that font.

There is also a KeyFinder menu. It contains the following commands:

---

*   Recall that desk accessories are small applications that may be launched from the Apple menu, over other applications in the Finder. They provide useful tools while you're working in another application.

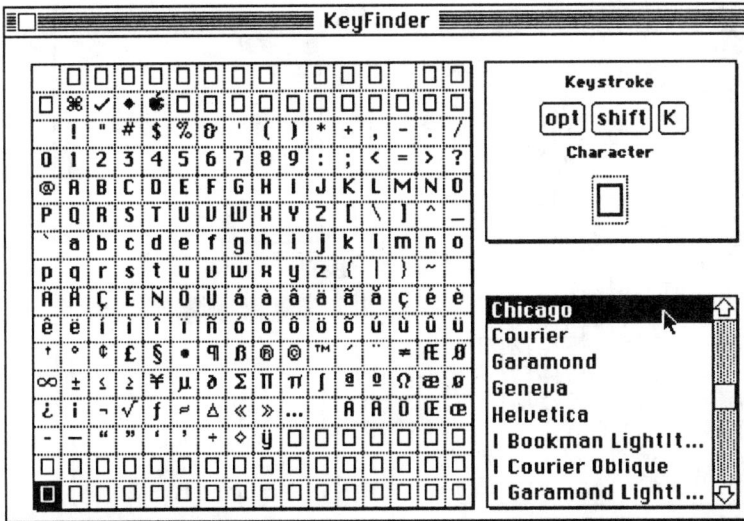

Figure 10.1 The KeyFinder window

About KeyFinder: Choosing this command displays a small panel giving credit to the authors of KeyFinder. Click once anywhere on the screen to send it away.

Swap Orientation: Changes the order in which characters are displayed in the matrix. Characters may be in their ASCII collating order from left to right in rows, or from top to bottom in columns. Figure 10.1 shows row order; Figure 10.2 shows column order.

You can toggle back and forth between these two views as you like. KeyFinder will "remember" the setting you chose last the next time you bring it up, so you don't have to reconfigure it every time you use it. This applies to all the options discussed below.

Real Font Size: Without this option checked, KeyFinder attempts to construct a 12-point version of the selected font out of whatever it can find. With the option checked, KeyFinder looks for a 24-point version in your System. If none is found, is decreases the size it's trying to find and goes after things again. When it actually finds an installed font, it uses that font to create an evenly scaled version to fit into the matrix. Basically, this option improves the display; although in some cases characters will extend outside of their squares and be clipped. A **Real Font Size** screen is shown in Figure 10.3. The single character displayed under the legend **Character** in the upper right panel shows the font size that KeyFinder has found to use.

Show ASCII: Normally, the ASCII control code characters (for things like Return and Line Feed and Form Feed and Ring Bell) are shown as empty

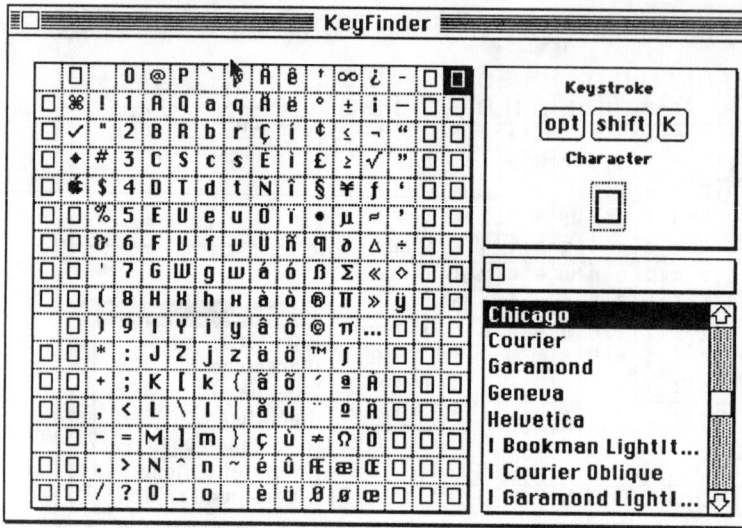

Figure 10.2 KeyFinder swapper in column order

boxes; an empty box in a font means there is no character corresponding to
that position in the font. Checking Show ASCII fills in the ASCII control
code boxes with the control code aliases as in Figure 10.4. This is actually
quite useful; you can get some applications to search for things like Returns
and Tabs if you know the ASCII code for them.

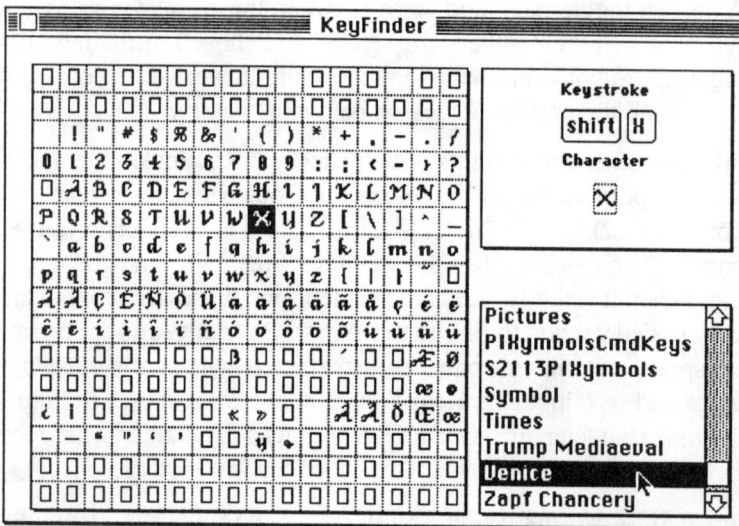

Figure 10.3 KeyFinder with Real Font Size option checked

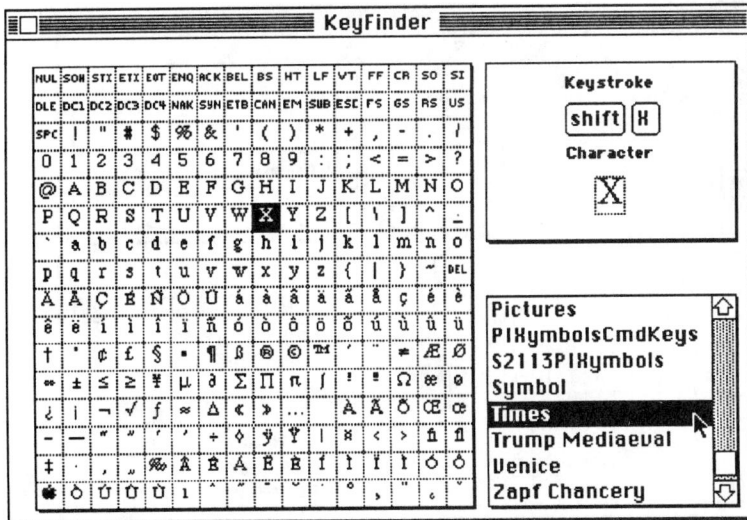

Figure 10.4 KeyFinder showing ASCII control codes

Of course, if you're going to do buttonheaded things like ask to see ASCII control codes, you probably want to know what the ASCII values are. You can do that.

Programmer Mode: This adds ASCII values to the rows and columns in the character matrix, and changes the upper-right panel to a display of the keystroke and ASCII values of the currently selected character in the matrix, as shown in Figure 10.5. In this orientation (by row), the first hexadecimal digit in a character is given next to the row it's in; the second digit is given next at the top of its column. Thus, the ASCII for "R" is $52. You can also find that out by clicking on the character; the upper right panel shows ASCII values in decimal, hexadecimal, and octal (base 8) notation for the character you've selected. By the way, you can also type a character to select it; typing "r" is the same as clicking on it in the matrix.

Text Edit: This adds a small text field to the KeyFinder window, directly below the character panel at the top right, as shown in Figure 10.6. You can type text into this field. You can also paste text into it from the Clipboard, and cut or copy text from it. This text may be pasted into other applications. (Note, however, that the characters may come across in whatever font you've currently selected in the *application*; **not** the one you chose in KeyFinder.)

The next two commands are used to configure a printer and to print the KeyFinder window. **Page Setup...** and **Print...** bring up dialog boxes that you should be quite familiar with if you've been using the Macintosh for any time

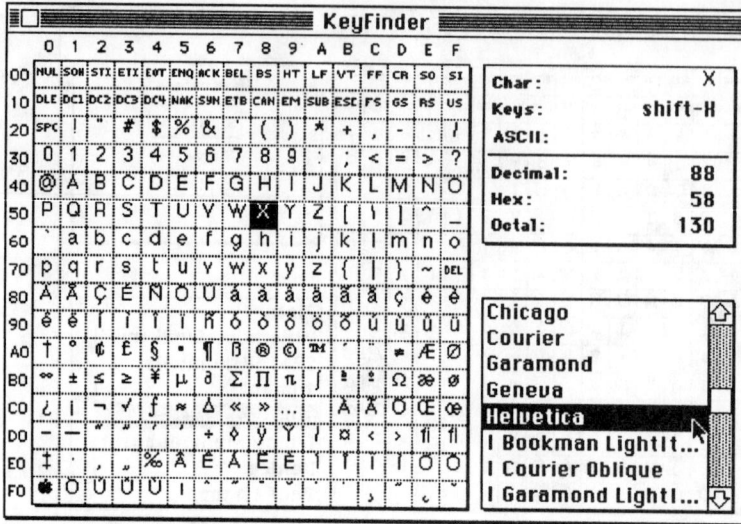

Figure 10.5 KeyFinder in programmer mode; with ASCII legends

at all. You can print key charts for all the fonts you frequently use and consult them without leaving your application.

Finally, the last command, **Quit,** returns you to whatever application you were in when you chose to run KeyFinder.

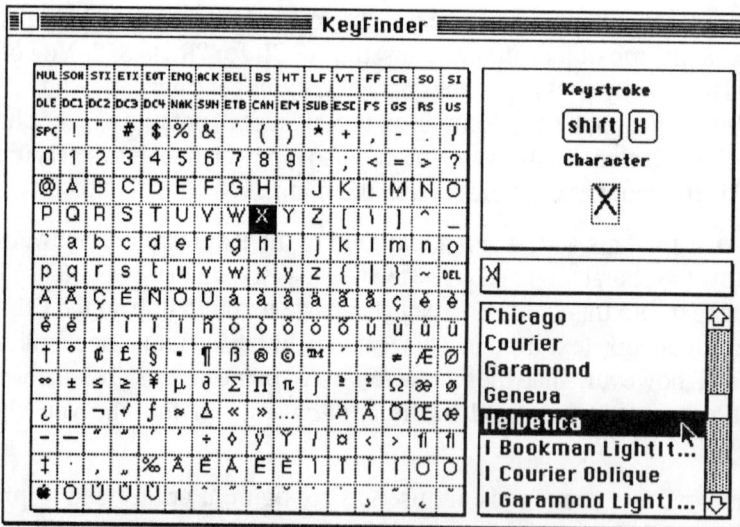

Figure 10.6 KeyFinder with text edit field active

Using KeyFinder

Using KeyFinder is just the simplest thing in the world. There are at least two ways you might want to use it: To find out how to get an unusual character in an unusual font, and to bring over a whole string of such characters without retyping, using the Clipboard. We'll see how to do both.

Finding Unusual Characters

One of the most interesting fonts available is shipped with all of Apple's newer laser printers. It's called Zapf™ Dingbats. A dingbat is just a noncharacter symbol. Printers call these extra characters "sorts." Zapf Dingbats contains a variety of sorts, including circled numerals, asterisks and stars, and arrows. Suppose we want to find a decent right-pointing arrow.

Well, first we choose KeyFinder from the Apple menu. The window appears, but doesn't get completely drawn right away. First, KeyFinder has to locate all your font files within the System and possibly elsewhere. This may take several seconds if you have a large number of fonts installed. KeyFinder opens up with the font Chicago selected, as in Figure 10.1.

We scroll down the list in the bottom right of the window till we see Zapf Dingbats, then we click on the name. The screen changes to a view of that font, like Figure 10.7.

All kinds of things are available in this font. (We really like the fat quotes on row 8.) It looks like there's a decent-enough arrow in the next to last column

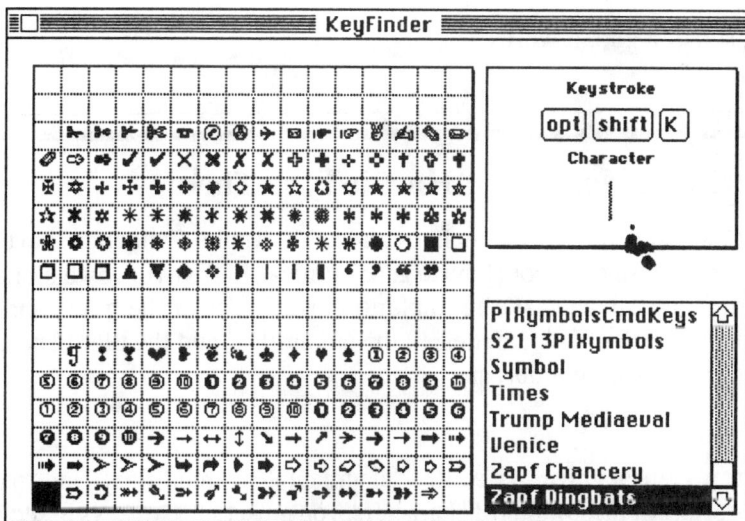

Figure 10.7 Symbols available in the font Zapf Dingbats

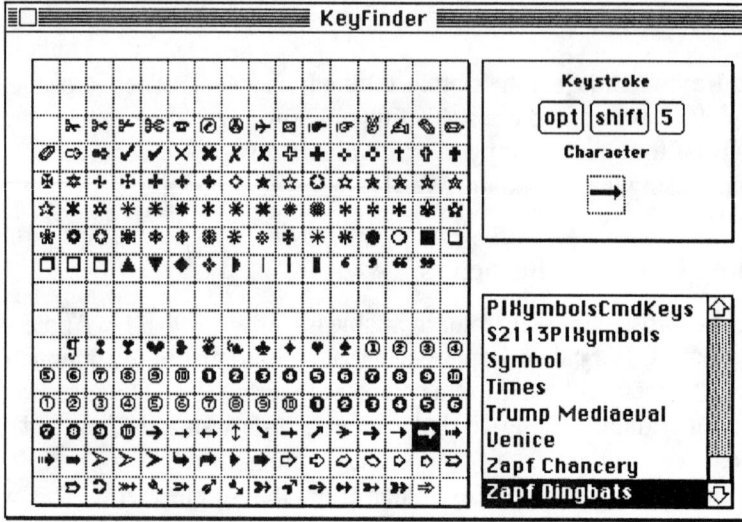

Figure 10.8 How to get a decent arrow

of the third row from the bottom. Let's click it to select it. We get the screen shown in Figure 10.8.

So it turns out, if we switch fonts to Zapf Dingbats and press the "5" key while holding down both Option and Shift, we get this arrow (shown in the upper right at 24 points). Let's try it.

➡

Well, son of a gun, it works.

▼ Diacritical Marks and How toType Them

Macintosh font designers, in harmony with Apple Computer, have been reasonably consistent about how to get diacritical marks over vowels, and even over some consonants. We're thinking in particular of the grave and acute accents, the umlaut (a.k.a diaresis), the circumflex, and the tilde. The classic examples of each, in order, are

à é ü î ñ

which are read "a grave," "e acute," "u umlaut," "i circumflex," and "n tilde."

To get any of these kinds of characters, you must type two keys in sequence; the first key with the modifier Option held down. (KeyFinder indicates this by separating the keys shown to get the character in the upper right panel.) The grave accent is easy; it shows up on the keyboard, next to the numeral 1 key. The "a grave" is given by

Option-` a

where the hyphen indicates two keys that must be pressed together. To get "e grave", you press

Option-` e

and so on. The procedure is similar for the other combinations, except those diacritical marks are not shown on the screen. Remember the character they're principally associated with, though. When you think of the acute accent, you usually think of the letter e. So to get a letter u with an acute accent, type

Option-e u

to get ú. When you think of the umlaut, you think of the letter u. To get that short word for Christmas, type

N o Option-u e l

to get Noël. (In English, the diaresis indicates a vowel pronounced in a syllable separate from the preceding vowel; No ël is a two-syllable word, as is na ïve.) And so on. The rule of thumb: Hold down the Option key and type the character the diacritical mark is associated with, then type the character you want the mark to appear over.

Copying Characters from KeyFinder

If you're working with but one font in your application and need to find out several characters, you can actually assemble them in KeyFinder and then copy them to your application.

Again we bring up KeyFinder. This time, we make sure that the option **Text Edit** is checked in the **KeyFinder** menu. The screen looks like Figure 10.9.

We're going to make up one doozy (should that be spelled "Dusy," since it refers to that fine old automobile, the Dusenberg?) of a last name. Instead of typing it, though, we click out its letters on the KeyFinder matrix, as shown in Figure 10.10.

Instead of writing down all the keystrokes used to get this (who could remember them all), we just select the name in the KeyFinder text edit field, **Copy** from the **Edit** menu, switch back to our application, and choose **Paste**. Voilà:

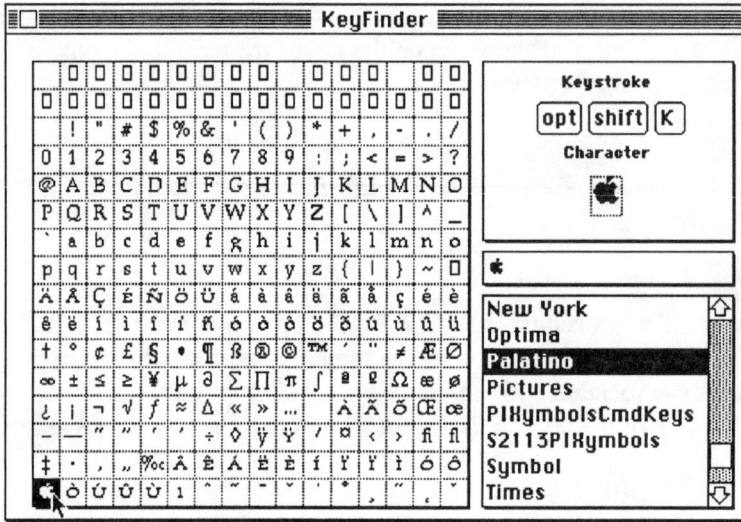

Figure 10.9 Using the text edit field

Béñaråö

You can even copy some of the ASCII control codes from the text edit field. Copying and pasting a Form Feed (FF) for example, inserts a hard page break in Microsoft Word.

KeyFinder can save you lots of time and effort, but it's only half the Norton desk accessory story. We think you'll agree that the other Norton DA is quite a find.

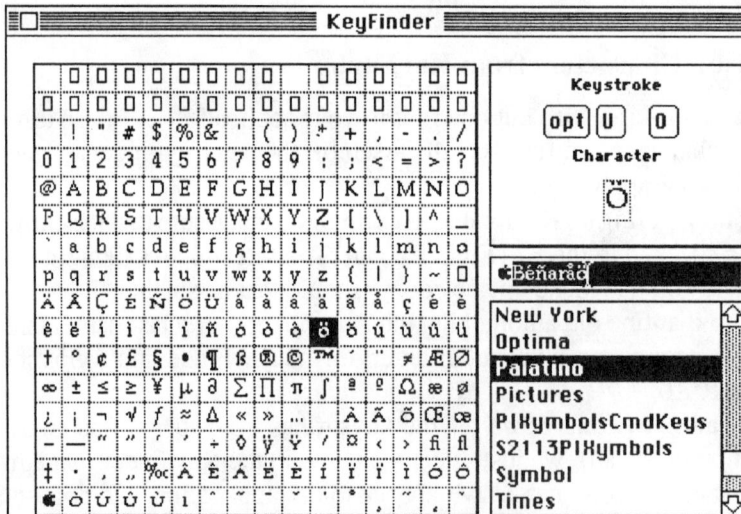

Figure 10.10 An interesting last name

Now That You've Found It, What're You Going To Do with It?

How well do you have your files organized? You know, it's a paradox, but the better your disk is organized, the harder it can be to locate documents and applications. And, the worse your disk is organized, the harder it can be to locate files. What gives?

Well, if you have lots of very logically named folders, with folders within folders, and files organized according to project and document type and whatnot, chances are you find yourself opening window after window to get at things. Nesting folders very deeply makes it a little tedious to get at files. That's one kind of hard.

The converse is true: If, in the most trivial case, you have no folders at all (other than the System folder, which you must have), then you can have literally hundreds of files at root level. Finding something there can be like looking for a needle in a haystack. And don't laugh; we know people who keep their hard disks in this condition. That's another kind of hard.

Even if your case is somewhere in between, finding a file in the Finder (that's what it's for, after all) is not necessarily as easy as it could be. Think of a simple case: You keep all your applications in a folder named "Applications," which is at root level (appears in the disk window). Each application is in its own folder inside "Applications." This means that if you want to launch, say, PageMaker or Multiplan, you have to double-click to open the disk window, double-click to open "Applications," and double-click to open the PageMaker (or whatever) folder before double-clicking on the application's icon. Lots of double-clicking, that, and it leaves you with three open windows, at least two of which you probably don't care beans about and which get in the way if you're using Multifinder.

Who wants to go to all that trouble just to launch an application? And that's only what can happen (or really, used to happen) when you know where something is. What happens if you forget? That memo to the boss I wrote last week: Is it in my Personal folder? Is it in the project folder? Which project was I working on when I wrote it? Did it end up in the application's folder? On a relatively large disk you could go snooping around for quite a while before finding that memo, probably leaving quite a trail of open windows behind you.

Well, this kind of spelunking hasn't been necessary for years, not since Apple Computer introduced its Find File desk accessory. This DA would look for files by name, show you where they were, and even move them to the desktop for you. That's about all it could do. Suppose you didn't want to move the file to the desktop? After all, if you're like us, you have lots of files that you work with all the time. Who wants them all mucking up the desktop just so you can work with them? Well, you could open up all those windows to get to files. That's no good either; you have to do it every time you want to get at something.

"Look," you might say to Find File, as if it were a loyal but not-so-intelligent canine. "You found the file. Now do something with it! I don't want to move it: I want to look at it, I want to open it, I want to work with it. And I want to do it *now*." Find File would stare back at you with a puzzled expression and a slightly cocked head.

You need a new friend. Let us introduce you to Fast Find.

Norton Fast Find

Fast Find is one of the two Norton DAs included with the Norton Utilities for the Macintosh. Superficially similar to Apple's Find File, which you get free with your paid subscription to the System, Fast Find is much faster, more flexible, and more powerful. You easily search any and all mounted disk volumes. You can peek inside files to make sure they're the ones you want. You can even copy their data to the Clipboard. Best of all, you can open documents and launch applications directly from Fast Find, just by double-clicking on their names. Without moving them or altering your windows or your desktop—which we think is pretty neat, because we do it all the time.

Choosing Fast Find from the Apple menu opens the window shown in Figure 10.11.

There are six operating areas on this window. Starting in the upper-left corner, you see icons for all mounted disks—in this case, the hard disk partitions "Athena II" and "Alexandria." Click on a drive icon to search that drive. Below the drive icons is a progress bar; during searches, it shows how far Fast Find has made it through the disks it's searching. Below the progress

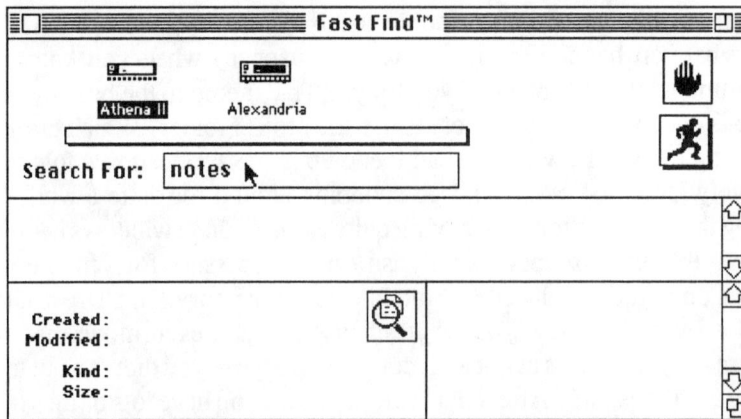

Figure 10.11 The Fast Find window

bar is a text field, in this case containing the word "notes." This is where you type the name of the file you wish to find. You don't have to type the complete name; any part of the filename—even just a letter or two—will work.

In the upper-right corner of the window are two buttons. Clicking the bottom one starts a search; clicking the top one stops it. The human figure in the lower button is animated while a search is proceeding. (If you don't want to spend CPU power making the little guy run, hold down the Option key while you click on him. Or, hold down the Shift key after you click.)

In the center of the window is a scrolling list; here is where the names of found files are displayed. Below this area are two more panels. The one in the lower-left corner displays information about the currently selected file. The icon with the magnifying glass is the View button; pressing it opens a window showing you the selected file's data. The file's icon type is shown below this button (this space is blank in Figure 10.11). Finally, the right corner displays the path to the file: the folder it's in, the folder its folder is in, and so forth back to the disk window. If the path is too long to fit in the space provided, you can scroll up and down with the scroll bar at the very right.

Of course there's a Fast Find menu, and of course we're going to tell you what's in it.

About Fast Find...: Credit where credit is due. Click to dismiss.

The next command toggles between **Search Folder** and **Search Drives**.

Search Folder: Restricts searches to a folder that you select. If you know a file is in a particular folder, you can narrow the search in this way and save time, especially on a large hard disk.

Search Drives: This command is only active if you've restricted a search to a particular folder and if that folder's icon is selected. Choosing it brings back the drive icons and expands the scope of searches back to entire volumes, or multiple volumes.

Move to Desktop: Moves the selected file to the Finder Desktop.

Select All Drives: Searches all mounted volumes in order.

View Document: Same as the magnifying glass button at the bottom of the screen. Opens a window revealing the selected file's data. Interesting in the case of text documents; useless in the case of graphics—for now.

Open Document: Launches a selected application or opens a selected document. Same as double-clicking on a file icon in the Finder.

Quit: Leaves Fast Find behind.

That's what's in it. Now let's use it.

Using Fast Find

It's no secret: We use Fast Find to launch applications. It is very nice to be able to do so in Multifinder. We don't have to switch to the Finder and then find the application icon, buried as it is in the application's folder. We just pull down Fast Find, type in the application's name (or even just a part of it), wait until the application shows up in the scrolling list, click to select it, and double-click to launch it. We've probably done that a couple of hundred times in the writing of this book.

Fast Find is good for other things, too. Right off the bat, we can think of three usage examples that ought to give you a clear notion of Fast Find's utility.

Find!

Sometime you just want to find something to know that it's there. Is this the diskette with the Dayton spreadsheet, the one I prepared for Sue? Where are my notes?

Speaking of notes, we used to keep lots of them. Wonder if they made it over to this new drive we're using. Let's find out.

We choose Fast Find from the Apple menu, type "notes", and click the running man "Start" button.

After about seven seconds, we see a screen like Figure 10.12.

The number "7" to the left of the progress bar shows that seven possible matches to "notes" were found. You can see from the three examples shown that "notes" can appear anywhere in the file's name, and can be capitalized. We click on a name to select it. This file was created back in 1986; it's a document of unknown type, about 3K long. The path shows that it is in the "tybr" folder

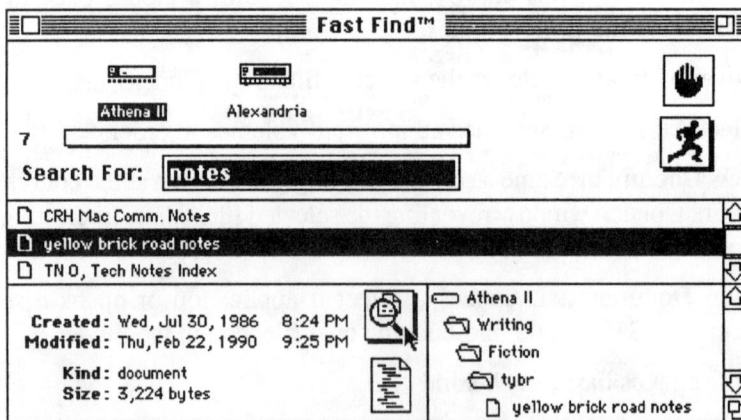

Figure 10.12 Seven "notes" files found

(we know what this means and we're not going to tell you), which is inside "Fiction," which is inside "Writing," which is at root level. Think of opening all those folders!

View and Copy!

Here's another one. Suppose you want some figures, or other such data, from a file. You're not even sure which file has the right stuff. Well, you can use Fast Find to locate the correct file, and even to copy the data you want, without opening the file or launching its application. Heck, you don't even need a copy of the application.

Taking the example in Figure 10.13, we click on another file's name.

This time, to see what's in the selected file, we click the magnifying glass button. (You can also choose View Document from the **Fast Find** menu, same thing.) We see a screen like Figure 10.14.

Interesting. If we want, we can drag a selection across this text, choose Copy from the Edit menu, quit Fast Find, and paste the text into another document in that document's application.

Open and Launch!

Finally, there's our favorite way to use Fast Find. If you double click on the selected file's name, Fast Find will launch its application (if necessary) and open the document. Note, to be sure, that this feature only works if (a) you open Fast Find in the Finder or (b) you are running under MultiFinder. Under the

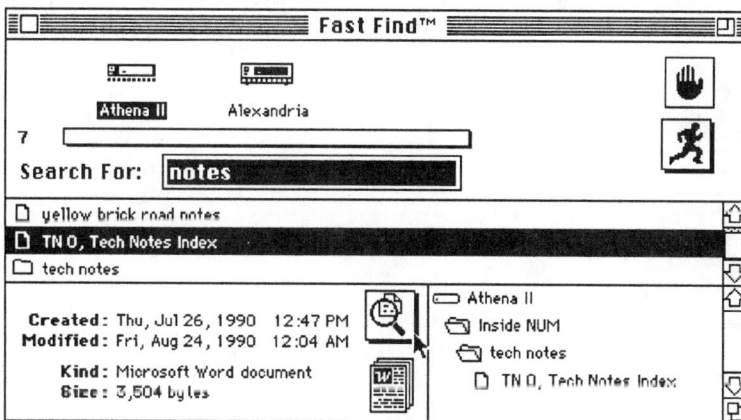

Figure 10.13 What's in here?

```
.7.................................!..........................................................................⇧
...........F...l.x..............  *...!........................................................
#0  Tech Notes Index

This is an index of all the Norton Utilities for the Macintosh Internal Technical Notes.
_____

_____

Number  Title  Last Update
0  Tech Notes Index  8/23/90
1  HFS Data Structures  7/24/90
 1a  Boot Blocks  7/24/90
 1b  Volume Information Block  7/24/90
 1c  BTree Node  7/24/90                                        ⇩

TN 0, Tech Notes Index                        [  Done  ]
```

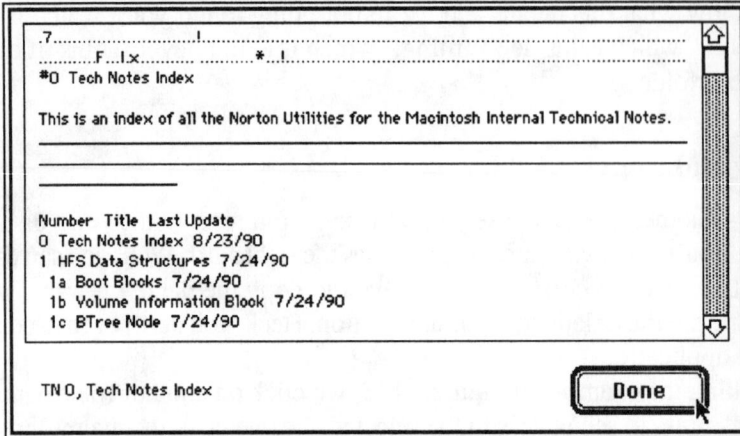

Figure 10.14 A view of the document's data

regular Finder, you can't launch one application from within another; you have to quit the first application before choosing Fast Find.

Now aren't you glad you got to know each other?

Review

This was a chapter about desk accessories. We saw how to use KeyFinder—a replacement for Key Caps—to locate strange characters in bizarre fonts, and even paste them into applications. We introduced Fast Find—a replacement for Find File—and saw how to locate, view and copy, and open files using it.

The next chapter covers our last new topic, before we return briefly to the Disk Editor. In Chapter 11, we introduce a member of the Norton Utilities for the Macintosh that can enhance just about every application you currently own.

11

Smooth Operator

Getting Directory Assistance

Introduction

To us, it seems that the way computers make you do things, and the way you really want to do them, are frequently at odds. Even on the Mac, though less so than with other systems. Think about it: You've got all that Macintosh power at your fingertips, but it isn't completely available every time you want it. Take dialog boxes. Even under Multifinder, you can't switch out of them to do something else. You have to Cancel.

And when would you want to "do something else?" Any number of times. Try saving a new file onto a crowded floppy disk. There you are, in the **Save** dialog box. You press Return. The disk is full. What do you do? Under Multifinder, you can exit the dialog box, switch to the Finder, and delete some files from the disk. But what if you crash before the new file is saved? Kiss it goodbye. Running under the regular Finder, the problem is even worse: You can't quit the application to go delete files without first saving the file. If you don't save, again the file is as good as gone.

Ever outsmart yourself? You lock a file via the checkbox in the file's Finder **Get Info** window. Then, at a later date, you attempt to open the file. The file is locked. You have to leave the **Open...** dialog box, maybe even leave the application, unlock the file, and start over.

You want to save a new document into the same folder as some other important document, but you can't remember where that important document is. So you scroll and click and click and scroll, searching every conceivable folder in the **Save** dialog box's scrolling list. You could just leave the dialog box and use Fast Find. But is that really the easiest way?

It isn't. None of the Mac's functionality ever goes away; it's simply a question of access. You need something that gives you access to the power to find, copy, unlock, and delete files. To create new folders. To let you see when files and folders were last modified. All from within the Save and Open dialog boxes in *any* application. So who're you going to call?

Calling Directory Assistance

Directory Assistance is an INIT (sometimes called "startup document") that modifies the standard **Open** and **Save** dialog boxes, adding two pop-up menus and a status line. Designed to work with virtually every application on the market, Directory Assistance lets you duplicate files (so that you can work with a copy and not the original, among other things), delete files, see their Get Info windows, and find files fast. In fact, Directory Assistance is even faster than Fast Find, so that if you want to open another file from within an application, it's better to search for the file using Directory Assistance that it is to look for it using the Norton Fast Find DA!

Directory Assistance also lets you choose how you want to display file and folder names in the scrolling list. You can mix files and folders, or you can have all folders grouped together at the head or tail of the list. You can sort by date, and see a status line showing the time of last modification of the selected file or folder. What's more, Directory Assistance will "remember" what file you've selected, so that when you return to a dialog box, the highlight is over the last file selected, and not at the top of the scrolling list. This is really handy if you're opening several files in order.

▼ Technically Speaking

Directory Assistance replaces two Macintosh Toolbox routines: SFGetFile and SFPutFile. These routines are used by almost every Macintosh application to open and save files, respectively. "Get" and "Put" draw the dialog boxes and negotiate the interaction with the File Manager. Some applications make modifications to the standard dialog box design, adding additional buttons and fields.

Directory Assistance takes over by patching the jump table. This is a data structure in RAM that maintains the addresses of the program code for various program routines. Directory Assistance substitutes its address for the addresses of SFGet and Put, whose code is contained in the Macintosh ROMs.

PNC has included "hooks" in the Directory Assistance code that allow other developers to access its functionality, linking it with their own routines. For more information, contact the Macintosh Development Manager at Symantec/ Peter Norton Group, 100 Wilshire Boulevard 9th Floor, Santa Monica, CA 90401.

When Directory Assistance is running, a typical Open... dialog box looks something like Figure 11.1.

All of Directory Assistance's functions are contained with the two pop-up menus that you see on either side of the path pop-up menu (the one you use to move back up to higher-level folders).

File Menu

New Folder: Brings up a small dialog box into which you type the name of the new folder (Figure 11.2). The newly created folder is put into the folder you're currently within; that is, the one whose name is shown on the path pop-up menu and whose contents are shown in the scrolling list.

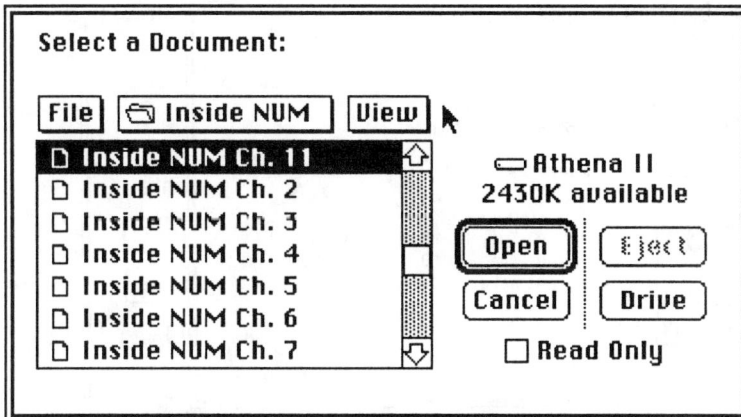

Figure 11.1 Open file dialog box with Directory Assistance on the case

Select a Document:

| File |

Name for new folder:

New Stuff

OK   Cancel

☐ App
☐ Ins
☐ NU
☐ Sys
☐ Utilities
☐ Writing

able

Cancel   Drive

☐ Read Only

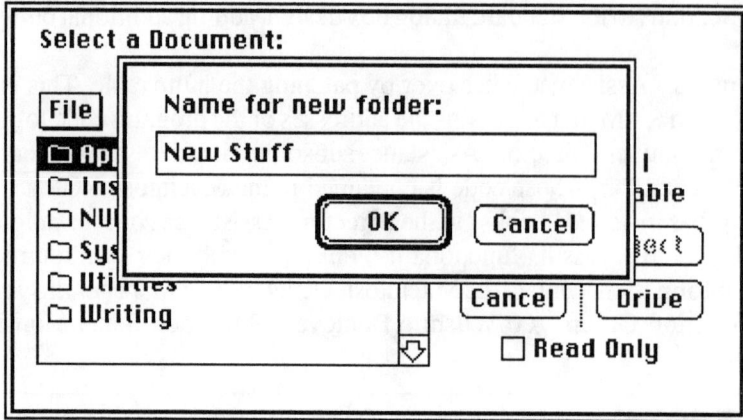

Figure 11.2 New Folder dialog box from Directory Assistance

Get Info: Selecting a file or folder name in the scrolling list and then choosing this command, brings up the file or folder's Get Info window, identical to the one accessed via **Get Info** in the Finder's **File** menu (Figure 11.3).

Notice in particular that Locked box; you can check and uncheck it at will directly within the dialog box, without exiting to the Finder.

Duplicate: Creates a copy of the currently selected file. The duplicate bears the name Copy of... and is placed in the same folder, as shown on the scroll list in Figure 11.4. If the name would be too long with the addition of the words "Copy of," then you're asked via a dialog box to choose another, shorter name.

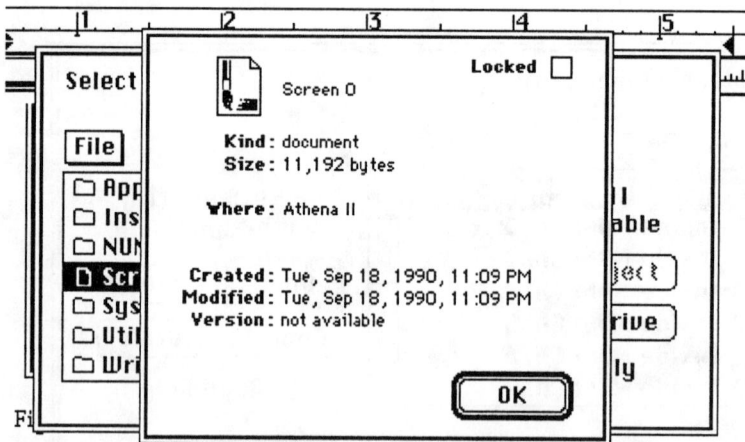

Select

| File |

☐ App
☐ Ins
☐ NU
☐ Scr
☐ Sys
☐ Uti
☐ Wri

Locked ☐

Screen 0

Kind: document
Size: 11,192 bytes

Where: Athena II

Created: Tue, Sep 18, 1990, 11:09 PM
Modified: Tue, Sep 18, 1990, 11:09 PM
Version: not available

OK

able

ect

rive

ly

Figure 11.3 Get Info window over Open dialog box

```
┌─────────────────────────────────────────────────────────┐
│ ╔═══════════════════════════════════════════════════════╗ │
│ ║  Select a Document:                                    ║ │
│ ║                                                        ║ │
│ ║  ┌──────┐ ┌───────────┐ ┌──────┐      ▶               ║ │
│ ║  │ File │ │⊂ Athena II │ │ View │                       ║ │
│ ║  └──────┘ └───────────┘ └──────┘                       ║ │
│ ║  ┌────────────────────────────┬─┐   ⊂ Athena II       ║ │
│ ║  │ ▢ Applications             │⬆│   2474K available   ║ │
│ ║  │ ▢ Copy of Screen 0         │ │                      ║ │
│ ║  │ ▢ Inside NUM               │ │   ┌──────┐  ┌──────┐ ║ │
│ ║  │ ▢ NUM 1.0                  │ │   │ Open │  │ Eject│ ║ │
│ ║  │ ▉ Screen 0                 │ │   └──────┘  └──────┘ ║ │
│ ║  │ ▢ Screen 1                 │ │   ┌──────┐  ┌──────┐ ║ │
│ ║  │ ▢ System Folder            │⬇│   │Cancel│  │Drive │ ║ │
│ ║  └────────────────────────────┴─┘   └──────┘  └──────┘ ║ │
│ ║                                      ☐ Read Only       ║ │
│ ╚═══════════════════════════════════════════════════════╝ │
└─────────────────────────────────────────────────────────┘
```

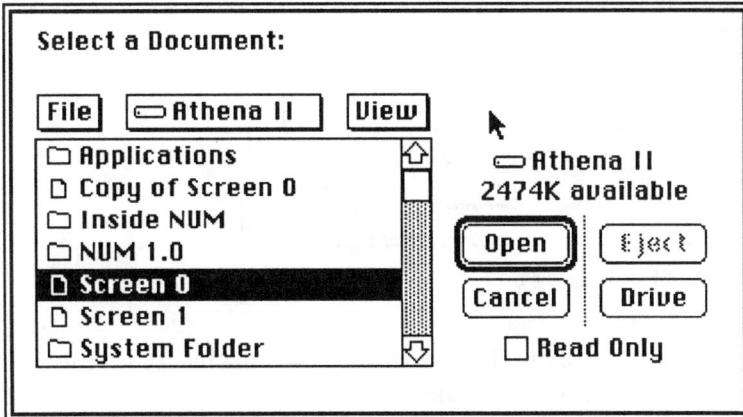

Figure 11.4 Duplicating a file

Delete: Erases the selected file. You are asked to confirm if this is really what you want to do (Figure 11.5).

You can skip this confirmation box if you want to; hold down the Option key while you select **Delete**.

Find...: Brings up a small dialog box into which you type the name of a file you wish to find, as shown in Figure 11.6.

When you click OK, the search commences within the currently open folder; it proceeds down into all the folders contained within it. If nothing is found within the folder or any of its daughters, then the search proceeds to the first folder's parent folder, etc. When a match is found, Directory Assistance immediately switches to show the contents of the folder containing the match, and selects the match as well.

Find Again: If the first search doesn't find the file you want, try try again. Selecting this command repeats a search with the previous name and starting

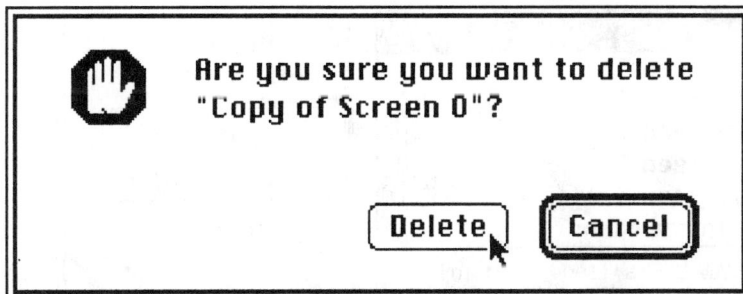

```
┌─────────────────────────────────────────────────────────┐
│ ╔═══════════════════════════════════════════════════════╗ │
│ ║                                                        ║ │
│ ║   ┌───┐    Are you sure you want to delete            ║ │
│ ║   │✋ │    "Copy of Screen 0"?                         ║ │
│ ║   └───┘                                                ║ │
│ ║                                                        ║ │
│ ║                    ┌────────┐  ┌──────────┐           ║ │
│ ║                    │ Delete │  │  Cancel  │           ║ │
│ ║                    └────────┘  └──────────┘           ║ │
│ ╚═══════════════════════════════════════════════════════╝ │
└─────────────────────────────────────────────────────────┘
```

Figure 11.5 Directory Assistance's Delete confirmation dialog box

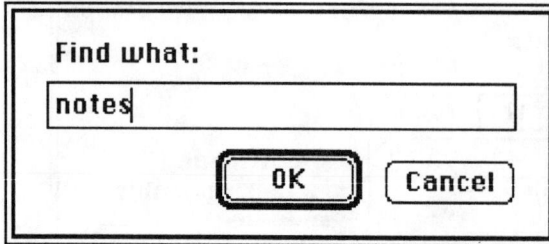

Figure 11.6 Find dialog box

at the current directory. This command is perhaps most convenient to access via its command-key equivalent, Command-A.

About...: Brings up a really snazzy and totally excessive credits screen, which will go away if you click the mouse button.

View Menu

This menu controls the order in which file and folder names are shown in the scrolling list.

by Name: This is the default Apple sorting order—alphabetically by name.

by Date: Sorts by date of last modification, with most recently created or modified files shown first, and olders ones last. The date and time of last modification are shown for the currently highlighted file or folder name, like the screen in Figure 11.7.

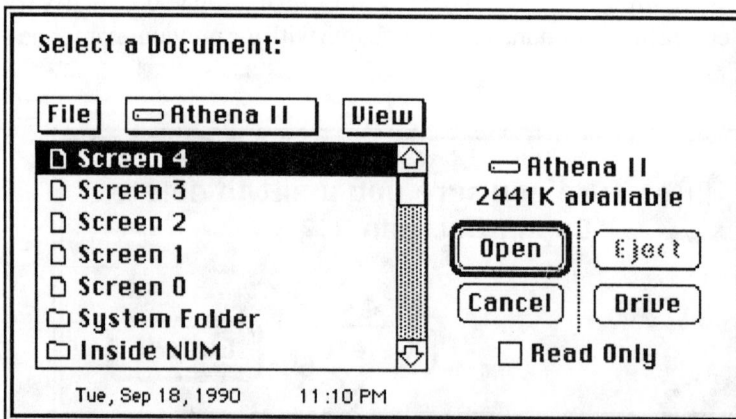

Figure 11.7 Files sorted according to date of creation/modification

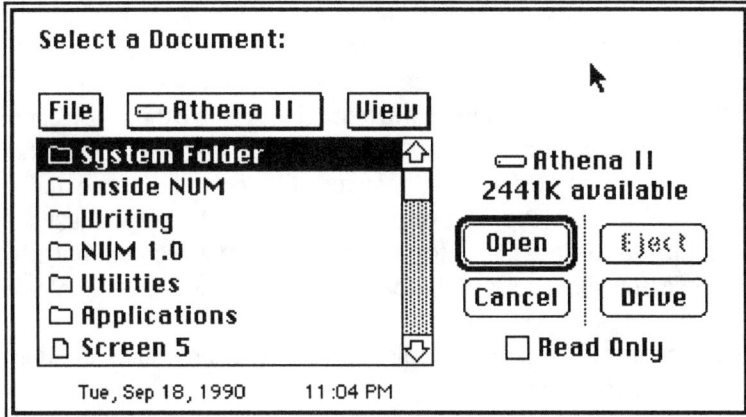

Figure 11.8 View by date with folders first

by Size: Sorts files and folders by their size in bytes, with larger files appearing first.

The last two options control where folders are shown in the scrolling list. This is important, so listen up (some reviewers have criticized NUM for not having this feature, which it in fact does have): If you want to return to the default Apple method of showing files and folder mixed together, then *un*check the currently checked option. Simply select it again.

Folders First: Puts folder names at the top of the scrolling list, like the screen in Figure 11.8.

Folders Last: Puts folder names at the end of the scrolling list, after any and all file names, like the screen in Figure 11.9.

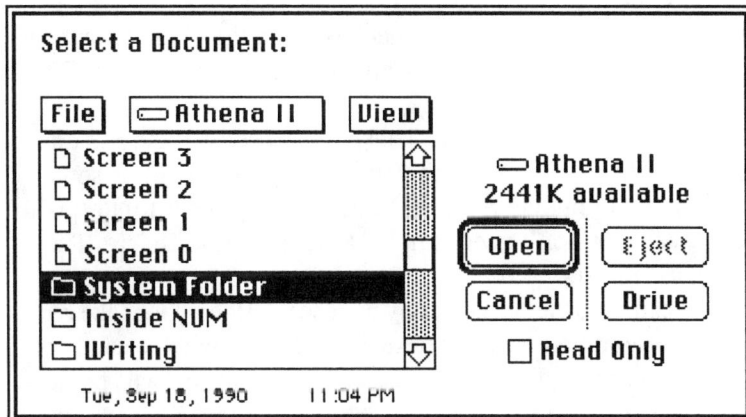

Figure 11.9 View by date with folders last

Remember, these two options are mutually exclusive: checking one unchecks the other. Selecting either one again, while it's already checked, unchecks it and returns you to the default, files 'n' folders mixed view.

Well, that's a lot of functionality in a small space. We think you can see how it all might come in handy. And not only when you want to **Open** or **Save** (not to mention **Save As**) files. After all, you can **Cancel** out of those dialog boxes without opening or saving. We've been known to select **Open** just so we can use Directory Assistance to delete one or more files. Our screen shot utility only allows 10 screen shots per disk before you have to start deleting old ones; we use Directory Assistance to do it.

Let's look at some other examples. Maybe we can create one that covers almost all the bases. Let's see . . . .

Hanging Up on the Finder

So here we are. We've been working for a while on a new document. Hmmmm. Maybe we ought to save a backup copy. Now what folder are those backup files in . . . .

No need to bother looking. We're already in the **Save As...** dialog box. We'll just use Directory Assistance.

After switching to our archive drive Alexandria, we choose **Find** from the Directory Assistance **File** menu. We type in NUM and press Return.

There it is (Figure 11.10).

We change to that folder (double-clicking on the selected name will do it) and choose **Save**.

Ooops. We can't save; this volume is getting too full. Looks like we'll have to clear up some room. Let's switch to View **by Size** (Figure 11.11), so we can easily find some big files to dump, if any are eligible.

A copy of the System! What the heck is that doing there? Maybe we ought to choose Get Info and find out more about this file. The screen in Figure 11.12 appears.

Check out the date on this file: This is an *old* copy of the System. Can't be too imporant, but . . . . Oh yeah, we were trying to get at some old desk accessories in an obsolete System. Must have dropped it into this folder by accident. Well, we don't need it now, so let's choose **Delete**. The screen in Figure 11.13 appears.

Now we can save the backup copy in peace. (When you make backups this way, which is admittedly a bit bizarre, you need to switch back to the original file. Otherwise, all additional work from this point on will be done on the backup.)

What could be easier than that?

File	🗁 Writing	View

🗀 Archives
🗀 Fiction
🗀 Hot Projects
🗀 **Inside NUM backup**
🗀 Personal

Save Current Document as:

Inside NUM Ch. 11

☐ Fast Save ☐ Make Backup

[File Format...] Normal

💾 Alexandria
2180K available

[Save] [Eject]

[Cancel] [Drive]

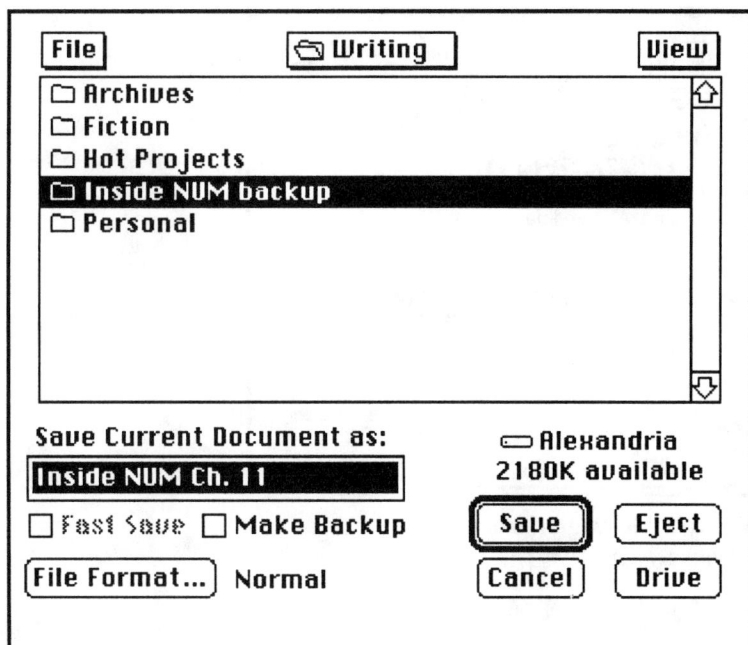

Figure 11.10 Using Find to locate a folder

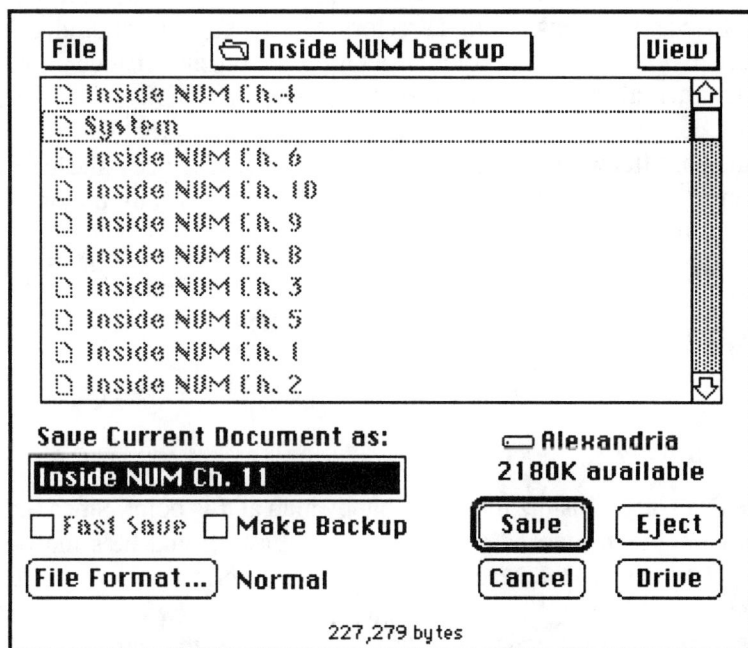

File	🗁 Inside NUM backup	View

🗋 Inside NUM Ch. 4
🗋 System
🗋 Inside NUM Ch. 6
🗋 Inside NUM Ch. 10
🗋 Inside NUM Ch. 9
🗋 Inside NUM Ch. 8
🗋 Inside NUM Ch. 3
🗋 Inside NUM Ch. 5
🗋 Inside NUM Ch. 1
🗋 Inside NUM Ch. 2

Save Current Document as:

Inside NUM Ch. 11

☐ Fast Save ☐ Make Backup

[File Format...] Normal

💾 Alexandria
2180K available

[Save] [Eject]

[Cancel] [Drive]

227,279 bytes

Figure 11.11 Clearing up room

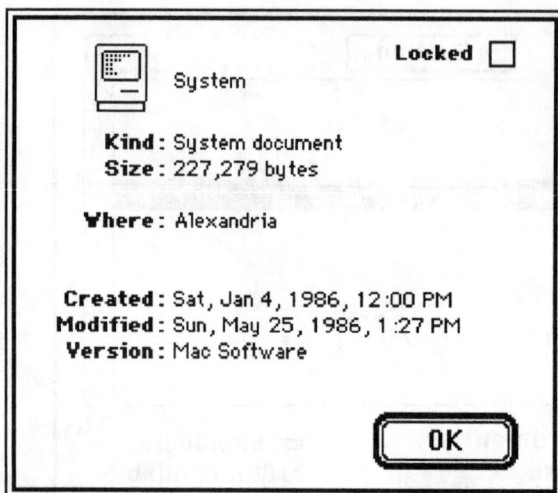

Figure 11.12 Getting information about this mysterious System

Review

This short chapter has covered Directory Assistance, a startup document that patches the **Open...**, **Save**, and **Save As...** dialog boxes found in almost all Macintosh applications. Using Directory Assistance, one can find, duplicate, and delete files, create new folders, get information, and change the filename sorting order, all without every leaving a dialog box.

This concludes our first-run coverage of the Norton Utilities for the Macintosh. After we meet the maker of Directory Assistance—the leader of the Norton Mac Pack, if you will—we'll take that long-promised closer look at using the Norton Disk Editor to modify files.

Meet the Makers

Gary Amstutz

You know Gary Amstutz must be a happy man at this point. Since the fall of 1989, he's gotten married (to actress Terri Easter), and he's managed the Norton Utilities for the Macintosh development effort to a very successful conclusion.

"My greatest satisfaction has been overcoming the barriers that other, mainly PC-based, companies have had in bringing their own Macintosh

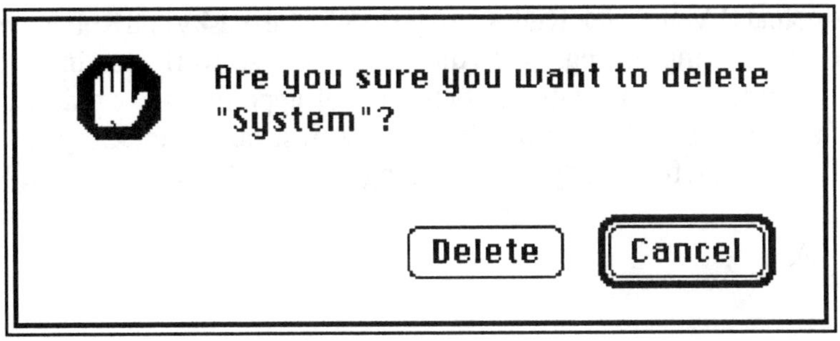

Figure 11.13 You bet we are!

products to market," Gary says. One of the most challenging aspects of the task was that, during the home stretch, PNC had another product almost ready to ship as well. The competition for resources was intense, especially given the pending merger with Symantec Corporation. Fortunately, everyone managed to pull together and get both products shipped within weeks of each other.

A 1976 graduate of St. Mary's college in San Antonio, Texas, Gary came to work for PNC in January of 1989, after moving to California from Tulsa, Oklahoma, his boyhood home. He took over the Norton Macintosh Utilities development effort in just a few months after starting.

Managing software development might seem unusual for someone who had 17 years training as a classical musician, and even spent three years on the road performing. "I almost went to Juilliard to study conducting, but I couldn't stand living in New York," he says. Still, we've seen other folks who have been drawn to computers from the music field, haven't we? Gary came to California with the intention of composing for film. His interest in MIDI led him toward software development. His artistic training gave him considerable sensivity toward interface issues.

"I want to go beyond what anyone else has done in terms of user friendliness. That's why we hired an artist for crucial parts of the interface to the Utilities, to make the product so much fun to use that it almost disguises the power."

When he's not at the office (which Terri says has been too often), Gary enjoys working in his MIDI studio at home. He still puts together the occasional demo tape. Asked about the future, he says "Computers and music are still moving closer together, especially given the recent emphasis on multimedia," and hints that we can look to this area for future refinements to the Norton Utilities for the Macintosh.

This concludes our series of profiles of the developers behind the Norton Utilities for the Macintosh. Many others were involved in the effort; we're sorry we couldn't profile them all. Among names we might mention are Dan Rollins, Donna Blakely, and Samuel Epstein. Diane Dzivilis deserves mention as principal QA engineer. Kudos also go to Kim Leznasky and Robert Perez for their work during testing. And Allen Reed, whose work was indispensible during product documentation, would be *so* disappointed if we didn't mention that he came up with the name "Directory Assistance" for Gary Amstutz's INIT. If we've left anybody out, we apologize. There's always the next edition.

12

A Closer Look

Using the Norton Disk Editor

Introduction

Have you ever seen Johnny Carson's Karnak routine on *The Tonight Show*? He "answers" questions in *hermetically* sealed envelopes, "having never before seen the question." Funny stuff. Whenever Ed McMahon gets down to the last question, he always makes a big deal of it: "I hold in my hand the *last* envelope."

We hold in our hands the last chapter of this book. In it, we return to the tool we introduced way back in Chapter 4, during our inside look at the structure of a Macintosh disk: The Norton Disk Editor. In Chapter 4, we explained only as much of the Disk Editor as was needed for the purposes of peeking into the various directory structures on a disk. Now, we're going to show you all of the resources that the Disk Editor makes available to you, and we're even going to show you how to use a few of them.

We say "a few." There are reasons for this, and taken together they comprise a set of warnings about using the Disk Editor. First of all, the Disk Editor has a great many features. It has more menu commands than any other part of the Norton Utilities for the Macintosh. So take your time.

Second, the Disk Editor is very powerful. This has an immediate and logical consequence: Being powerful, the Disk Editor is also potentially dangerous. You should recall that in Chapter 7, when we were showing you how to use Format Recover to restore directory damage, we used the Disk Editor to simulate scrambling or erasure of the catalog b-tree. What a mess we made. Format Recover was able to fix it, but doing the same kind of damage to documents and applications can make them useless. Where possible, back up files before you attempt to edit them. (We say "where possible" because some damaged files can't be opened or even copied. In these cases, it couldn't hurt to try fixing them. We're going to consider just such a case toward the end of the chapter.)

Finally, the topic of file editing and repair itself is a very, broad one. So broad, in fact, that it deserves a book all by itself, and maybe we'll write one some day. Although the kinds of repairs you can effect on files fall into some broad catagories, the particulars are as specific as the file formats themselves. This should suggest to you that there are about as many specific ways to fix files as there are types of files. Each file type has its own header, after all, and header damage can render files unopenable. One broad category—many ways to fix.

In one chapter, we cannot begin to introduce you to all the nuances of file editing. We can, however, introduce you to the tools and take you through a couple of nontrivial examples that will give you a feel for their use. With that, along with patience and prudence, you should do just fine.

Reviewing the Disk Editor Interface

The Disk Editor does not have its own button on the Norton Utilities for the Macintosh main menu screen. Instead, it is accessed via a menu command in the Utilities menu of that screen, and in every other application in the Utilities.

As you probably remember, the first thing you're asked to do when you launch the Disk Editor is to choose a volume to explore. Once you've done this, the Disk Editor reads information off the selected volume; then it opens a directory window showing its files and folders, like Figure 12.1.

This window is the main tool for finding and selecting folders and files to edit. File and folder names are shown in the large scrolling area. You double-click on the folder icons to toggle them open and closed. In Figure 12.1, all the folders are closed except the one for the root directory.

There are five buttons across the top of the window. **Edit File** opens a data window showing the contents of the selected file. (The button is dimmed, and therefore inoperative, when the highlight is over a folder name.) **Edit Info** brings up a dialog box in which you may change certain file and folder attributes, including the type and creator codes, and a set of Finder flags that

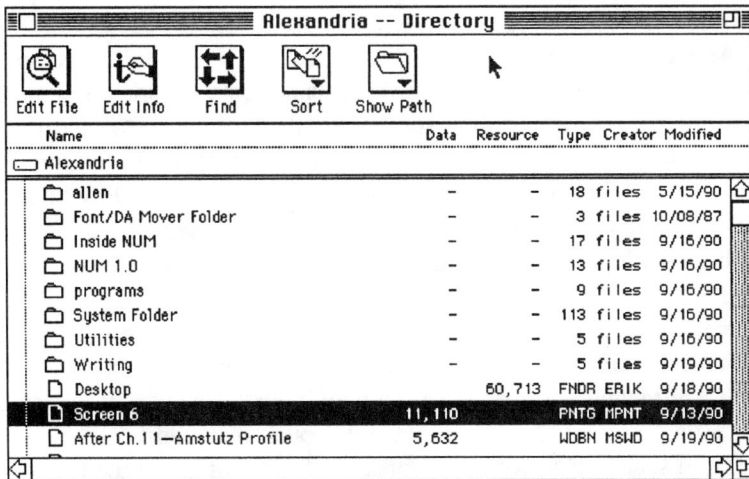

Figure 12.1 Norton Disk Editor directory window

we'll look at later. **Find** brings up a dialog box whereby you may locate a file or folder on the scrolling list by name. **Sort** is a pop-up menu; you can change the order in which file and folder names are displayed. **Show Path** is a pop-up menu showing the parent folder of the selected item, its grandparent folder (if any), etc., back up to root or disk window level.

If you choose Edit File, another type of window opens, like Figure 12.2. We saw the data window in Chapter 4 when we were looking at the hexadecimal data in the various data structures.

You edit data in this window. You can edit in either the hexadecimal area—the four columns at the left—or in the ASCII interpretation at the right. Click

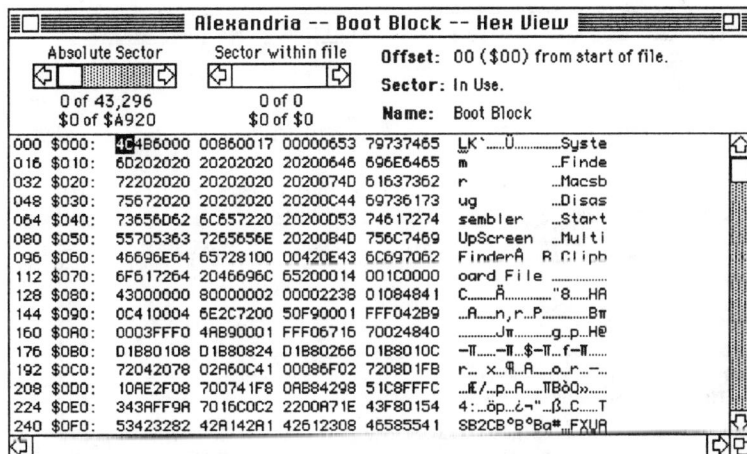

Figure 12.2 NDE data window showing boot block

the mouse pointer on the exact point you wish to edit; the cursor moves as you type. A legend at the far left shows what position within the current sector is occupied by the beginning of that row of data. (Data are shown in order from left to right, and then down.) The scroll bar at the far right shows additional data within the sector. (There are 512 bytes in a sector; only 256 are shown in the graphic above.) Scroll bars at the very top of the window allow you to move among absolute sectors on the disk (#0 being the first sector in the boot blocks according to this numbering scheme), and among sectors within the file being viewed.

There is another type of window in NDE: an interpreted view of any of the disk directory structures. We looked at each of these views in Chapter 4. The so-called *autoview* of the data for the boot blocks is shown in Figure 12.3.

Note that this view is just that: a view. You may not edit data. You can still move from sector to sector on the disk via the scroll bar at the top.

As we said before, the majority of NDE's commands are contained in the menus, and there are many of them. Starting at the top:

File Menu

Open File: This is the same as clicking on a filename in the directory window, and then clicking the **Edit File** button. However, in this case you select the file to open by means of a dialog box, as you would if you were opening a document within an application.

Note one critical difference between this and any other Open dialog box you've seen: You must choose whether to open the file's resource fork or its data fork (Figure 12.4).

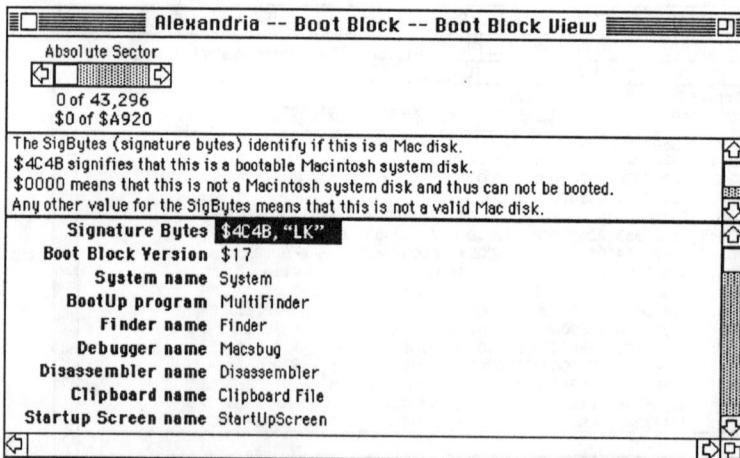

Figure 12.3 Autoview of boot blocks

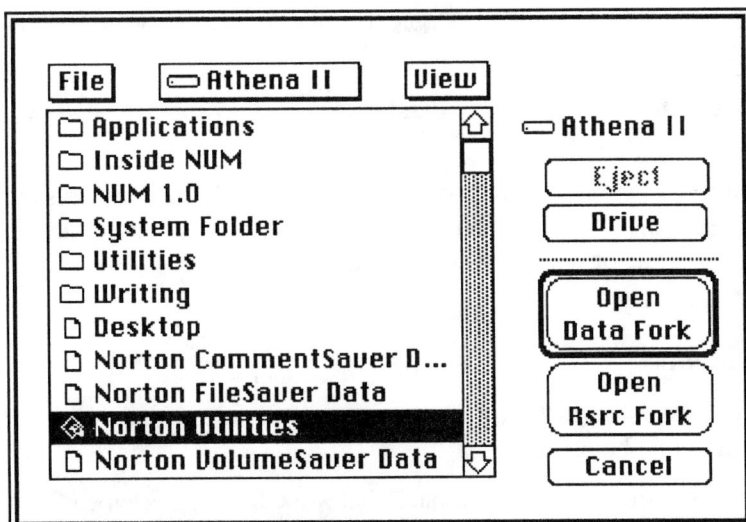

Figure 12.4 Open File dialog box

Open Volume: Lets you open a new directory window for a different (or even the same) disk volume. The same dialog box (Figure 12.5) appears that you see when you first launch the Disk Editor.

Close: Closes up and sends away the currently active window. Recall that the active window is uppermost and is totally unobscured by other windows, and that its title bar contains five parallel line segments on either side of the

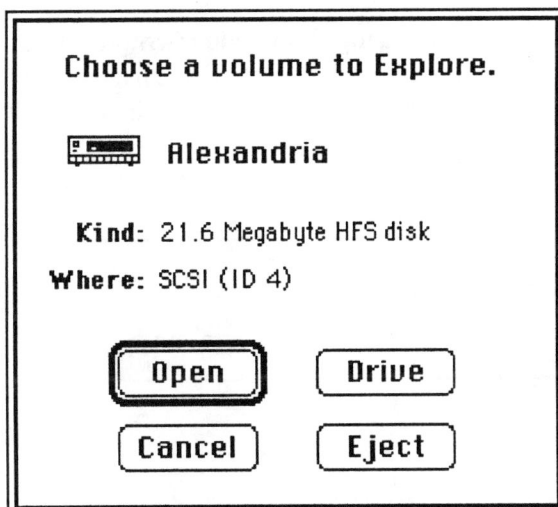

Figure 12.5 Open Volume dialog box

window's name. If other windows are open, the uppermost of these becomes active.

Page Setup: The familiar dialog box used to indicate how you want something printed.

Print: Yes, you can print data directly from NDE. Choosing this command brings up the Print dialog box associated with your current choice of printer. The contents of the active window are printed.

Edit Menu

The commands **Undo, Cut, Copy, Paste,** and **Clear** are for the benefit of DAs that you might be using.

Find: The first of many commands that work differently, depending on what kind of window is active. In a Directory window, **Find** brings up a dialog box like Figure 12.6 that lets you locate a file or folder by name.

If, on the other hand, you select Find when a data window is active, a different dialog box appears—one like Figure 12.7.

This command searches within the currently selected file for an exact match to the data you type in. You can type either the ASCII or the hexadecimal version of the data you want to find; as you type one version, the other is filled in for you. So that, if nothing else, this command can be used as a quick-and-dirty ASCII to Hex converter. Note the checkbox option to ignore case: When this box is checked, capital and small letters are treated the same for purposes of searching.

Find Again: Repeats a search using the previous criteria. In directory windows, searches for another file with a match to the name you typed. In a data window, searches for another exact match to the data string you entered.

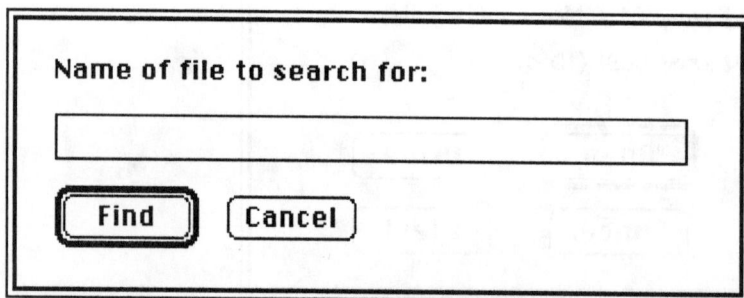

```
 ┌─────────────────────────────────────────────┐
 │                                             │
 │   Name of file to search for:               │
 │                                             │
 │   ┌─────────────────────────────────────┐   │
 │   │                                     │   │
 │   └─────────────────────────────────────┘   │
 │                                             │
 │   ┌─────────┐   ┌──────────┐                │
 │   │  Find   │   │ Cancel   │                │
 │   └─────────┘   └──────────┘                │
 │                                             │
 └─────────────────────────────────────────────┘
```

Figure 12.6 Find dialog box for directory windows

```
┌─────────────────────────────────────────────────────┐
│ ┌─────────────────────────────────────────────────┐ │
│ │                                                   │ │
│ │  Text to Search For:                              │ │
│ │                                                   │ │
│ │  ASCII  ┌─────────────────────────────────────┐  │ │
│ │         │                                     │  │ │
│ │         └─────────────────────────────────────┘  │ │
│ │                                                   │ │
│ │  Hex    ┌─────────────────────────────────────┐  │ │
│ │         │                                     │  │ │
│ │         └─────────────────────────────────────┘  │ │
│ │                                                   │ │
│ │      ╭─────────╮  ┌──────────┐                    │ │
│ │      │  Find   │  │  Cancel  │   ⊠ Ignore Case    │ │
│ │      ╰─────────╯  └──────────┘                    │ │
│ │                                                   │ │
│ └─────────────────────────────────────────────────┘ │
└─────────────────────────────────────────────────────┘
```

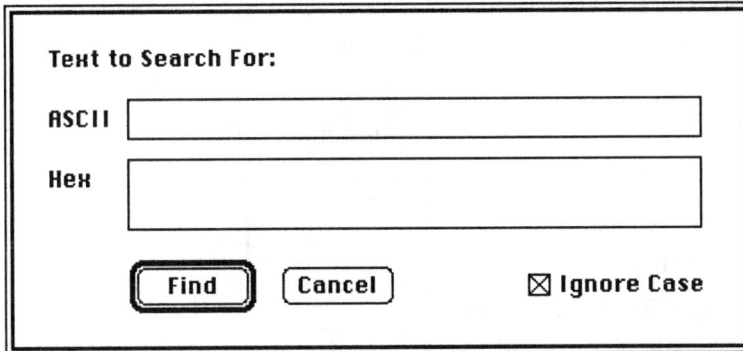

Figure 12.7 Find dialog box in data window

Objects Menu

The first six commands (**Boot Blocks, Volume Info Block, Extents Tree Header, Extents B-Tree, Catalog Tree Header, Catalog B-Tree**) are used to view the directory structures we talked about in Chapter 4. If the NDE Autoview option is *on* (via a checkmark option in the **View As** submenu, which is in the **Display** menu), then the selected directory structure is shown in an interpreted view, like Figure 12.3. If Autoview is off, the directory structure is shown in hexadecimal format in a data window, like Figure 12.2. Remember that you can edit within a data window; you can't edit in an Autoview window.

Directory: Opens up a directory window for the volume you're currently exploring.

The next three commands are used to move among sectors on a volume; they're roughly equivalent to the upper-left scroll bar on a data window.

Read Previous Sector: Active only within a data window; choosing this command moves you back one absolute sector. Equivalent to clicking once on the left arrow of either upper scroll bar.

Read Next Sector: Again, only active within a data window; choosing this command moves you forward one absolute sector. Equivalent to clicking once on the right arrow of either upper scroll bar.

Read Sector...: We used this command in Chapter 4 to locate unoccupied space, so we could leave a message there. Choosing it activates the dialog box shown in Figure 12.8.

First, note that you can choose whether to use hexadecimal or decimal notation for numbers you enter; do this by clicking the appropriate radio button at the top of the dialog box. The absolute sector number and block

```
┌─────────────────────────────────────────────┐
│                                               │
│   Read What:              ◉ Decimal           │
│                           ○ Hex               │
│                                               │
│   ◉ Sector Number        ┌──────────┐         │
│                          │  38295   │         │
│   ○ Allocation Block     └──────────┘         │
│                           ┌──────────┐        │
│   ○ Catalog B-Tree Node   │  38281   │        │
│                           └──────────┘        │
│   ○ Extents B-Tree Node   ┌──────────┐        │
│                           │          │        │
│   ○ Byte Offset within file└──────────┘       │
│                           ┌──────────┐        │
│                           │ 0        │        │
│   ╔═════════╗  ┌──────────┐└──────────┘       │
│   ║  Read   ║  │  Cancel  │                   │
│   ╚═════════╝  └──────────┘                   │
│                                               │
└─────────────────────────────────────────────┘
```

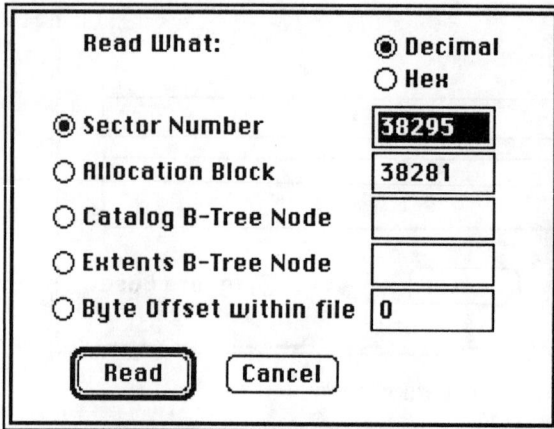

Figure 12.8 Read Sector dialog box

number of the sector currently being viewed (if any) are shown, as in Figure 12.8, and will change to the appropriate format if you click a radio button.

The five vertical radio buttons control what sector you transfer to. The first is used if you want to go to a particular absolute sector. The second, if you want to find a particular allocation block (blocks and sectors are only the same on smaller volumes; block numbering begins after the volume bit map). The third and fourth radio button options are used to find particular nodes within the catalog and extents b-trees, respectively. If you know the node number you want, but not what sector that node is in, use one of these ways of inputting the search data. The last option will take you into the file you're currently viewing in the data window by the specified number of bytes. Offset simply means "distance in bytes from the beginning."

When you click any of these radio buttons, the text box to the right of the line is highlighted. Type in the number you want at this point, and then click Read.

Write Sector: If you have made any changes to the sector currently being viewed in the data window, then this command is active. Choosing it saves your changes back out to disk. Be careful! What's done can't be undone, unless the change is made to a directory structure.

Display Menu

The first five commands are active only in the data window; the last three are active only in a directory window.

Resource Fork: If there is one, choosing this command switches the data window to a hex view of the current file's resource fork.

Data Fork: Switches to the beginning of the current file's data fork, if it has one.

With both of the previous commands, if either fork is empty, then the command is dimmed out and unavailable. That's one way of telling what forks a file has.

View in Hex: Used to force an Autoview window to the hexadecimal data window, which you can edit in. For example, if you choose Boot Blocks from the Objects menu, as a rule you'll see the interpreted view of the boot blocks. Choosing View in Hex at this point changes to the editable view that every other kind of file is shown in. (See Figure 12.2.)

View in ASCII: Switches the data window to an all-ASCII view of the selected sector or object (Figure 12.9). You can edit within this view as well, though some types of data can't be entered this way (e.g., control codes).

View As: This submenu controls the NDE Autoview feature. The seven options within are all mutually exclusive; selecting one disables the previous selection. With Autoview checked, NDE shows directory objects (those listed in the Objects menu) in the appropriate interpreted view. However, if the selected object is so badly damaged that NDE can't tell what it is any more, it will show the object in the hex data window.

Choosing any of the other options in this submenu will force the data window to an interpreted view in the style of the selected object. Confused? No need to be. If you choose Boot Blocks in View As, then NDE will attempt to

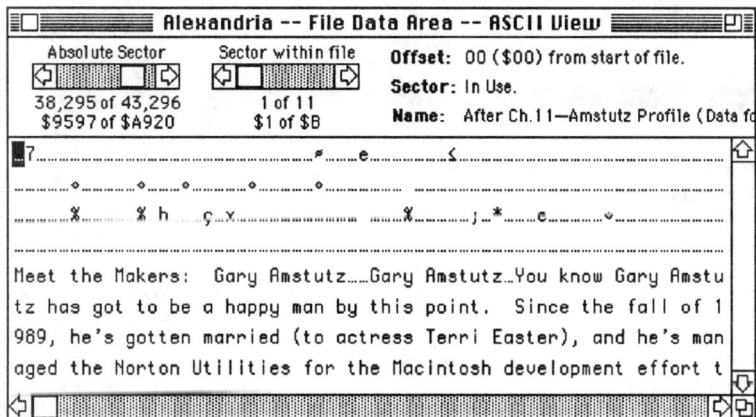

Figure 12.9 Data window in ASCII view

interpret any and all sectors on the disk as boot blocks, and the data window will show an interpreted boot blocks view, no matter what sector you choose to look at.

Why would you ever use this? If Autoview fails because the desired object is damaged. If you try to view, say, the catalog tree, and NDE shows it to you in hex (even though you have Autoview checked), then choose Catalog B-Tree from the View As submenu. Doing so forces the data window to an interpreted view of the catalog tree.

The final three commands (options, really) in the **Display** menu are used to control what you see in a directory window.

Current Folder: This is the default view, as in Figure 12.1. It starts out showing the contents of the disk window; click on a folder's name or icon to open it and show its contents.

All Files Flat: Eliminates (for viewing purposes only!) the folder hierarchy, and shows all files and folders on your disk in order, as in Figure 12.10. The exact order they're shown in depends, of course, on what option you've chosen via the **Sort** button at the top of the window.

All Files Outline: Shows all files and folders on the volume in a hierarchical view, with relationships indicated by lines and indentation. A folder's contents are shown in order beneath its name, and indented from it, as in Figure 12.11.

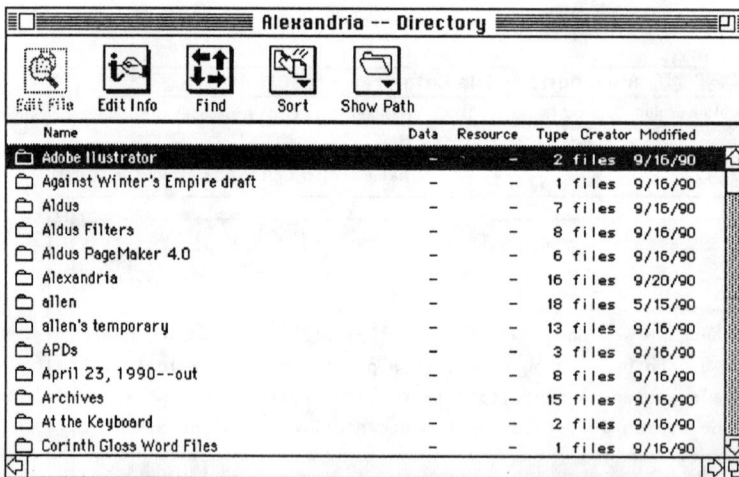

Figure 12.10 Volume Alexandria directory window, all files flat view

```
▣□▯▦▦▦▦▦▦▦▦▦  Alexandria -- Directory  ▦▦▦▦▦▦▦▦▦□▯▣
```

Name		Data	Resource	Type	Creator	Modified
📁 Performer 3.3		–	–	4 files		9/16/90
	🅰 Performer™ 3.3		723,542	APPL	MOUP	5/17/90
	🅰 TeachText		19,052	APPL	ttxt	4/30/88
	▯ 3.3 Update Notes Part One	26,942	4,284	ttro	ttxt	11/01/89
	▯ 3.3 Update Notes Part Two	21,294		ttro	ttxt	10/31/89
📁 SuperPaint		–	–	2 files		9/16/90
	🅰 SuperPaint		165,123	APPL	SPNT	5/28/87
	▯ SuperPaint Prefs		2,726	SPPF	SPNT	3/29/90
📁 Voyager		–	–	5 files		9/16/90
	📁 More Settings-Orbits	–	–	9 files		9/16/90
	▯ Apollo Asteroids	2,016		USET	UGER	11/27/89
	▯ Bright Asteroids	2,016		USET	UGER	11/27/89
	▯ Bright Comets	2,016		USET	UGER	11/27/89

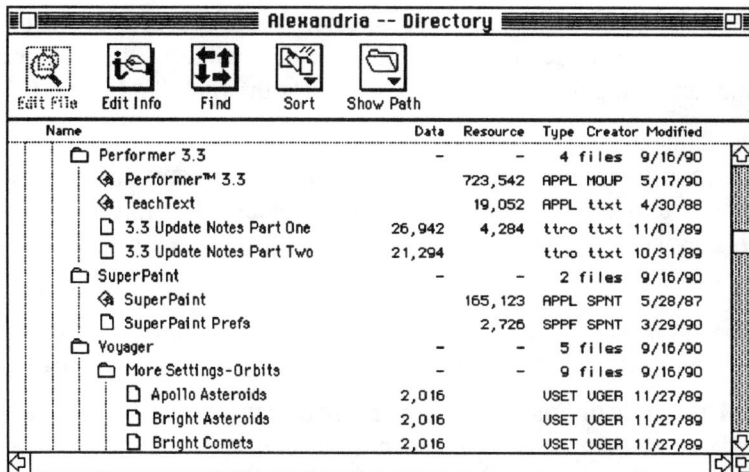

Figure 12.11 Volume Alexandria directory window, all files outline view

Information Menu

There are but two commands in this menu. The first toggles according to what's currently selected—if you're in a directory window—or according to whether you are viewing or editing a file in the data window. The two possibilities are

Folder Information: Brings up a dialog box showing the attributes of the folder currently selected on the directory window, like Figure 12.12. You can change or edit any of these parameters. They're explained below.

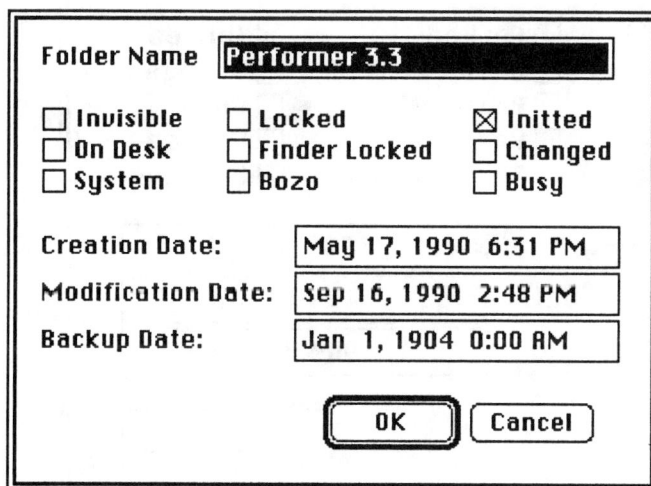

```
┌─────────────────────────────────────────────────┐
│                                                   │
│   Folder Name  ▐Performer 3.3              ▌       │
│                                                   │
│   ☐ Invisible   ☐ Locked         ☒ Initted       │
│   ☐ On Desk     ☐ Finder Locked  ☐ Changed       │
│   ☐ System      ☐ Bozo           ☐ Busy          │
│                                                   │
│   Creation Date:     ┌─────────────────────────┐ │
│                      │ May 17, 1990  6:31 PM   │ │
│   Modification Date: ┌─────────────────────────┐ │
│                      │ Sep 16, 1990  2:48 PM   │ │
│   Backup Date:       ┌─────────────────────────┐ │
│                      │ Jan  1, 1904  0:00 AM   │ │
│                                                   │
│              ┌────────┐  ┌────────┐              │
│              │   OK   │  │ Cancel │              │
│              └────────┘  └────────┘              │
│                                                   │
└─────────────────────────────────────────────────┘
```

Figure 12.12 Folder Information dialog box

File Information: If you have selected a file's name in the directory window, or if you are editing a file in the data window, then choosing this command brings up an attributes dialog for the file, like Figure 12.13.

Recall that the Type and Creator codes are used by the Finder to distinguish applications from documents and, in the case of documents, to determine what application to launch in order to open the document. The 15 Finder attributes, which may be set or unset by checking the boxes next to their names, are explained below:

Invisible: File or Folder's icon is not shown on the desktop, although its name may be visible in **Open** and **Save** dialog box scrolling lists.

On Desk: File or Folder's icon is shown directly on the desktop along with disk icons, and not inside its parent folder.

System: File is a Macintosh system file (e.g., Finder, Clipboard, etc.). Such files can't be renamed.

Bundle: File has an icon associated, or bundled, with it.

No Inits: In the case of INITs and CDEVs (control panel devices), this bit is set if the file contains no other INIT resources within it. If the file is an application, then it is to be opened read-only when used on a network.

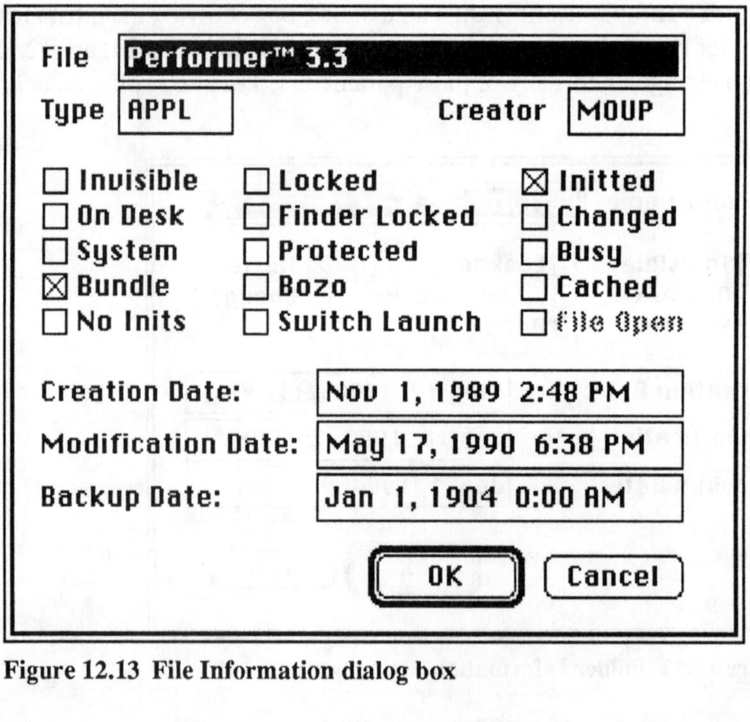

Figure 12.13 File Information dialog box

Locked: File cannot be modifed when this bit is set.

Finder Locked: As above, but Joe User can change. Checking the Locked box in a File's Get Info window sets this bit.

Protected: File can't be copied, duplicated, or moved. Period.

Bozo: An early form of copy protection; so called because any Bozo could break it by flipping this bit back to zero.

Switch Launch: For applications: Attempts to make the file's resident volume the current system volume upon launch.

Inited: Finder has "seen" file during startup or after.

Changed: File or folder has been modified since we spoke last.

Busy: Someone else is talking to file.

Cached: File's data is stored in RAM cache (set via Control Panel).

File Open: Somebody else is looking at file; hands off.

If you try to change the attributes shown in the chart while running under MultiFinder, you may be ignored.

Disk Information: Brings up a small window with information about the volume you're exploring, like Figure 12.14.

If the current volume is one that NDE recognizes, it will tell you things like what device number the drive uses, its blocks size, how many platters that are, etc.

The **Utilities** menu you know about: That's how you transfer to other NUM modules. So now our task is done.

We realize that this tour of NDE's menus presents you with an awful lot of information to digest at one sitting. In all such cases, the best way to get the point home is via an example or two. To which topic we now devote ourselves.

Using the Disk Editor

There are two simple tasks that we can think of that will get you started on using the Norton Disk Editor to do real stuff. We've done both successfully ourselves. We can also think of another interesting exercise or two that we can leave you with, after outlining the general principles. Our point is not to completely train you in the use of NDE, but to show you some of what it's good for.

```
┌──────────────────────────────────────┐
│ ▤□▤▤▤▤    Disk Information   ▤▤▤▤▤     │
├──────────────────────────────────────┤
│                                        │
│  ┌──────────────────────────────────┐ │
│  │  Information about "Athena II"   │ │
│  └──────────────────────────────────┘ │
│                                        │
│  ┌──────────────────────────────────┐ │
│  │   ▣▭▭▭    Athena II              │ │
│  │                                  │ │
│  │      Kind : 21.6 Megabyte HFS disk│ │
│  │      Used : 19,827,200 Bytes (19.4 Meg)│
│  │      Free : 2,332,160 Bytes (2.3 Meg)│ │
│  │     Files : 392 Files, 56 Folders │ │
│  │     Where :                      │ │
│  │                                  │ │
│  │   Created : Sep 16, 1990 12:45 PM│ │
│  │  Modified : Sep 20, 1990  3:45 AM│ │
│  │ Backed up : Jan  1, 1904  0:00 AM│ │
│  └──────────────────────────────────┘ │
│                                        │
│  ┌──────────────────────────────────┐ │
│  │     SCSI device :                │ │
│  │   SCSI Block Size :              │ │
│  │   Total Drive Size :             │ │
│  │    Allocation Size :             │ │
│  │        Cylinders :               │ │
│  │           Heads :                │ │
│  └──────────────────────────────────┘ │
└──────────────────────────────────────┘
```

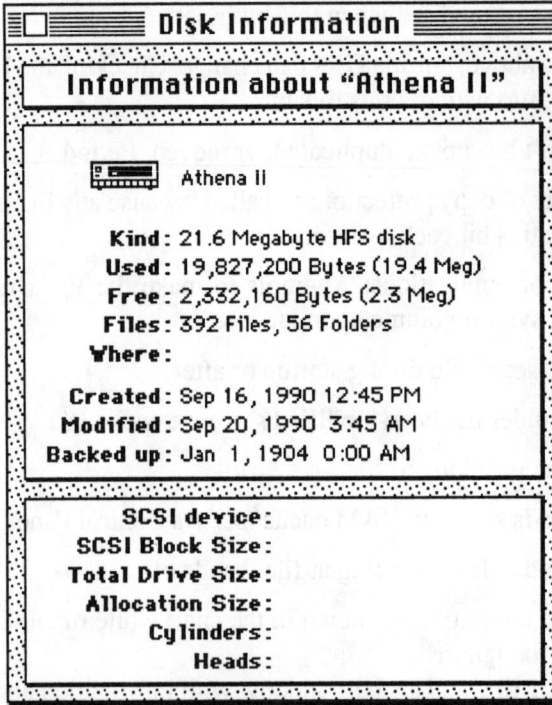

Figure 12.14 Disk Information window

Inevitable Word of Caution

It bears repeating that the Norton Disk Editor is powerful, and therefore dangerous. You can inflict the most amazing damage on individual files, folders, and yes, entire volumes. Do not edit anything until you've made a backup copy of it! If, heaven forfend, you should happen to mess things up worse than they were, a backup will at least get you back up to where you started.

If you've been editing sectors and you get the "Do you want to save changes to this sector?" message, and you suddenly become unsure, do the right thing: Throw the changes out.

OK, enough said. Now to work.

Changing a File's Attributes

We have heard it said that door locks, whether on houses or cars, are there merely to keep the honest people out. Thieves have no qualms about breaking them. The same thing is true, we think, of sensitive data on your disks. You mostly need security to foil the curiosity of your honest co-workers, not to thwart industrial espionage. (Not to make light of a serious subject. In some places you need bars on the windows, and in some offices you need password-protected disks.)

If you can accept the premise that security's main effect is to protect the honest from temptation, then you'll agree that the level of protection needed is not very great. You can provide just a touch of security to sensitive files very easily using the Norton Disk Editor, without any inconvenience to yourself. This small measure of security is based on the old adage "Out of sight, out of mind."

By changing a single attribute, you can make files and folders invisible to the Finder. This won't make them invisible within applications, so that those who are determined to pry (and know what they're doing) will be able to find things. However, making icons invisible keeps them out of the way of people who might just happen to be clicking through your folders to see what you have.

After launching the Norton Disk Editor and choosing to explore the volume on which our about-to-be-hidden folder resides, our first task is to find the folder in the directory window. The easiest way to do that is to click the **Find** button on the screen shown in Figure 12.15.

We enter the name (or portion thereof) of the folder we want to protect, then we click Find. The Disk Editor searches for matches. If any are found, they are all displayed in the directory window (Figure 12.16). No other files or folders are shown.

(To return to a view of the complete disk, select **Current Folder** from the **Display** menu.)

OK, NDE has found two folders with the word "personal" in their names. To find out where each of these folders is located, we select its name and then hold down the **Show Path** button. Now, let's protect the first folder. Its name is already highlighted, so we simply click the **Edit Info** button at the top of the directory window. A screen like Figure 12.17 appears.

To make the folder invisible within the Finder, we just click the **Invisible** checkbox (it's the first one) and then click **OK**, as shown in Figure 12.18.

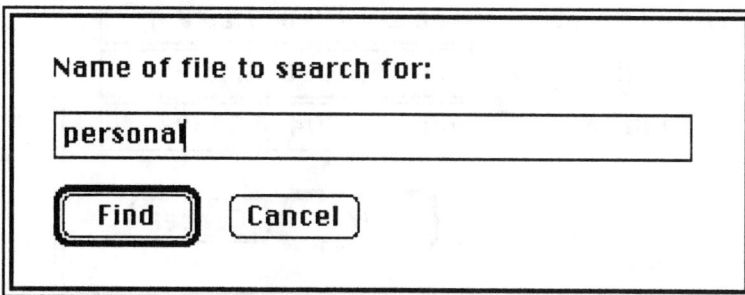

```
┌──────────────────────────────────────────────────┐
│                                                    │
│    Name of file to search for:                     │
│                                                    │
│   ┌────────────────────────────────────────────┐  │
│   │ personal                                     │  │
│   └────────────────────────────────────────────┘  │
│                                                    │
│   ╔═══════════╗   ┌───────────┐                    │
│   ║   Find    ║   │  Cancel   │                    │
│   ╚═══════════╝   └───────────┘                    │
│                                                    │
└──────────────────────────────────────────────────┘
```

Figure 12.15 Finding something private

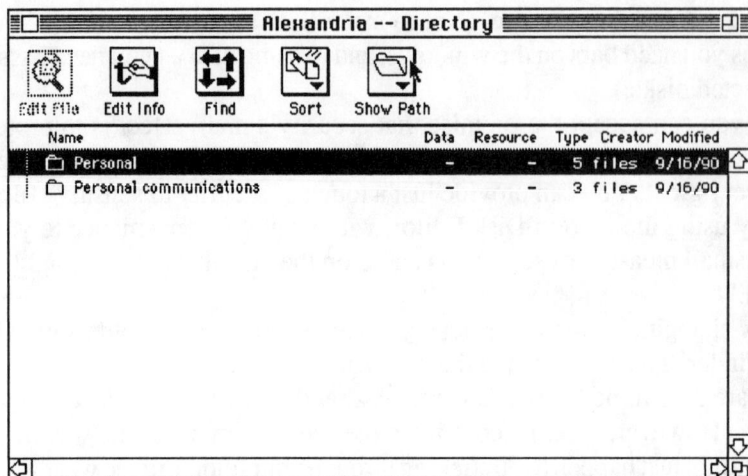

Figure 12.16 Two folders found

To test the effect of this small (one bit) change, we leave NDE temporarily and return to the Finder. From pressing Show Path, we determined that "Personal" was in the Writing folder on volume Alexandria. We open that folder's window (Figure 12.19).

However, if we choose Open... from an application's file menu (Figure 12.20).

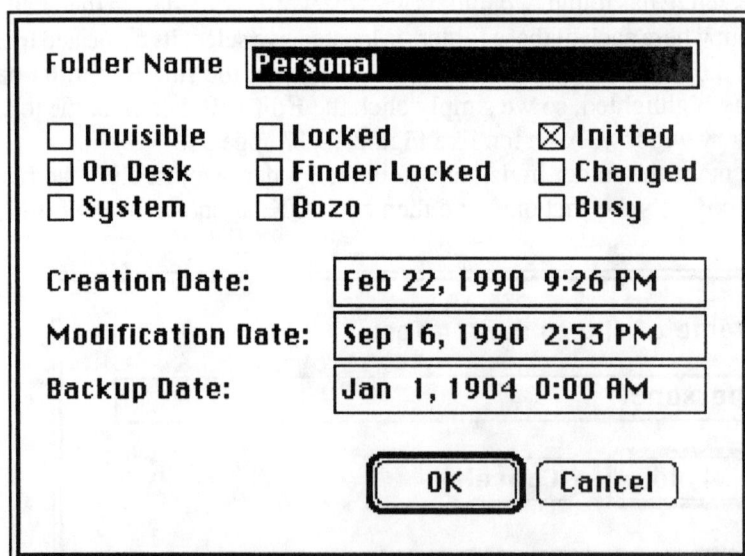

Figure 12.17 Attributes and other information for the Personal folder

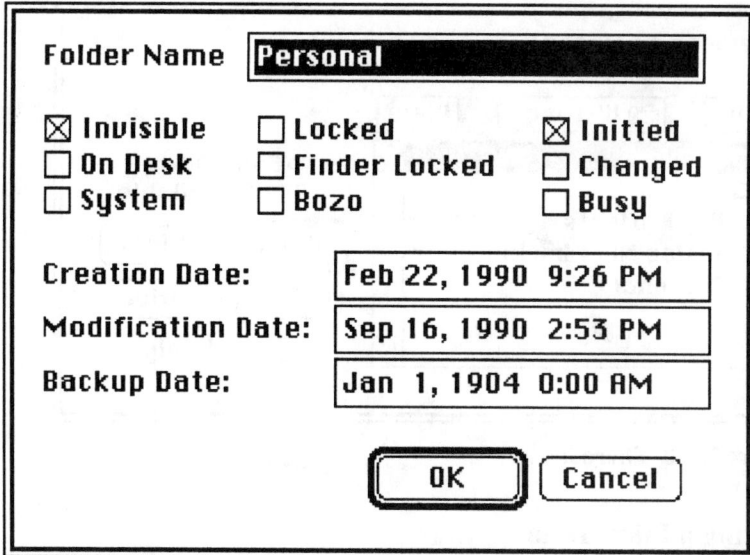

Figure 12.18 Folder "Personal" will now be invisible to the Finder

We see that "Personal" hasn't really gone anywhere. From within an application, it can still be viewed and opened, and any files within it can be opened as well.

Exercise   Can you think of any other ways to protect folders and files using Edit Info? Try experimenting with various attribute combinations.

We've done some editing from a directory window; now, let's try our hand at some honest to goodness hexadecimal editing. In this case, though, we will use but a single key to input new data.

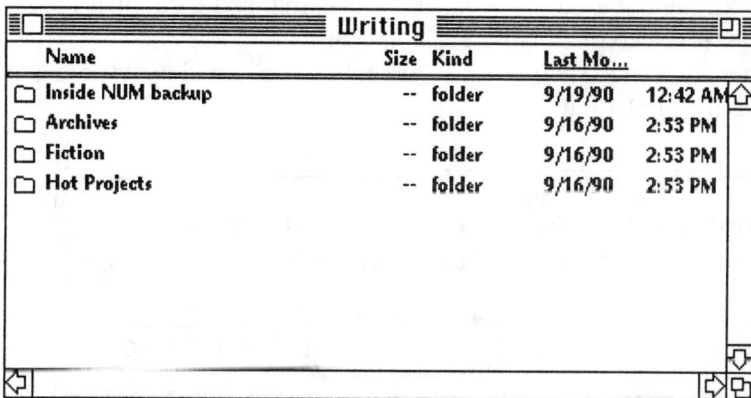

Figure 12.19 Oh where, oh where, has our Personal folder gone?

```
┌──────────────────────────────────────────────────────────┐
│  Select a Document:                                        │
│                                                            │
│  ┌──────┐ ┌──────────────┐ ┌──────┐                       │
│  │ File │ │ 🗀 Writing    │ │ View │                       │
│  └──────┘ └──────────────┘ └──────┘                       │
│  ┌────────────────────────────┬──┐                        │
│  │ 🗀 Archives              │⇧│   ⊂⊃ Alexandria          │
│  │ 🗀 Fiction              │  │   1934K available        │
│  │ 🗀 Hot Projects         │  │                          │
│  │ 🗀 Inside NUM backup    │  │  ┌─────────┐ ┌─────────┐  │
│  │ 🗀 Personal             │  │  │  Open   │ │  Eject  │  │
│  │                         │  │  └─────────┘ └─────────┘  │
│  │                         │⇩│  ┌─────────┐ ┌─────────┐  │
│  └────────────────────────────┴──┘  │ Cancel  │ │  Drive  │  │
│                                  └─────────┘ └─────────┘  │
│                                  ☐ Read Only              │
└──────────────────────────────────────────────────────────┘
```

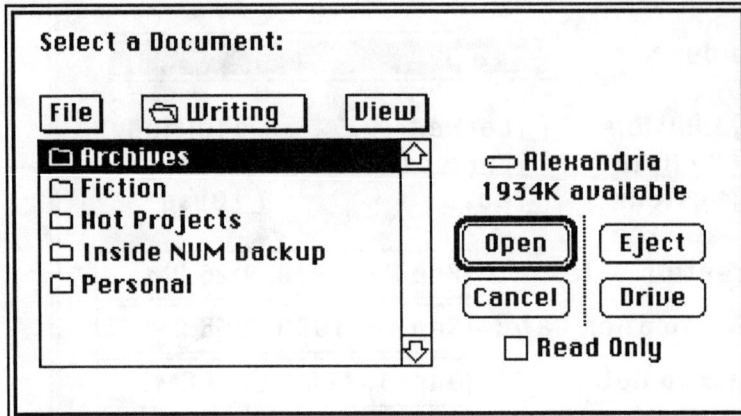

Figure 12.20 There it is!

Editing a File's Data

There are some Macintosh alert boxes that put a sinking feeling in the pit of your stomach the minute they appear, like Figure 12.21.

This message usually means that something nasty has happened to the file's data. The Mac knows this because the data in one or more sectors doesn't jive with the "checksum" values for those sectors. You can't copy or open the file as long as this inconsistency remains.

One way to remedy the problem is to wipe the problem sector(s) clean. Although you'll lose data in the process, in these cases it's a choice between losing 500 or more characters or the entire file.

To attempt this kind of fix, launch the Disk Editor, choosing the volume on which the damaged file resides. Find the file's name in the directory window (Figure 12.22).

Next, highlight the file's name by clicking, and then click the **Edit File** button. A screen like Figure 12.23 appears.

One thing you'll notice—the Disk Editor has turned up its nose at this file, just as the Finder did.

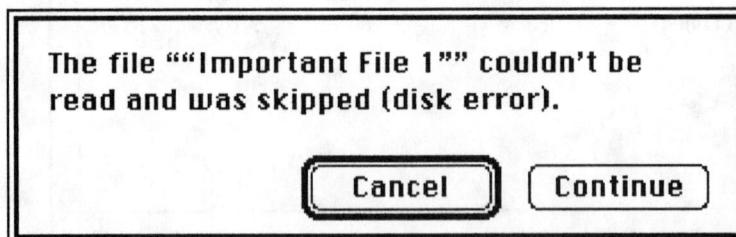

```
┌──────────────────────────────────────────────────────────┐
│                                                            │
│   The file ""Important File 1"" couldn't be                │
│   read and was skipped (disk error).                       │
│                                                            │
│                                                            │
│              ┌──────────────┐   ┌──────────────┐           │
│              │   Cancel     │   │   Continue   │           │
│              └──────────────┘   └──────────────┘           │
└──────────────────────────────────────────────────────────┘
```

Figure 12.21 Uh Oh

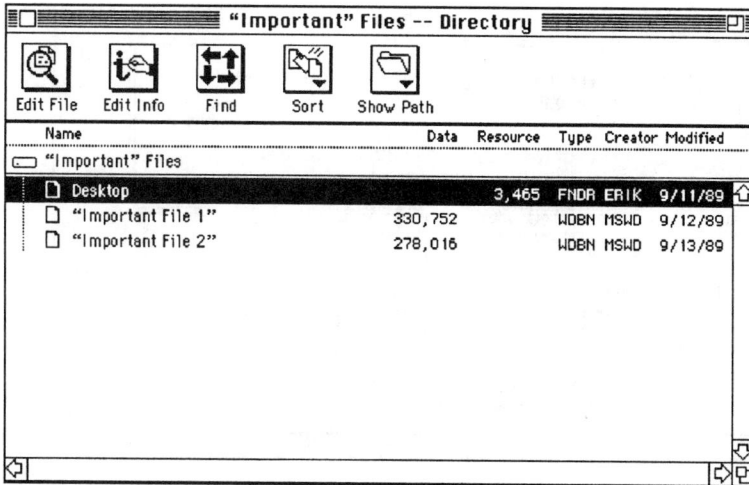

Figure 12.22 First, find the damaged file

The next steps can be slightly tedious in the case of a long file like the one in Figure 12.23. Essentially, you step through the file one sector at a time until you find the bad one(s). Click the right arrow on the "Sector Within File" scrollbar at the top. Don't click too fast, or you'll end up skipping sectors. How do you know when you've found bad sectors? The Disk Editor tells you. (See Figure 12.24.)

At this point, the thing to do is wipe the sector clear. With the insertion rectangle in the hex data (rather than the ASCII), hold down the zero key until the whole thing has been zerod out. Now click the file scroll bar again to move forward. An alert box appears; go ahead and save the sector changes.

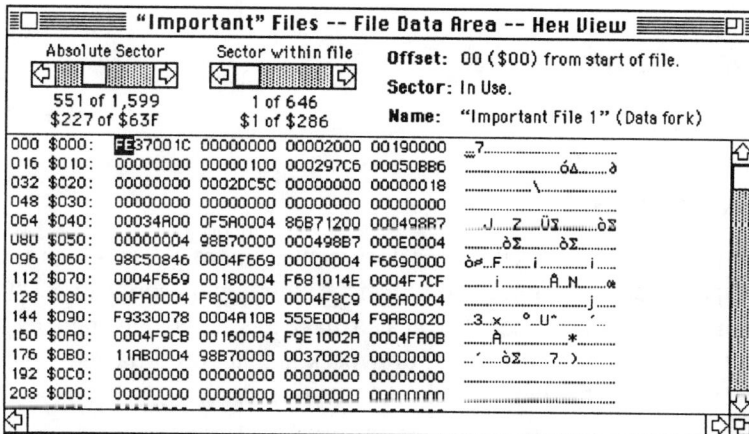

Figure 12.23 Editing a damaged file

```
                "Important" Files -- File Data Area -- Hex View
     A|                                                          rt of file.
  ◁|                                                                        |
  1,|            ✋      Error reading sector (bad data mark                 |)
     $|                  checksum).
 000 $|
 016 $|    ┌──────────┐                                                      ⇧
 032 $|    │    OK    │   (Norton Disk Editor: Error Number 350)
 048 $|    └──────────┘
 064 $040:    00140500  18001414  05001800  14140580  ..........................H
 080 $050:    18001414  05001800  151C0500  18001414  ..........................
 096 $060:    04001000  14040010  00140400  10001404  ..........................
 112 $070:    00100014  08801C00  151C0000  02040010  ...........Ä..............
 128 $080:    00160A3A  FFFFFFFF  FFFF17E6  00000000  .......:..................
 144 $090:    00001002  D01105FA  1500000F  0500011A  ........-.................
 160 $0A0:    B84417E7  00000000  00001002  D0110384  ⊤D.................-....Ñ
 176 $0B0:    1500000F  0500011A  B84417E8  00000000  .............⊤D..........
 192 $0C0:    00001002  D01101C2  1500000F  05000119  ........-....⌐...........
 208 $0D0:    504414E9  00000000  00001002  D01500C8  PD................-....»
 224 $0E0:    0F050001  195044FF  FFFFFFFF  0DEF0000  ......PD..................
 240 $0F0:    00000000  11016815  00000AF0  00000000  .........h...............
  ◁|                                                                    ⇨⇩
```

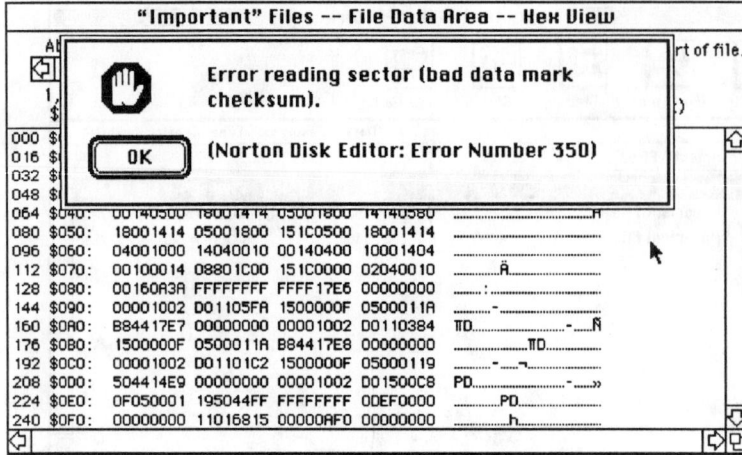

Figure 12.24 A-ha! A bad sector

Sometimes only one sector is damaged. It's a good idea to keep looking once you find one. Any other damage is likely to be close by. If you go more than about 24 sectors without finding more damaged ones, chances are you've found them all. It's rare for a file to have more than one damaged spot.

We have used this method successfully to repair a damaged PageMaker file. On the other hand, we have had it fail as well. The worse the damage (more sectors bad), the less likely it is that you'll be able to fix. If there is physical damage to the media, you probably won't be able to fix the file. If you get a message that NDE "can't find a sector," then give up immediately: the media has been damaged so that one or more sectors have had their address information destroyed. Without that, the disk hardware can't locate the sectors or their data.

Other Disk Editor Tasks

We leave these as exercises for you.

Directory Tasks

To provide additional security for documents, you might consider changing their type and creator codes. This will make their regular applications "ignore" them in the Open dialog box. If you also make them invisible, then they won't be seen in the Finder, either. The drawback is that you'll have to change the codes back, using the Disk Editor, before you can open the file(s) again.

You could also alter a file or folder's last modification date, making it later than the date of last backup. The file will be backed up in an incremental backup by most software even if it hasn't changed.

The "Locked" attribute is different than "Finder Locked" in that "Finder Locked" can be reset much more easily, via the Get Info window. Set "Locked" to protect a file more securely from modification.

File Editing

Sometimes files are rendered unopenable by a damaged header. We have seen messages like "This is not a so-and-so file" when attempting to open documents damaged in this way. Compare the first sector in the damaged file with the first sector in two intact files of the same type. (You need two so you can see how far from the beginning the data should remain the same.) If you notice a discrepancy, then you can correct the damaged file so that its header is the same as the other two.

Finally

As a last test of your prowess, we have thought of a continuation of an exercise we started in Chapter 4. Recall that we located an unused sector and left a small message in it. Could you turn such a sector into a file without using UnErase? You could use the Norton Disk Editor to insert a leaf record for the sector into a leaf node of the catalog b-tree. You need to know the format for a leaf record; such data formats are given in Appendix B, "Macintosh Data Structures." We'll outline the entire procedure for you.

Locate an unallocated sector using the volume bit map. Determine the allocation block number of the unused sector. Verify that it is indeed unused by transferring directly to it using NDE's Read Sector command. Record the block number. Leave a message within it if you like.

Switch to the catalog b-tree. Find a lead node that has less than two file records in it. Switch to View in Hex. Now, making sure to start at the appropriate offset (i.e., just after the end of the last record, so that you don't destroy any of its data, and so that the Mac interprets your data correctly), type an exact copy of the existing leaf record. Using the appropriate chart from Appendix B, make changes in two fields; give the "file" a unique name, and change its extent information to the allocation block that you found previously, the empty one where you may possibly have just left a message. Quit the Disk Editor and restart your Macintosh.

If an icon for your new "file" shows up in the appropriate window after startup, then you've succeeded in creating a new file, just as the Macintosh OS's File Manager does. Now you've really earned your NDE stripes!

Review and Salut

In this chapter we reviewed the Norton Disk Editor. We went into more detail than we did in Chapter 4, where we first introduced it. We looked at the three types of windows used in the Disk Editor: directory windows, for locating files and folders; autoview windows, for examining directory structures like the b-trees; and data windows, for directly editing files. We also went through all the commands available in NDE's menus.

We saw how to use NDE to make a file or folder invisible on the desktop. We used its editing capabilities to wipe out a bad sector in a file. We then left you with some other examples of its use, including a final challenge in which you use the Disk Editor to "create" a file from scratch. This final exercise uses most of the fundamental concepts in this book. Success indicates you understand the inner workings of the Macintosh very well.

And that, dearest friends, brings us to the very end. We have enjoyed having you along on this tour of the Norton Utilities for the Macintosh. We hope that you have learned some important things about the Mac that you didn't know before, and that this knowledge will aid you in future endeavors. We also hope you have a better "feel" for the Utilities themselves. If this book inspires you to continue exploring on your own, and if it increases the value you get out of the Norton Utilities for the Macintosh, then it will have been well worth our effort to write it. Best wishes!

Appendix A

Glossary

What! You didn't know every one of the words we just threw at you? Not to worry. We've compiled a list of them here, along with what we hope are cogent definitions. (Many of the glossary entries below appear in the *Apple Publications Glossary, Version 3.0*, ©1988 by Apple Computer, Inc. To them we tender our sincere thanks.)

allocate: To reserve an area of memory or disk space for use.

Apple menu: The menu farthest to the left in the menu bar, indicated by an Apple symbol, from which you choose **desk accessories.**

application program: Software that performs a specific task, such as word processing, database management, or graphics. Also called simply an *application.*

ASCII: Acronym for *American Standard Code for Information Interchange* (sometimes pronounced "ASK-ee"). A standard that assigns a unique binary number of exactly one byte's length to each text character and control character. ASCII code is used for representing text inside a computer and for transmitting text between computers or between a computer and a peripheral device.

233

attribute: See **file attributes** and **volume attributes**.

backup: (n.) A copy of a disk or of a file on a disk. It's a good idea to make backups of all your important disks and to use the copies for everyday work, keeping the originals in a safe place. (Some program or startup disks cannot be copied.)

bad sector: An area of a disk that is unreadable. Bad sectors can be caused by **physical** problems (e.g., scratches or fingerprints) or **logical** problems. Speed Disk can locate bad sectors on your hard disk and render them harmless with its Verify Media or Verify Media First commands. See "sector."

bit: A contraction of *binary digit.* The smallest unit of information that a computer can hold. The value of a bit (1 or 0) represents a simple two-way choice, such as yes or no, on or off, positive or negative, something or nothing, Democrat or Republican.

block: (1) A logical unit of data storage or transfer, typically 512 bytes; can be larger on high-capacity disks. (2) A contiguous region of computer memory of arbitrary size, used by an application to store data. Also called a *memory block.*

boot: Another way to say *start up.* A computer boots by loading a program into memory from an external storage medium such as a disk. Starting up is often accomplished by first loading a small program, which then reads a larger program into memory. The program is said to "pull itself up by its own bootstraps"—hence the term *bootstrapping* or *booting.* There are those who claim that the original term referred to the necessity of kicking the old, alligator-clip-wired computers to get them going, but these folk are seldom taken seriously.

boot block: (1) An area on a formatted disk that signals the computer that the disk contains an application to be started up. (2) The first block of a file system, or the first two logical blocks of a volume. The boot block contains the system's startup instructions.

boot device: The peripheral device that reads an operating system's initial startup instructions.

boot disk: See **startup disk.**

buffer: (1) An area of memory set aside for the specific purpose of holding data until it is needed. (2) A "holding area" of the computer's memory where information can be stored by one program or device and then read at a different rate by another.

bundle: A resource that links files with their appropriate icons so that the Finder can correctly launch applications and open files.

button: A pushbutton-like image in dialog boxes where you click to designate, confirm, or cancel an action.

byte: A unit of information consisting of a fixed number of **bits.** One byte consists of a series of eight bits and can take any value between 0 and 255 ($00 and $FF hexadecimal). The value can represent an instruction, a number, a character, or a logical state. See also **kilobyte, megabyte.**

cache: A holding area in main memory where write information for block input/output is temporarily stored.

Cancel button: A button that appears in a dialog box. Clicking it cancels the command.

case-sensitive: Able to distinguish between uppercase characters and lowercase characters. A Find command is case-sensitive, for example, if typing and produces different results from typing AND in a text box.

catalog: A list of all files stored on a disk. Synonymous with **directory.**

Catalog B-Tree: A data structure that contains essential bookkeeping information for an HFS disk, including the physical locations of files and their sizes.

character: Any symbol that has a widely understood meaning and thus can convey information. Some characters—such as letters, numbers, and punctuation—can be displayed on the monitor screen and printed on a printer. See also **control character.**

character code: An integer representing the character that a key or key combination stands for.

character key: Any of the keys on a computer keyboard—such as letters, numbers, symbols, and punctuation marks—used to generate text or to format text; any key except Caps Lock, Command, Control, Esc, Option, and Shift. Character keys repeat when you press and hold them down.

checkbox: A small box associated with an option in a dialog box. When you click the checkbox, you may change the option or affect related options.

Chooser: A desk accessory that lets you configure your computer system to print on any printer for which there's a printing resource on the current startup disk. If you're part of an AppleTalk network system, you use the Chooser to connect and disconnect from the network and choose among devices connected to the network. You can also specify a user name that the system uses from time to time—when you're printing on a LaserWriter, for example.

Clear: A command in the Edit menu that removes selected material without placing it on the Clipboard. You can use the Undo command immediately after using Clear to reverse the action.

Clear key: A key located in the numeric keypad section of certain keyboards whose usage is similar to the Escape key; it often cancels a command or a dialog box.

click: (v.) To position the (mouse) pointer on something, and then press and quickly release the mouse button. (n.) The act of clicking.

Clipboard: The holding place for what you last cut or copied; a buffer area in memory. Information on the Clipboard can be inserted (pasted) into documents.

color wheel: A dialog box accessed in the Control Panel desk accessory or, for example, in Norton Speed Disk or Layout Plus. The color wheel lets you adjust hue, saturation, and brightness.

Command key: A key that, when held down while another key is pressed, causes a command to take effect. The Command key is marked with a propeller-shaped symbol. On some machines, the Command key has both the propeller symbol and the Apple symbol on it.

configuration: (1) A general-purpose computer term that can refer to the way you have your computer set up. (2) The total combination of hardware components—central processing unit, video display device, keyboard, and peripheral devices—that make up a computer system. (3) The software settings that allow various hardware components of a computer system to communicate with one another.

configure: To change software or hardware actions by changing settings.

contiguous: In one piece. Memory or disk space may be contiguous. Contiguous disk files can be accessed more quickly than fragmented ones; Speed Disk eliminates fragmentation to ensure that files are contiguous. Compare with **fragmented**.

control character: A nonprinting character that controls or modifies the way information is printed or displayed.

control key: See **modifier key**.

Control Panel: A desk accessory that lets you change the speaker volume, the keyboard repeat speed and delay, mouse tracking, color display, and other features.

Control Panel device (cdev): Application accessed by means of the **Control Panel.** The Norton Utilities for the Macintosh include two Control Panel devices—FileSaver and DiskLight.

copy-protect: To make a disk uncopyable. Software publishers frequently try to copy-protect their disks to prevent them from being illegally duplicated by software pirates. Compare **write-protect.** See also **lock.**

CPU: Central Processing Unit. Circuitry within the computer that performs arithmetic and logical tasks. The "brain" of the system.

crash: To cease to operate unexpectedly, possibly destroying information in the process.

crashed drive: A drive that won't mount. See also **mount.**

creator code: See **file creator code.**

current startup disk: The disk that contains the system files the computer is currently using. The startup disk icon always appears in the upper-right corner of the Finder's desktop.

cursor: (1) A symbol displayed on the screen marking where the user's next action will take effect or where the next character typed from the keyboard will appear. (2) The term used to refer to the pointer on the screen.

cut: To remove something by selecting it and choosing Cut from a menu. What you cut is placed on the Clipboard. In other editing applications, "Delete" serves the same function.

cut and paste: To move something from one place in a document to another in the same document or a different one. It's the computer equivalent of using scissors to clip something and glue to paste the clipping somewhere else.

data: Information, especially information used or operated on by a program. The smallest unit of information a computer can understand is a **bit.**

data fork: The part of a file that contains data, accessed via the File Manager.

decimal system: The commonly used form of number representation, in which numbers are expressed in the base-10 system, using the 10 digits 0 through 9. Compare **hexadecimal system.**

default: A value, action, or setting that a computer system assumes, unless the user gives an explicit instruction to the contrary. For example, unless instructed otherwise, Speed Disk will Verify Media and Verify Files before optimizing. Default values represent the safest, most common, or likely settings to use.

delete: To remove something, such as a character or word from a file, or a file from a disk. Keys such as the Backspace key and the Delete key can remove one character at a time by moving to the left. The Cut command removes selected text and places it on the Clipboard; the Clear command removes selected text without placing it on the Clipboard. (The Undo command can reverse the action of Clear and of the Backspace or Delete key if it is used immediately.)

Delete key: A key that moves the insertion point backward, removing the previously typed character, or that removes the current selection. Its function is identical to that of the Backspace key on the original Macintosh keyboards.

deselect: To perform some action (such as clicking a button) that causes an object to be not selected. A deselect command has an effect opposite to that of a **select** command. For example, deselecting a device such as a printer is to place it into a condition in which it will not receive data.

desk accessory: A "mini-application" that is available from the **Apple menu** regardless of which application you're using—for example, the Control Panel, Norton Fast Find, and Norton KeyFinder are all desk accessories. Desk accessories are files of type DFIL and creator DMOV, and can be installed using the Font/DA Mover.

desktop: Your working environment on the computer—the menu bar and the gray area on the screen. You can have a number of documents on the desktop at the same time. At the Finder level, the desktop displays the Trash and the icons (and windows) of disks that have been accessed.

Desktop file: A resource file in which the Finder stores the version data, bundle, icons, and Get Info comments for each application on the volume.

destination volume: The duplicate volume, as opposed to the source (original) volume. When you are making a copy of a file or a volume, the destination volume is the volume onto which you are copying. Compare **source volume.** See also **volume.**

device driver: A program that manages the transfer of information between the computer and a peripheral device. For example, the SCSI device driver is the program code stored in the boot blocks of a disk that manages communication between an application and data on the SCSI device.

dialog box: (1) A box that contains a message requesting more information from you. Sometimes the message warns you that you're asking your computer to do something it can't do or that you're about to destroy some of your information. In these cases, the message is often accompanied by a beep. (2) A box that a Macintosh application displays to request information or to report that it is waiting for a process to be completed.

dimmed: Used to describe words or icons that appear in gray. For example, menu commands appear dimmed when they are unavailable; folder icons are dimmed when they are open.

directory: A file used internally by the Finder and other parts of the operating system that contains a list of all the names and locations of other files stored on a disk. The directory is an internal representation of the Finder's folders. A directory is sometimes called a *catalog.*

directory dialog box: A type of dialog box you use to work in the hierarchical file system from within an application. Such dialog boxes appear whenever you choose the Open or Save As commands from within an application. Norton Directory Assistance adds greater flexibility and control to standard directory dialog boxes.

directory hierarchy: The collection of all files on the currently mounted file systems. Hierarchy refers to the logical structuring of files within folders (within other folders).

disabled: Describes a menu item or menu that cannot be chosen; the menu item or menu title appears dimmed. A disabled item in a dialog or alert box has no effect when clicked. See also **dimmed**.

disk: A flat, circular, magnetic surface, serving as a medium for storing information.

disk drive: The device that holds a disk, retrieves information from it, and saves information to it.

disk drive light: A light that comes on when your disk drive is loading from or storing on a disk. Norton DiskLight supplements this light by displaying a configurable, on-screen icon representing your hard disk or floppy disk. DiskLight is quite convenient if you've placed your hard disk on the floor or in some other location where you can't see the disk drive light.

document: Whatever you create with an application program—information you enter, modify, view, or save. See also **file.**

double click: (n.) Two clicks in quick succession, interpreted as a single command. The action of a double click is different from that of a single click. For example, clicking an icon selects the icon; double-clicking an icon opens it.

drive: (n.) (1) See **disk drive.** (2) A button in certain dialog boxes that allows you to access information from a different drive (volume).

driver: See **device driver.**

edit: To change or modify. For example, to insert, remove, replace, or move text in a document.

Edit menu: A menu in most Macintosh applications that lists editing commands—like Copy, Cut, and Paste.

eject: To remove a disk from a disk drive.

Enter key: A key that confirms an entry or sometimes a command.

error message: A message displayed or printed to tell you of an error or problem in the execution of a program or in your communication with the system. An error message is often accompanied by a beep.

Escape key: See **Esc key.**

Esc key: A key that generates the escape character. In many applications, pressing Esc allows you to return to a previous menu or to stop a procedure.

extent: A piece of a file. Data within a single extent is in contiguous blocks.

Extents B-Tree: A data structure containing records of fragmented files: where they begin, where each fragment is stored, and how large each fragment is. Extents past three in each fork are managed in this structure. The first three extents are managed in the catalog b-tree.

field: A data item separated from other data by blanks, tabs, or other specific delimiters.

file: Any named, ordered collection of information stored on a disk. Application programs and documents you create are examples of files. You make a file when you create text or graphics, give the material a name, and save it to disk; in this sense, *file* is synonymous with **document.** A Macintosh file consists of a **data fork** and a **resource fork.**

file attributes: Information indicating whether a file is locked, invisible, etc.

file creator code: A four-digit sequence contained in a file that specifies which application created it. Compare with **file type**.

file management: A general term for copying files, deleting files, and other chores involving the contents of disks.

File Manager: The part of the operating system that supports file input and output.

File menu: A menu in most Macintosh applications that lists commands that affect whole documents—commands like Save, Print, and Quit.

filename: The name that identifies a file. The maximum character length of a Macintosh filename is typically 31 characters. Compare **pathname.**

file server: A specially equipped computer that allows network users to store and share information. AppleShare software, Macintosh computers, and one or more hard disks make up a file server on an AppleTalk network system.

file system: Part of the operating system that manages how files and folders are organized and retrieved.

file type: (1) In a directory listing, the code that characterizes the contents of a file and indicates how the file may be used. (2) A four-character sequence, specified when a file is created, that identifies the type of file. Examples of file types are TEXT, APPL, and MPST. Compare with **file creator code.**

Finder: The application that maintains the Macintosh desktop and starts up other programs at the request of the user. You use the Finder to manage documents and applications, and to get information to and from disks. You see the desktop when you start up your computer, unless you have specified a different startup application.

floppy disk: A disk made of flexible plastic, as opposed to a hard disk, which is made of magnetically coated metal. The term *floppy* was originally applied to disks with thin, flexible disk jackets, such as 5.25-inch disks, which were literally floppy and could be easily bent. With 3.5-inch disks, the disk itself is flexible, but the jacket is made of hard plastic. Both kinds, however, are called floppy disks.

folder: A holder of documents, applications, and even other folders on the desktop. Folders (called subdirectories in some operating systems) allow you to organize information in any way you want.

font: A complete set of characters in one design, size, and style. In traditional typography usage, *font* may be restricted to a particular size and style or may comprise multiple sizes, or multiple sizes and styles, of a typeface design.

Font/DA Mover: An application that allows you to add or remove fonts and desk accessories from a disk's System file or from a font or desk accessory file.

font family: A complete set of characters for one typeface design, including all styles and sizes of the characters in that font. For example, the Geneva font family includes 9-point to 36-point characters in italic, bold, outlined, and other styles.

fork: (n.) One of the two parts of a Macintosh file: the *data fork* contains data accessed via the Macintosh File Manager, and the *resource fork* contains data used by the application, such as menus, fonts, and icons. (v.) To create a new process.

format: (v.) To divide a disk into tracks and sectors where information can be stored. Blank disks must be formatted before you can save information on them for the first time. Formatting can be *low level*, in which brand-new hard disks (or floppies, whether brand-new or not) are made ready to store data, or *high level*, where a directory is created (or destroyed, in the case of accidentally formatting a data-containing hard disk) by system software. Format Recover used together with FileSaver provides a remedy for the latter case. Often referred to as *initialize*.

fragmented: In several pieces. Memory or disk space can be fragmented. Speed Disk eliminates disk fragmentation when it optimizes a volume.

free space: The portion of memory or of a disk that is not allocated to (used by) any file.

"happy Macintosh": An icon displayed when a valid system folder is found on a valid volume during startup. Compare with **"sad Macintosh."**

hard disk: A disk made of metal and sealed into a drive or cartridge. A hard disk can store very large amounts of information compared to 3.5-inch floppy disks.

hard disk drive: A device that holds a hard disk, retrieves information from it, and saves information to it. Hard disk media made for microcomputers are permanently sealed into the drives.

hexadecimal system: The representation of numbers in the base-16 system, using the 10 digits 0 through 9 and the six letters A through F. For example, the decimal numbers 0, 1, 2, 3, 4, . . . 8, 9, 10, 11, . . . 15, 16, 17 would be shown in hexadecimal notation as 00, 01, 02, 03, 04, . . . 08, 09, 0A, 0B, . . . 0F, 10, 11. Hexadecimal numbers are a convenient representation of the computer's internal memory organization. Two hexadecimal digits are exactly equivalent to one byte. Hexadecimal numbers are usually preceded by a dollar sign ($). Thus, $FF means 11111111 in binary.

hierarchical file system (HFS): A feature of system software that lets you use folders to organize documents, applications, and other folders on a disk. Folders (sometimes called subdirectories) can be nested in other folders to create as many levels as you need.

highlight: To make something visually distinct. For example, when you select a block of text using a word processor, the selected text is highlighted—it appears as light letters on a dark background, rather than dark-on-light. Highlighting is accomplished by inverting the display.

hyperlink: A connection between related items in databases. The Norton Utilities for the Macintosh has an on-line help system that allows users to click on specially marked text to access hyperlinks in order to see material about related concepts.

icon: An image that graphically represents an object, a concept, or a message. Icons on the outside of the computer can be used to show you where to plug cables, such as the disk drive icon on the back panel that marks the disk drive connector. Screen icons in mouse-based applications represent disks, documents, application programs, or other things you can select and open.

information window: The window that appears when you select an icon and choose Get Info from the File menu. It supplies information such as size, type, and date; and it includes a comment box for adding information. What you write into the comment box is frequently called "Finder Comments." Format Recover can restore this after a desktop is rebuilt.

initialize: Has two meanings, depending on what kind of disk is being talked about. *Floppy Disks*: To prepare a blank disk to receive information by organizing its surface into tracks and sectors. *Hard Disks*: To create and or reset the bookkeeping and directory information. See **format**.

initialized disk: A disk that has been organized into tracks and sectors by the computer and is therefore ready to store information.

installation: The process of copying files from floppy distribution diskettes to a hard disk and setting appropriate configuration information.

installed font: A font in a specific size that you install in the System file of a startup disk by using installation software or the Font/DA Mover.

interface: (n.) The devices, rules, or conventions by which one component of a system communicates with another. Also, the point of communication between a person and a computer.

K: See **kilobyte.**

keyboard shortcut: A keystroke that you can use instead of a mouse action to perform a task. For example, pressing the Command and the X keys at the same time is the same as choosing the Cut command from the Edit menu.

kilobyte (K): A unit of measurement consisting of 1024 (2^{10}) bytes. Thus, 64K memory equals 65,536 bytes. The abbreviation *K* can also stand for the number 1024, in which case *Kbyte* is used for kilobyte. See also **megabyte.**

launch: To open or run an application or program.

local area network (LAN): A group of computers connected for the purpose of sharing resources. The computers on a local area network are typically joined by a single transmission cable and are located within a small area such as a single building or section of a building.

lock: To prevent documents, files, or entire disks from being altered. Files can be locked with software commands; for example, to lock a document select it and choose Get Info from the File menu, then click the Locked check box in the upper-right corner of the Info window. An entire disk can be physically locked by sliding the small tab on the back of the plastic case of a 3.5-inch disk, or by using a write-protect tab on the disk jacket of a 5.25-inch disk; in this sense *lock* is synonymous with *write-protect*. Compare **unlock.**

locked file: A file whose data cannot be changed.

locked volume: A volume whose data cannot be changed. Volumes can be locked by either a software flag or a hardware setting.

logical: Governed or specified by software. Compare with **physical**.

Macintosh File System (MFS): A nonhierarchical (single-level) file system that was used on the original Macintosh computer and preceded the currently used HFS (Hierarchical File System). Note: Most current formatted 400K single-sided disks use MFS. Unfortunately, the Norton Utilities for the Macintosh only address HFS disk problems. Compare with **Hierarchical File System.**

main menu: The top level of options in a program having several levels of options. Making a choice from a main menu takes you to another menu.

megabyte (MB): A unit of measurement equal to 1024 kilobytes, or 1,048,576 bytes. See also **kilobyte.**

media: See **bad sector.**

memory: A hardware component of a computer system that can store information for later retrieval. See also **main memory, random-access memory, read-only memory, read-write memory.**

memory block: A contiguous, page-aligned region of computer memory of arbitrary size, allocated by the Memory Manager. Sometimes simply called a *block*.

menu: A list of choices presented by a program, from which you can select an action. In the desktop interface, menus appear when you point to and press menu titles in the **menu bar.** Dragging through the menu and releasing the mouse button while a command is highlighted chooses that command.

missing symbol: A character (often a square) that is drawn in the case of a request to draw a character that's missing from a particular font.

mount: To install a file system onto the directory hierarchy. Compare **unmount.**

mounted volume: A volume that has been inserted into a disk drive and has had descriptive information read from it by the File Manager.

MultiFinder: A first-generation multitasking operating system for Macintosh computers that makes it possible to have several applications open at the same time, including background applications that let you perform one task while the computer performs another. Well, sort-of.

network: A collection of interconnected, individually controlled computers, together with the hardware and software used to connect them. A network allows users to share data and peripheral devices such as printers and storage media, to exchange electronic mail, and so on.

on-line help: Assistance you can get from an application program while it's running.

on-line volume: A mounted volume with its volume buffer and descriptive information contained in memory.

open: To make available. You open files or documents in order to work with them. A file may not be read from or written to until it is open. In the desktop interface, opening an icon causes a window with the contents of that icon to come into view. You may then perform further actions in the window when it's active.

operating system: (1) A program that organizes the actions of the parts of the computer and its peripheral devices. (2) Low-level software that controls a computer by performing such basic tasks as input/output, memory management, and interrupt handling. Sometimes abbreviated OS.

Option key: A modifier key that gives a different meaning or action to another key you press or to mouse actions you perform. For example, you can use it to type foreign characters or special symbols contained in the optional character set.

optimize: To improve the performance of something. Norton Speed Disk, for example, optimizes your hard disk by eliminating fragmentation, making free space contiguous, and by prioritizing files.

parent folder: The folder that an item (file or other folder) is contained in.

partition: A segment of a volume created either by software or by hardware.

pathname: A description of the exact location of a file in a file system, including its parent folder, grandparent, etc.

physical: Governed or specified by hardware. Compare with **logical**.

program disk: A disk that contains an operating system and a self-starting application program.

prompt: A message on the screen that tells you of some need for response or action. A prompt is usually in the form of a symbol, a message, a dialog box, or a menu of choices.

RAM: See **random-access memory.**

RAM cache: Random-access memory you can designate to store certain information an application uses repeatedly. Using the RAM cache can greatly speed up your work, but may need to be used sparingly or not at all with applications that require large amounts of memory. You set the RAM cache in the Control Panel and in certain other applications.

random-access memory (RAM): The part of the computer's memory that stores information temporarily while you're working on it. A computer with 2MB RAM has two megabytes of memory available to the user (minus the amount occupied by the operating system). Information in RAM can be referred to in an arbitrary or random order, hence the term *random-access.* Information in RAM is temporary, gone forever if you switch the power off without saving it on a disk or other storage medium.

raster: A single horizontal line on a video screen or in a printer's output. Rasters are draw left to right and are assembled top to bottom to form a complete image.

Read Me document: A plain text document that is included on application and system software disks and provides you with late-breaking information about the product. See **TeachText.**

reboot: See **restart.**

resource fork: The part of a file that contains information used by an application, such as menus, fonts, and icons. An executable file's code is also stored in the resource fork. Sometimes called a *resource file*. Compare with **data fork.**

restart: To start your computer again, by choosing the Restart command from the Special menu of the Finder. It is necessary to restart when you place new startup documents (INITS) in your System folder—DiskLight and FileSaver, for example—in order to launch them.

Return key: A key that causes the cursor or insertion point to move to the beginning of the next line in a text editor or word processor. It's also used in some cases to confirm a command.

run: (1) To execute a program. When a program runs, the computer performs the instructions. (2) To load a program into main memory from a peripheral storage medium, such as a disk, and execute it. See **launch**.

"sad Macintosh": An icon that indicates a serious problem encountered during startup preventing further progress. Consult the Emergency Procedures section for further information.

save: To store information by transferring it from main memory to a disk. Work not saved disappears when you switch off the computer or when the power is interrupted.

scroll: (1) To move a document or directory in its window so that a different part of it is visible. (2) To move all the text on the screen upward or downward, and in some cases sideways.

SCSI: An acronym for *Small Computer System Interface* (pronounced "SKUH-zee" by most, "SEX-zee" by some; go figure). An industry standard interface that provides high-speed access to peripheral devices.

SCSI device: A device, such as a hard disk or tape backup unit, that uses the Small Computer System Interface.

sector: Part of a **track** on a disk; when a disk is formatted, its recording surface is divided into tracks and sectors.

select: (v.) (1) To designate where the next action will take place. To select using a mouse, you click an icon or drag across information. In some applications, you can select items in menus by typing a letter or number at a prompt, by using a combination keypress, or by using arrow keys. (2) To enable a device to receive data.

Shift-click: A technique that allows you to extend or shorten a selection by positioning the pointer at the end of what you want to select and holding down the Shift key while clicking the mouse button.

Shift-drag: A technique that allows you to select multiple objects by holding down the Shift key while you drag to enclose the objects in a rectangle.

Shift key: A key that, when pressed, causes the subsequent letter you type to appear in upper case or the top symbol on a two-character key to be produced. The Shift key can also modify mouse actions. See **Shift-click, Shift-drag.**

signature: A sequence of bytes contained in the header that uniquely identifies an application or document to the Finder and to data-recovery applications like UnErase. Compare with **file creator code**.

source: (n.) The original volume. When you are making a copy of a file or a volume, the source volume is the volume you are copying from; the **destination** volume is the disk you're placing the copy on. (adj.) Describes files that are being copied or translated as well as the disk or folder containing source files.

source volume: The original volume, as opposed to the duplicate (destination) volume. When you are making a copy of a file or a volume, the source volume is the volume from which you are copying. Compare **destination volume.** See also **volume.**

standard file dialog: See **directory dialog box.**

startup disk: A disk with all the necessary program files—such as the Finder and System files contained in the System folder for the Macintosh—to set the computer into operation. Sometimes called a *boot disk.*

startup document: A small program loaded into memory at startup time. Startup documents are located in the System folder. The Norton Utilities for the Macintosh include two startup documents—Directory Assistance, File Saver, and DiskLight. Also called *INIT.*

startup drive: The disk drive from which you started your application.

subdirectory: A directory within a directory; a file (other than the volume directory or root directory) that contains the names and locations of other files. Equivalent to *folder* in the Macintosh operating system.

system disk: A disk that contains the operating system and other system software needed to run applications.

System file: A file Macintosh computers use to start up and to provide systemwide information.

System folder: A special folder containing the System file, the Finder, and system resources, such as fonts, desk accessories, control panel devices, etc. The system folder has a small Macintosh icon on it to distinguish it from other folders.

system startup information: Certain configurable system parameters that are stored in the first two logical blocks of a volume and read in at system startup. See **boot blocks**.

TeachText: An application on the System Tools disk that lets you read **plain text documents.**

text: (1) Information presented in the form of readable characters. (2) The display of characters on a display screen.

text box: The place or places in any dialog box where you can type information.

tracks: A series of concentric circles that are magnetically drawn on the recording surface of a disk when it is formatted. Tracks are further divided into 8 to 12 consecutive *sectors*. A track corresponds to one ring of constant radius around the disk.

Trash: An icon on the desktop that you use to discard documents, folders, and applications.

unlock: To remove the restriction on the use of a disk or a file so that it can once again be changed, deleted, or renamed. Compare **lock.**

unmount: To remove a file system from the directory hierarchy.

unmounted volume: A volume that hasn't been inserted into a disk drive and had descriptive information read from it, or a volume that previously was mounted and has since had the memory used by it released.

version: A number indicating the release edition of a particular piece of software.

vertical retrace interrupt: A period of time during a Macintosh's operation, occurring while the electron beam that "paints" the screen is being pulled back up to the top after reaching the bottom raster. During this period, all active tasks are interrupted so that the Mac's CPU can take care of system housekeeping tasks. Occurs 60 times per second.

virtual memory: Memory space that is separate from the main memory (physical RAM) and is instead located in auxiliary memory media (usually disks). The ability of a system to address virtual memory space is important for multitasking operating systems and applications too large to be handled in RAM alone.

virus: A program intended to alter data in an invisible fashion, usually for destructive or "mischievous" aims; viruses are often transferred across local area networks, electronic bulletin boards, or by infected (floppy) disks. The Norton Disk Doctor diagnoses certain viruses.

volume: A general term referring to a storage device or to part of a storage medium formatted to contain files; a source of or a destination for information. A volume can be an entire disk or only part of a disk. Its information is organized into files.

volume attributes: Information contained on volumes and in memory indicating whether the volume is locked, whether it's busy (in memory only), and whether the volume control block matches the volume information (in memory only).

volume bitmap: A portion of every initialized disk that keeps track of occupied and free disk space. Speed Disk displays a graphic depiction of the volume bitmap to indicate fragmentation and to show what happens during optimization.

volume information block: A nonrelocatable block that contains volume-specific information including the volume name, size, number of files and folders, amount of free space, etc.

write: To transfer information from the computer to a destination external to the computer (such as a disk drive, printer, or modem) or from the computer's processor to a destination external to the processor (such as main memory).

Appendix B

Macintosh Data Structures

The following tables show the exact meaning of each field within certain critical Macintosh HFS data structures. We start with an overview of HFS disks and their typical layout.

Overview of an HFS disk

Take for example a typical 40-megabyte hard disk. The overall picture of the disk would look like this:

Sector #	Contents
0–1	Boot Blocks
2	Volume Information Block
3–13	Volume Bit Map
14	Extents B-Tree Header
15–691	Extents B-Tree
692	Catalog B-Tree Header
693–1369	Catalog B-Tree
1370–79997	File data area
79998	Backup copy of Volume Info Block
79999	Last sector on disk

251

Allocation Block Size

Note that there are 80,000 sectors on a 40-megabyte hard disk (512 bytes per sector), and the disk has 40,000 blocks (1024 bytes per allocation block). The allocation block size usually follows this pattern:

Disk Size	Sectors on disk	AlBlSize	SectorsPerAlBlk
0–32 meg	0–65,535	512 bytes	1
32–64 meg	65,536–131,071	1024 bytes	2
64–96 meg	131,072–196,607	1536 bytes	3
96–128 meg	197,608–262,143	2048 bytes	4
128–160 meg	262,144–327,679	2560 bytes	5
160–192 meg	327,680–393,215	3072 bytes	6
192–224 meg	393,216–458,751	3584 bytes	7
256–288 meg	458,752–524,287	4096 bytes	8
288–320 meg	524,288–589,823	4608 bytes	9
320–352 meg	589,824–655,359	5120 bytes	10
(600 meg)	(1,228,800)	(9728 bytes)	19
(1.2 gig)	(2,457,600)	(19456 bytes)	38
(default)	(x)	[1+(x÷65536)]*512	[1+(x÷65536)]

Logical versus Physical

All references to "sector number" in this document refer to logical sectors within an HFS volume, with the exception of the discussion of the SCSI Partition Table and the SCSI Driver Descriptor Map, where "sector number" refers to raw absolute sectors on the SCSI device.

Disks and Drives, Volumes and Partitions

Technically speaking, "disk" and "drive" refer to the disk media in a physical sense, while "volume" and "partition" are used in a logical sense. Since most Macintosh drives are partitioned into a single volume, "disk" or "drive" is often used when "volume" or "partition" is intended.

Boot Blocks

The Boot Blocks occupy sectors 0 and 1 on all Macintosh volumes and contain information used during the boot process. The Boot Block data structure (shown below) is located in the first part of sector zero. The rest of sector zero and all of sector one contain executable boot code. If the volume is not a bootable volume (a partition, for example), the Boot Blocks will normally be empty.

Offset		Type	Alias	Comment	
$00	0	uint	sigBytes;	/* $4C4B—LK—Larry Kenyon	*/
$02	2	ulong	bootCodeOffset;	/* branch instruction to start of boot code	*/
$06	6	uint	bootBlkVersNum;	/* version number of the boot block	*/
$08	8	uint	flags;	/*	*/
			value == $0001 to allocate secondary sound buffer (TN 113)		
			value == $FFFF to allocate both secondary video & sound buffers (TN 113)		
$0A	10	char	systemName[16];	/* system filename (all Pascal strings)	*/
$1A	26	char	finderName[16];	/* program to run when quit an application	*/
				/* (usu Finder)	*/
$2A	42	char	debuggerName[16];	/* name of debugger (usu Macsbug)	*/
$3A	58	char	dissassemblerName[16];	/* dissassembler (usu Dissassembler)	*/
$4A	74	char	startupScreenName[16];	/* startup screen name (usu Startup)	*/
$5A	90	char	bootupProgName[16];	/* program to run after bootup (usu Finder)	*/
$6A	106	char	clipboardName[16];	/* clipboard file (usu Clipboard File)	*/
$7A	122	uint	maxFiles;	/* number of FCBs to allocate, ÷2 or ÷4	*/
$7C	124	uint	eventQueueSize;	/* number if elements in event queue	*/
$7E	126	ulong	heapSize128;	/* system heap size on 128K Mac	*/
$82	130	ulong	heapSize256;	/* system heap size on 256K Mac	*/
$86	134	ulong	heapSize512;	/* system heap size on 512K Mac and larger	*/
$8A	138	char	*bootCode;	/* the rest of the sector and the next sector	*/

Volume Information Block

The Volume Info Block is always at sector 2 on Mac HFS disks. If the Volume Info Block is missing or damaged, then the disk will be unmountable. The VIB changes frequently and is updated often; it is probably the one sector most vulnerable to damage during a crash.

Offset		Type	Alias	Comment		
$00	0	uint	drSigWord;	/* $4244—BD—Big Disk		*/
$02	2	ulong	drCrDate;	/* date & time drive last formatted		*/
$06	6	ulong	drLsMod;	/* date & time of last modification		*/
$0A	10	uint	drAtrb;	/* flags		*/
	vLocked		0x8000	bit 15	volume locked by software	
	vCopyProt		0x4000	bit 14	volume is copy protected	
	cleanUmount		0x0100	bit 8	clean unmount	
	vWrProt		0x0080	bit 7	volume locked by hardware	
	vBusy		0x0040	bit 6	volume is busy	
	bit2		0x0004	bit 2	set if disk inconsistencies when mount	

```
        bit1              0x0002  bit 1    set if disk inconsistencies when mount
        bit0              0x0001  bit 0    set if disk inconsistencies when mount
$0C 12  uint   drNmFls;           /* number of files in the root directory      */
$0E 14  uint   drVBMStart;        /* sector of start of volume bit map. Usu 3.  */
                                  ?* (see drAlBlSt)                             */
$10 16  uint   drAllocPtr;        /* new File Allocation Pointer                */
$12 18  uint   drNmAlBlks;        /* number of allocation blocks on volume      */
$14 20  ulong  drAlBlkSiz;        /* allocation block size                      */
$18 24  ulong  drClpSiz;          /* default clump size                         */
$1C 28  uint   drAlBlSt;          /* first sector represented in bit map. eg 16.*/
                                  /* (see drVBMStart)                           */
$1E 30  ulong  drNxtCNID;         /* next unused file number or DirID           */
$22 34  uint   drFreeBks;         /* number of unused allocation blocks         */
$24 36  uchar  drVN[28];          /* volume name (pascal string)                */
$40 64  ulong  drVolBkUp;         /* date and time of last backup               */
$44 68  uint   drSeqNum;          /* index into set of backup disks             */
$46 70  ulong  drWrCnt;           /* volume write count                         */
$4A 74  ulong  drXTClpSiz;        /* clump size of extents tree                 */
$4E 78  ulong  drCTClpSiz;        /* clump size of catalog tree                 */
$52 82  uint   drNmRtDirs;        /* number of folders in root directory        */
$54 84  ulong  drFilCnt;          /* total number of files on volume            */
$58 88  ulong  drDirCnt;          /* total number of directories on volume      */
$5C 92  DrFndrInfo drFndrInfo;    /* finder Info (TN129)                        */
$5C 92  ulong  blessedFolderID;   /* dirID of the blessed folder                */
$60 96  ulong  startupAppDirID;   /* dirID containing startup application       */
$64 100 ulong  finderFolderChain; /* dirID of first folder in Finder's chain of */
                                  /* opened folders.                            */
$68 104 char   unknown;           /*                                            */
$69 105 char   filler;            /* filler                                     */
$6A 106 char   filler2[18];       /* to make 32 byte struct.                    */
$7C 124 uint   drVSSize;          /* size of volume cache                       */
$7E 126 uint   drVCBMSize;        /* size of VBM cache                          */
$80 128 uint   drCtlCSize;        /* size of common cache for the volume in mem.*/
$82 130 ulong  drXTFlSize;        /* length of extents tree                     */
$86 134 ExtRecdrXTExtRec;         /* first 3 extents descriptors for extents tree*/
$86 134 uint   start1;            /* starting allocation block of first extent  */
$88 136 uint   length1;           /* length of extent in allocation blocks      */
$8A 138 uint   start2;            /*                                            */
$8C 140 uint   length2;           /*                                            */
$8E 142 uint   start3;            /*                                            */
$90 144 uint   length3;           /*                                            */
$92 146 ulong  drCTFlSize;        /* length of catalog tree                     */
$96 150 ExtRecdrCTExtRec;         /* first 3 extents descriptors for catalog tree*/
$96 150 uint   start1;            /* starting allocation block of first extent  */
$98 152 uint   length1;           /* length of extent in allocation blocks      */
$9A 154 uint   start2;            /*                                            */
$9C 156 uint   length2;           /*                                            */
$9E 158 uint   start3;            /*                                            */
$A0 160 uint   length3;           /*                                            */
$A2 162 char   *theRest;          /*                                            */
```

B-Tree Node

The HFS B-Tree structure is currently used for both the Extents and Catalog trees, as well as the Desktop Manager files, Desktop DB, and Desktop DF. The node size is always 512 bytes, so each node occupies an entire sector.

There are three basic node types, each of which is described individually on the following pages:

HeaderNode

Index Node

Leaf Node

This is the basic structure of one node of an HFS B-Tree.

Offset		Type	Alias	Comment
$00	0	ulong	fLink;	/* forward link to next node on this level (relative */ /* sector number) */
$04	4	ulong	bLink;	/* backward link to previous node on this level */
$08	8	uchar	nodeType;	/* $FF == leaf node, $00 == index node */ /* $01 == BTH node, $02 == 2nd VBM */
$09	9	char	level;	/* level of this node (1 == levelOfLeaf) */
$0A	10	uint	numRecs;	/* number of records contained in this node */
$0C	12	uint	filler;	
$0E	14	[data]		/* The node data starts here. */
$1D8	472	int	offset20;	/* offsets pointing to the individual records */
$1DA	474	int	offset19;	
$1DC	476	int	offset18;	
$1DE	478	int	offset17;	
$1E0	480	int	offset16;	
$1E2	482	int	offset15;	
$1E4	484	int	offset14;	
$1E6	486	int	offset13;	
$1E7	488	int	offset12;	
$1EA	490	int	offset11;	
$1EC	492	int	offset10;	
$1EE	494	int	offset9;	
$1F0	496	int	offset8;	
$1F2	498	int	offset7;	
$1F4	500	int	offset6;	
$1F6	502	int	offset5;	
$1F8	504	int	offset4;	
$1FA	506	int	offset3;	
$1FC	508	int	offset2;	
$1FE	510	int	offset1;	

B-Tree Header Node

This is the structure of a header node for an HFS B-Tree. The BTH node itself has a standard B-Tree node structure, and the B-Tree Header Record is the first record in the header node, starting at byte $0E.

The HFS B-Tree maintains an internal bitmap, located in the third record of the header node, to record which of its nodes are currently in use. Since the header node itself is always in use, the bitmap of an empty BTree will always have at least one bit set (the first bit, which can be found as a $80 at byte $F8). A second bitmap, when needed, comprises the single record of an additional node, the node number of which is stored in the fLink field of the header node.

Offset			Type	Alias	Comment	
	($00)	(0)	ulong	fLink;	/* fLink to overflow BTH BitMap (usu NULL)	*/
	($04)	(4)	ulong	bLink;	/* bLink. (not used in BTH)	*/
	($08)	(8)	uchar	nodeType;	/* $01 == BTH node	*/
	($09)	(9)	char	level;	/* level of this node (1 for BTH)	*/
	($0A)	(10)	uint	numRecs;	/* number of records contained in this node	*/
	($0C)	(12)	uint	filler;		
$00	($0E) 0	(14)	uint	BTHTreeDepth;	/* Depth of the tree	*/
$02	($10) 2	(16)	ulong	BTHRootNode;	/* node number of root node	*/
$06	($14) 6	(20)	ulong	BTHNumLeafRecords;	/* number of leaf records in tree	*/
$0A	($18) 10	(24)	ulong	BTHFirstLeafNode;	/* node number or first leaf node	*/
$0E	($1C) 14	(28)	ulong	BTHLastLeafNode;	/* node sector number or last leaf node	*/
$12	($20) 18	(32)	uint	BTHNodeSize;	/* size of each node (usu 512 bytes == 1	*/
					/* sector)	*/
$14	($22) 20	(34)	uint	BTHMaxKeyLen;	/* maximum size of a key in this tree	*/
$16	($24) 22	(36)	ulong	BTHNumNodes;	/* number of nodes in the tree (leaf	
					/* and index)	*/
$1A	($28) 26	(40)	ulong	BTHFreeNodes;	/* number of free nodes in the tree	*/
	($F8)	(248)	uchar	BTreeBitMap[256];	/* Bit Map for keeping track of used	*/
					/* nodes	*/

Extents B-Tree Data Structures

The following are componants within an Extents B-Tree node.

Extents Key

This is the structure of an Extents Key, which prefixes each record in the Extents Tree.

Offset		Type	Alias	Comment
$00	0	char	xkrKeyLen;	/* length of the key ($07 in Extents Tree) */
$01	1	uchar	xkrFkType;	/* fork type of this extent $00==data, $FF==rsrc */
$02	2	long	xkrFNum;	/* file number that this extent represents */
$06	6	int	xkrFABN;	/* Allocation Block Number within file */

Extents Tree Index Record

This is the structure of an Index Record in an Extents Tree Index Node.

Offset		Type	Alias	Comment
$00	0	char	cdrType;	/* always 0 for Index Record */
$01	1	char	cdrResrv2;	/* filler */
$02	2	int	downLink;	/* node number of downlink */

Extents Tree Leaf Record

This is the structure of an Extent Record in an Extents Tree Leaf Node.

Offset		Type	Alias	Comment
$00	0	uint	start1;	/* starting allocation block of this extent */
$02	2	uint	len1;	/* length in blocks of this extent */
$04	4	uint	start2;	/* (Three extents are held in each Extent Record). */
$06	6	uint	len2;	
$08	8	uint	start3	
$0A	10	uint	len3;	

Catalog B-Tree Data Structures

The following are components of a Catalog B-tree node.

Catalog Key

This is the structure of a Catalog Key, which prefixes every Index node in the Catalog Tree.

Offset		Type	Alias	Comment
$00	0	char	ckrKeyLen;	/* length of key ($25 in index node, dynamic in leaf)*/
$01	1	char	ckrResrv1;	/* filler */
$02	2	long	ckrParID;	/* parent ID of the file or folder (or dirID of thread) */

```
$06  6    char   ckrCName[];      /* file name or folder name (""for thread)        */
$xx  x    char   filler;          /* only if needed to force next field to even byte */
```

Note: ckrCName is always 32 characters long in an Index node. In a Leaf node, the filenames are packed.

Catalog Tree Index Record

This is the structure of an Index record in a Catalog Tree Index node.

Offset		Type	Alias	Comment
$00	0	char	cdrType;	/* always 0 for Index Record	*/
$01	1	char	cdrResrv2;	/* filler	*/
$02	2	int	downLink;	/* node number of downlink	*/

Catalog Tree Leaf Record

Catalog Tree Leaf Records can be one of four types:

Name	cdrType
Directory Record	1
File Record	2
Thread Record	3
File Thread Record	4 (System 7.0, a.k.a. "alias")

These are described individually on the following pages.

Catalog Tree Directory Record

The structure of a Directory Record of a Catalog Tree Leaf Node is given here.

Offset		Type	Alias			Comment
$00	0	uchar	cdrType;			/* always 1 for directory record */
$01	1	uchar	cdrResrv2;			/* filler */
$02	2	uchar	dirFlags;			/* flags, see also PB->ioFlAttrib */
			filFlagsLocked	0x01	bit 0	/* Finder locked*/
			filFlagsIsAliased	0x02	bit 1	/* the file has an alias pointing to it (Sys 7) */
			filFlagsBit2	0x04	bit 2	/* rsrc Fork Open (PB) */
			filFlagsBit3	0x08	bit 3	/* data fork open (PB) */
			filFlagsBit4	0x10	bit 4	/* is Directory (PB) */
			filFlagsBit5	0x20	bit 5	
			filFlagsCopyProt	0x40	bit 6	/* file is copy protected */
			filFlagsRecordUsed	0x80	bit 7	/* file is opened (PB) */
$03	3	uchar	ioACUser			/* AppleShare Privileges */

	privNoSearch		0x01	bit 0	/* if set, user can't see folders*/		
	privNoRead		0x02	bit 1	/* if set, user can't see files */		
	privNoWrite		0x04	bit 2	/* if set, user can't make changes */		
	privBit3		0x08	bit 3			
	privBit4		0x10	bit4			
	privBit5		0x20	bit5			
	privBit6		0x40	bit6			
	privNotOwner		0x80	bit7	/* if set, user is not owner of the folder */		

$04	4	uint	dirVal;		/* number of files in this directory	*/
$06	6	ulong	dirDirID;		/* directory ID (file number) of this directory	*/
$0A	10	ulong	dirCrDat;		/* folder creation date	*/
$0E	14	ulong	dirMdDat;		/* folder modification date	*/
$12	18	ulong	dirBkDat;		/* folder backup date	*/
$16	22	DInfo	dirUsrInfo;		/* finder info	*/
$16	22	Rect	frRect;		/* folder's rectangle	*/
$1E	30	int	frFlags		/* flags. Not all of these make sense for folders	*/

frFlagsOnDesk	0x0001	bit 0	/* folder is on desktop	*/
frFlagsColor1	0x0002	bit 1	/* was BFOwnAppl	*/
frFlagsColor2	0x0004	bit 2	/* was Reserved02	*/
frFlagsColor3	0x0008	bit 3	/* was Reserved03	*/
frFlagsBit4	0x0010	bit 4	/* was frFlagsNeverSwitch	*/
frFlagsBit5	0x0020	bit 5	/* was frFlagsAlwaysSwitch	*/
frFlagsBit6	0x0040	bit 6	/* was frFlagsCached	*/
frFlagsBit7	0x0080	bit 7	/* was sharedOpen/readOnly	*/
frFlagsInitted	0x0100	bit 8	/* folder has been seen by Finder	*/
frFlagsChanged	0x0200	bit 9		
frFlagsBusy	0x0400	bit 10		
frFlagsBozo	0x0800	bit 11	/* was noCopy	*/
frFlagsSystem	0x1000	bit 12		
frFlagsBit13	0x2000	bit 13	/* was frFlagsBundle	*/
frFlagsInvisible	0x4000	bit 14	/* folder is invisible	*/
frFlagsLocked	0x8000	bit 15	/* not Finder Lock	*/

$20	32	Point	frLocation;		/* folder's location	*/
$24	36	int	frView;		/* folder's View	*/
$26	38	DXInfo	dirFndrInfo;		/* more finder info	*/
$26	38	Point	frScroll;		/* position of scroll bars of the folder	*/
$2A	42	ulong	frOpenChain;		/* chain of open folders	*/
$2E	46	int	frUnused;		/* filler	*/
$30	48	int	frComment;		/* resource ID for GetInfo comment for the folder	*/
$32	50	ulong	frPutAway;		/* folder where came from (if on desk)	*/
$36	54	uchar	dirResrv[16];		/* used internally	*/
$46	70	start of next key				

Color Bits in dirUsrInfo.frFlags

	Color1	Color2	Color3
Black			(no bits set)
Light Blue		x	
Green	x		

Red		x	x
Brown	x		
Pink	x		x
Dark Blue	x	x	
Orange	x	x	x

File Record

The structure of a File Record of a Catalog Tree Leaf Node is given here.

Offset		Type	Alias			Comment	
$00	0	char	cdrType;			/* always 2 for file record	*/
$01	1	char	cdrResrv2;			/* filler	*/
$02	2	char	filFlags;			/* flags, see also PB->ioFlAttrib	*/
			filFlagsLocked	0x01	bit 0	/* Finder locked */	
			filFlagsIsAliased	0x02	bit 1	/* file has an alias pointing to it (Sys 7) */	
			filFlagsBit2	0x04	bit 2	/* rsrc fork open (PB) */	
			filFlagsBit3	0x08	bit 3	/* data fork open (PB) */	
			filFlagsBit4	0x10	bit 4	/* is Directory (PB) */	
			filFlagsBit5	0x20	bit 5		
			filFlagsCopyProt	0x40	bit 6	/* file is copy protected */	
			filFlagsRecordUsed	0x80	bit 7	/* record is used (FileRecord) */	
			filFlagsRecordUsed	0x80	bit 7	/* either fork open (PB) */	
$03	3	char	filTyp;			/* file type, always 0 in HFS	*/
$04	4	FInfo	filUsrWds;			/* Finder Info aka PB->ioFlFndrInfo	*/
$04	4	OSType	fdType;			/* file type	*/
$08	8	OSType	fdCreator;			/* file creator	*/
$0C	12	int	fdFlags;			/* finder flags	*/
			fdFlagsOnDesk	0x0001	bit 0	/* file is on desktop */	
			fdFlagsColor1	0x0002	bit 1	/* was BFOwnAppl */	
			fdFlagsColor2	0x0004	bit 2	/* was Reserved02 */	
			fdFlagsColor3	0x0008	bit 3	/* was Reserved03 */	
			fdFlagsNeverSwitch	0x0010	bit 4	/* never switch launch this file */	
			fdFlagsAlwaysSwitch	0x0020	bit 5	/* always switch launch this file */	
			fdFlagsCached	0x0040	bit 6	/* resEdit—"shared" */	
			fdFlagsSharedOpen	0x0080	bit 7	/* aka NoInits or readOnly */	
			fdFlagsInitted	0x0100	bit 8	/* file has been seen by Finder */	
			fdFlagsChanged	0x0200	bit 9		
			fdFlagsBusy	0x0400	bit 10		
			fdFlagsBozo	0x0800	bit 11	/* was noCopy */	
			fdFlagsSystem	0x1000	bit 12		
			fdFlagsBundle	0x2000	bit 13		
			fdFlagsInvisible	0x4000	bit 14		
			fdFlagsLocked	0x8000	bit 15	/* not Finder Lock */	
$0E	14	Point	fdLocation;			/* file's location	*/
$12	18	int	fdFldr;			/* file's folder (MFS only)	*/

```
           fTrash          -3       /* in trash window        */
           fDesktop        -2       /* on Desktop   */
           fDisk            0       /* in disk window         */
$14   20   ulong    filFlNum;       /* file number                                    */
$18   24   uint     filStBlk;       /* first allocation block of data fork            */
$1A   26   ulong    filLgLen;       /* logical EOF (file size)                        */
$1E   30   ulong    filPyLen;       /* physical EOF                                   */
$22   34   uint     filRStBlk;      /* first allocation block of rsrc fork            */
@24   36   ulong    filRLgLen;      /* logical EOF (file size)                        */
$28   40   ulong    filRPyLen;      /* physical EOF                                   */
$2C   44   ulong    filCrDat;       /* file's creation date                           */
$30   48   ulong    filMdDat;       /* file's modification date                       */
$34   52   ulong    filBkDat;       /* file's last backup date                        */
$38   56   FXInfo   filFndrInfo;    /* finder info                                    */
$38   56   int      fdIconID;       /* resource ID of the file's icon                 */
$3A   58   int      fdUnused[4];    /* filler                                         */
$42   66   int      fdComment;      /* resource ID of the file's comment file         */
$44   68   long     fdPutAway;      /* home directory of the file (if on desktop)     */
$48   72   uint     filClpSize;     /* file's clump size (0 if uses default clump size) */
$4A   74   ExtRec   filExtRec;      /* first 3 extents records for data fork          */
$4A   74   uint     start1;         /* starting allocation block if first extent      */
$4C   76   uint     length1;        /* length of extent in allocation blocks          */
$4E   78   uint     start2;
$50   80   uint     length2;
$52   82   uint     start3;
$54   84   uint     length3;
$56   86   ExtRec   filRExtRec;     /* first 3 extents records for rsrc fork          */
$56   86   uint     start1;         /* starting allocation block if first extent      */
$58   88   uint     length1;        /* length of extent in allocation blocks          */
$5A   90   uint     start2;
$5C   92   uint     length2;
$5E   94   uint     start3;
$60   96   uint     length3;
$62   98   ulong    filResrv;       /* used internally                                */
$66  102   start of next key
```

Color Bits in filUsrWds.fdFlags

	Color1	Color2	Color3
Black				(no bits set)
Light Blue			X
Green		X	
Red		X	X
Brown	X		
Pink	X		X
Dark Blue	X	X	
Orange	X	X	X

Catalog Tree Thread Record

The structure of a Thread Record of a Catalog Tree Leaf Node is given here.

Offset		Type Alias	Comment	
$00	0	uchar cdrType;	/* always 3 for thread record	*/
$01	1	uchar cdrReserv2;	/* filler	*/
$02	2	uchar thdResrv[8];	/* used internally	*/
$0A	10	ulong thdParID;	/* parent directory ID for this directory	*/
$0E	14	uchar thdCName[32];	/* directory name of thread	*/
$2E	46	start of next key		

File Thread Record (System 7.0)

The structure of a File Thread Record (or Alias Record) of a B-Tree Leaf node is given here.

Offset		Type Alias	Comment	
$00	0	uchar cdrType;	/* always 4 for file thread record	*/
$01	1	uchar cdrReserv2;	/* filler	*/
$02	2	uchar thdResrv[8];	/* used internally	*/
$0A	10	ulong thdParID;	/* parent directory ID for this alias record	*/
$0E	14	uchar thdCName[];	/* file name of the alias	*/
$2E	46	start of next key		

Appendix C

Hints and Tips

Directory Assistance

The Find... command in Dir Asst is fast. It is simple, but it is the fastest way to navigate from one folder to another in Open and Save dialog boxes.

Even though there is no "Folders Mixed" command in the view menu. You can get back to the normal alphabetical view by turning off the checkmarks for both the "Folders First" and "Folders Last" menu items.

You can cycle in reverse order through the drives that you have mounted by holding down the option key when hitting the drive button (or opt-Tab).

Fast Find

Undocumented Features

Command-T brings up a types&creators search dialog.
Option-click on start button, you get no animation (faster).
Holding down space while searching disables animation.
Option-click on item in Get Info will show path of creator.

The Fast Find text viewer can be used to pull important text out of a damaged file that can't be opened.

Many people use Fast Find as a file launcher. It is quicker than trying to scrounge around the Finder for the application. You can also open documents straight from Fast Find.

FileSaver

To reinstall the FileSaver data files, you need to uninstall and hit OK, then reinstall and hit OK.

Just because you are running the FileSaver INIT doesn't mean that all your drives are protected. You must specifically choose which ones to protect via the FileSaver cdev. If you reboot and you don't see the FileSaver cursor, or you see it flash on the screen for a fraction of a second, you are probably not protected. The cursor should be on the screen for at least a second or two (per hard drive).

If FileSaver delete protection is enabled, then when you throw a file away in the Finder, FileSaver will make a copy of the file's housekeeping information and store it away in a safe place (for UnErase to use later if you want to get the file back). [Actually, this is done when you Empty the Trash, not immediately when you throw the file away.] This extra step to save away the file information is worthwhile to protect against accidentally deleting the wrong file, but takes a bit of extra time. This extra time is not noticeable unless you are throwing away hundreds of files at the same time (a big folder, for example). If you are certain that you are throwing away the "right" folder, you can temporarily disable FileSaver by holding down the command key when you empty the trash; this may speed up emptying the trash.

Help

If the help engine is launching the wrong version of the help file (e.g., an old version, or a copy on a server instead of on your local hard disk) you can hold down cmd-opt-shift when opening help to choose where the help file is located.

Main Menu

When launching Speed Disk or Layout, if it is launching the wrong version of SpeedDisk or Layout (e.g., an old version, or a copy on a server instead of on your local hard disk) you can hold down cmd-opt-shift to re-ask for file to launch.

Norton Disk Doctor

If you are trying to run NDD on a disk that keeps getting ejected before you have a chance to open it (e.g., you get a message that "the desktop file could not be created"), you are probably in MultiFinder and the Finder ejecting the disk before NDD can have a look at it. Reboot under Finder only and try again.

NDD report quirk—Num Files On Disk: This is the true number of files including hidden files (e.g., the desktop file). The Finder subtracts the desktop file in the GetInfo dialog for drives so its number will often be one lower.

In the NDD report, for bytes on disk and free space, the Finder says "529K" but NDD says "541,184 bytes." These are both correct because a K is 1024 bytes, not 1000, and 529*1024=541,184.

Norton Disk Editor

Pressing Command-Shift-**Drive** when choosing which drive to edit will show more things to edit, including partitions that are normally hidden, like the part of the disk that stores the disk driver. You can also edit an entire physical SCSI drive (regardless of its partitioning schemes) this way. This feature may allow you to get at damaged partitions that are otherwise unreadable. [A/UX partitions, too.]

Holding down the option key when clicking on the drive button in most drive dialogs allows you to go backwards through the drive list.

When you Open a volume to edit, NDE will scan the disk for certain pieces of information (disk housekeeping information) and will read that info into memory and keep it around for quicker access. If you switch into MultiFinder and move some files around or delete some files off the disk that you are looking at with NDE, NDE won't know about the changes. This is not a big problem, but can be confusing if you see a file in NDE that you thought you just deleted. You can get around this by quitting NDE and restarting the program, or you can Open Volume... again, and hold down the option key when you click Open. This will re-read the disk housekeeping information into NDE's buffers. If for some reason you do not want NDE to read any of this information (this can be helpful when trying to edit a severely damaged disk whose housekeeping information has been damaged or overwritten), you can hold down Command-Shift-Option when Opening the disk the first time.

When you use any navigation keys to move around the hex view in NDE (e.g., arrow keys, home, page up, return, etc.) the keys will perform their expected actions. If, however, you want to type one of those keys into the sector, hold down the option key when you hit the key and the key's ASCII value will be entered at the cursor position. (The cursor must be in the ASCII half of the window, not the hex half).

After executing a Find command in the Directory view of the Disk Editor, the directory window will contain the list of files that were found. If you want to get back to the full directory listing, you can do so by choosing "Directory" again from the Objects menu.

General

If you have a crashed hard disk, or a hard disk that has erased files that you want to recover, and you were running the Desktop Manager INIT on that hard disk, do not boot a disk with Finder that doesn't also have the desktop manager INIT running. If you do, there is a chance that the Finder will try to rebuild an old-style desktop on that disk and in doing so could overwrite the data that you are trying to recover.

Appendix D

Problems and Solutions

The following is a list of a few incompatibilities that the Norton Utilities for the Macintosh have with other software. Included are the affected software, the symptoms, and possible ways around the problems. Some of these difficulties may already have been rectified by the time you read this.

Directory Assistance 1.0

Excel 1.5, SAM 2.x

Symptoms   When you hold down the command key in an Open dialog (without any other keys, just the command key), Excel will beep continuously. When you do the same thing in a Select Folder dialog in SAM, SAM will interpret the command key alone as a command-A and choose the selected folder.

Workarounds   Type very quickly when using the command key.

DiskLight 1.0

After Dark 2.0

Symptoms Machine will hang after screen saver kicks in and has been running for a few seconds to a few minutes. This happens very intermittently.

Workarounds Don't run DiskLight and After Dark on the same machine.

Fast Find 1.0

Rival 1.1

Symptoms

When the user selects a file that was found, the file icon and file information in the info panel is generic (e.g., "document" instead of "MacWrite document").

The user cannot launch documents by double clicking on them (you get an open dialog box asking "Find the application to launch this document...").

Workarounds Get upgrade to Rival, version 1.1.1 or above (1.1.3 is now shipping 8/20/90).

FileSaver 1.0

TOPS 3.0

Symptoms If Filesaver is installed on a TOPS server volume, it will take a very long time to unmount the TOPS volume (can be 3–5 minutes) and the user will eventually get an error 46 from FileSaver.

Workarounds

Hold down the command key when you unmount the TOPS volume (so that FileSaver doesn't try to update the TOPS volume). Do this right before shutting down too, so the drive won't be updated with all the rest at shutdown time.

Don't share entire TOPS volumes—only share the folders that you need.

Turn off FileSaver protection on the server machine for the server drive that is mounted remotely. (Remove the invisible FileSaver data files).

Do not run the FileSaver INIT on the local machine.

Word Perfect 1.0.5

Symptoms   When WordPerfect does a periodic save of opened files, the first save works fine; the second periodic save results in a FileSaver Init error 95. You click **OK** and the message reappears. On second **OK** the file saves properly.

Workarounds   Either don't run FileSaver or don't use periodic save option in Word Perfect.

KeyFinder 1.0

DataDesk Keyboard (Non-ADB)

Symptoms   Certain keys when pressed don't show up like they should (e.g., Home, End).

Workarounds   Nothing known.

Installer 1.0

Icon Colorizer

Symptoms   When installing, Installer will eject a disk and then ask for the same disk back again.

Workarounds

Follow the instructions and stick the disk back in—it won't happen that many times.

Turn off Icon Colorizer before running the Installer.

Layout Plus 1.0

Rival 1.1

Symptoms   When booting Layout Plus under MultiFinder, the user gets a message that the Finder cannot be opened.

Workarounds

Get upgrade to Rival, version 1.1.1 or above (1.1.3 is now shipping).

Run Layout Plus under Finder only.

Norton Disk Doctor 1.0

Virex 1.7.1

Symptoms   Machine crashes with ID 01 sometime during Analyzing Files step.

Workarounds   Disable Virex before running NDD.

Speed Disk 1.0

MicroTech Hard Drives (and others)

Symptoms   When you click on the optimize button, you get the message "This drive has weak sectors. Your data is safe. Cannot optimize."

Workarounds   Go to Expert Level, turn off Verify Data, and try again. If problem persists, the drive may legitimately have weak sectors and the user should back up the data and reformat the drive.

PLI Turbo 40 Syquest Drive (and perhaps others)

Symptoms   When you run old versions of the PLI driver software (we think 1.1 to 1.5), Speed Disk will find many bad sectors in the Verify Media scan and will not optimize the drive. After that happens and you quit Speed Disk, some applications on that disk will stop working (disk error -36 when you are trying to launch applications, or duplicate files, or open folders . . .). Drive works fine again after reboot.

Workarounds   Update the disk to a new version of the PLI driver (1.8 seems to fix the problem).

Index

W